THE RIGHT TO ORGANIZE AND ITS LIMITS

THE BROOKINGS INSTITUTION

The Brookings Institution—Devoted to Public Service through Research and Training in the Social Sciences—was incorporated on December 8, 1927. Broadly stated, the Institution has two primary purposes: the first is to aid constructively in the development of sound national policies; and the second is to offer training of a supergraduate character to students of the social sciences.

The responsibility for the final determination of the Institution's policies and its program of work and for the administration of its endowment is vested in a self-perpetuating board of trustees. It is the function of the trustees to make possible the conduct of scientific research under the most favorable conditions, and to safeguard the independence of the research staff in the pursuit of their studies and in the publication of the results of such studies. It is not a part of their function to determine, control, or influence the conduct of particular investigations or the conclusions reached, but only to approve the principal fields of investigation to which the available funds are to be allocated, and to satisfy themselves with reference to the intellectual competence and scientific integrity of the staff. Major responsibility for "formulating general policies and co-ordinating the activities of the Institution" is vested in the president. The by-laws provide also that "there shall be an advisory council selected by the president from among the scientific staff of the Institution."

Authors of studies published by the Institution have had the advice, criticism, and assistance both of an administrative officer and of a co-operating committee selected from the staff. In manuscript accepted for publication, the author has freedom to present his final interpretations and conclusions, although they may not necessarily be concurred in by some or all of those who co-operate with him or by other members of the staff. The Institution in publishing the work assumes the responsibility that it meets reasonable tests of scholarship and presents data and conclusions worthy of public consideration.

THE RIGHT TO ORGANIZE
AND ITS LIMITS

*A Comparison of Policies in the United States
and Selected European Countries*

BY

KURT BRAUN

Prof. Econ.

Howard U.

Wash. D.C.

Washington, D. C.
THE BROOKINGS INSTITUTION
1950

PREFACE

The membership of American unions has increased about fivefold in the last fifteen years and the economic and political power of the unions has grown correspondingly. This is partly a natural development, but it has also greatly been fostered by recent public labor policy, designed to protect and strengthen unionism. The resulting growth of labor power in due course brought demands for revisions of our basic labor law to meet the needs of the changed situation. Legislation was first passed in some states, and then in 1947 the Taft-Hartley Act was enacted by the federal government.

The passing of these statutes, however, did not signify the end of efforts to revise the law governing the rights and duties of unions. The legislators recognized that the determination of labor policy is a continuing and developing process. Congress, accordingly, decided that the problems involved should receive more extended study. It established joint congressional committees to watch the Taft-Hartley Act in operation and to examine the whole field of labor-management relations for the purpose of making recommendations, especially concerning future legislation. Thus the whole question of the rights and duties of organized labor is still a significant problem.

In efforts to solve this problem, it is believed that much valuable information can be gained from examining how comparable problems have been handled in foreign countries. A number of western European governments have dealt for a long time with labor issues with which American governments are now concerned. Moreover, they have tended to determine their policies toward concerted labor activities in the light of the same basic principles by which this country has been guided. The author, therefore, has undertaken a systematic, comparative study of the rights and duties assigned to organized labor in the United States and selected European countries. It also covers prevailing management and union policies to the extent necessary to clarify the background of public policies.

The present volume is based on this study and analyzes the position taken by the various governments with respect to the exercise by workers of the fundamental rights to form, join, and operate organized groups. The second part is devoted chiefly to an analytical, comparative survey of public policies with regard to compulsion to organize—one of the most hotly debated issues involved in labor organization. In view of the primary purpose of the study, which is to present material to those who are striving for improvements in our own country, the emphasis of the discussion is placed upon general principles which have been used here as well as abroad, and upon their various interpretations, possibilities of application, and effects. Since today's basic problem is no longer the recognition of freedom to act in concert as such but rather the limits within which this freedom may be properly exercised, the attention, further, is focused on efforts which have been made to delimit its legitimate scope.

The author has interviewed and corresponded with many domestic and foreign government officers, leading employers, labor leaders, economists, and members of the legal profession. He has, further, canvassed a considerable number of domestic and foreign documents, issued by public authorities and private organizations, court decisions, law books, and relevant private publications. In addition, he has utilized personal observations and experiences obtained as a practitioner in Europe and in the United States.

HAROLD G. MOULTON

President

June 1950

ACKNOWLEDGEMENTS

Much of the material for this volume has been obtained in conversations or through correspondence with officials of embassies, foreign and domestic government agencies, employers' associations, and unions. The author wishes to acknowledge his indebtedness to all these individuals, organizations, and public authorities. Their number is so great as to make it impossible to mention all of them by name.

Special thanks, however, are due to Professor A. Amiaud, University of Paris; Mr. D. C. Barnes, Assistant Secretary, Ministry of Labour and National Service, London; Mr. Ernest A. Bell, International Secretary, British Trades Union Congress; Mr. Erik Brodén, Director, Swedish Employers' Confederation; Professor Herman Finer, University of Chicago; Mr. Marcel Flory, First Secretary, French Embassy, Washington; Lord Chief Justice Goddart, London; Mr. Robert Kean, O.B.E., Member of the General Purposes Committee and Council of the British Employers' Confederation; Mr. Edouard Lambert, *Directeur du Travail,* French Ministry of Labor; Mr. Lars Gunar Ohlsson, Chief, Legal Department, Swedish Ministry of Social Affairs; Mr. Louis G. Silverberg, Director of Information, National Labor Relations Board; Mr. Gaston Tessier, President, French Confederation of Christian Workers; Mr. Gustav Vahlberg, Joint President, Swedish Confederation of Trade Unions; and Mr. Pierre Waline, Member of the Board of Directors, National Council of French Employers.

The author deeply appreciates the kindness of Mr. E. F. Rimensberger, Labor Attaché, Legation of Switzerland, Washington, who has made valuable suggestions and has been of great help in various other respects. The friendly assistance of the office of the Labour Attaché, British Embassy and the Embassy of Sweden in Washington, as well as the French Embassy, Information Division, New York, and many members of their staffs is gratefully acknowledged. The author, further, desires to thank both the Geneva and Washington offices of the International Labour Office for their aid and co-operation.

The author is under special obligation to Mr. Frederick F. Blachly, a retired member of the Brookings Institution, who gave him access to an unpublished study on federal administration which furnished much valuable material on the internal management of the federal personnel administration.

Kurt Braun

CONTENTS

ix

TABLE OF ABBREVIATIONS

A_____Atlantic Reporter (United States)

1918 A.C. 120_____English Law Reports, Appeal Cases, 1918 volume, page 120

AD dom 73 (1937) Decisions of the Swedish Labor Court, volume 1937, no. 73

A.F. of L._____American Federation of Labor (United States)

Ala._____Alabama

A.L.R._____American Law Reports Annotated

am._____amended

Ann. Code_____Annotated Code

BGE 51_____Decisions of the Swiss Federal Court (Bundesgericht), vol. 51

Cass-civ._____French Court of Cassation, Civil division

C.C.H. Lab.Cas.___Commerce Clearing House, Labor Cases (United States)

cert. den._____certiorari denied. Petition to review a decision denied by the Supreme Court of the United States.

C.I.O._____Congress of Industrial Organizations (United States)

Cong._____Congress of the United States

D. 1916.I.26_____Dalloz, Jurisprudence Générale, Recueil Périodique et Critique de Jurisprudence, de Législation et de Doctrine (French collection of annotated court decisions and laws), 1916 volume, first part, page 26.

Del._____Delaware

East_____East, King's Bench Reports (United Kingdom)

169 Fed. (2d) 1___Federal Reporter, 2d series, vol. 169, p. 1

Fed. Reg._____Federal Register (United States)

Fed. Supp._____Federal Supplement series, containing decisions of the federal district courts (United States)

Ga._____Georgia

Gaz. Pal._____La Gazette du Palais (French Law Reporter)

H.B._____House Bill (United States)

H.J. Res._____House Joint Resolution (United States)

H. Rept._____House of Representatives Report (United States)

Ia._____Iowa

I.L.O._____International Labor Office

J.O._____Journal Officiel de la République Française
(Official Journal of the French Republic)

L.1947_____laws of 1947

L.B._____Legislative Bill (United States)

L.C.C._____London County Council

L.R._____Law Reports (United Kingdom)

LRRM_____Labor Relations Reference Manual
(United States)

Mass._____Massachusetts or Massachusetts Reporter

N.C._____North Carolina

N.E._____Northeastern Reporter (United States)

N.H._____New Hampshire or New Hampshire Reports

NLRB._____National Labor Relations Board
(United States)

66 NLRB 380____Decisions of the National Labor Relations
Board, volume 66, p. 380 (United States)

N.W.L.B._____National War Labor Board (United States,
World War II)

N.Y._____New York or New York Court of Appeals Reports

N.Y. Supp._____New York Supplement Reporter

Op. Att. Gen._____Opinion of the Attorney General
(United States)

P._____Pacific Reporter (United States)

Pa._____Pennsylvania

Q.B._____Queen's Bench Reports (United Kingdom)

RAGE 4_____Decisions of the German Supreme Labor Court
(Reichsarbeitsgericht), vol. 4

rel._____release

Rev. Quest. Prud._Revue "Questions Prud 'homales"
periodical dealing with the work of the French
labor courts

RGBl_____German official law gazette

RGZ 104_____Decisions of the German Supreme Court
(Reichsgericht) in civil matters, vol. 4

Ry._____railway

S.B._____Senate Bill (United States)

Sir 22.1.148 or
S 22.1.148_____Recueil Général des Lois et des Arrêts, fondé par
J. B. Sirey (French collection of annotated
court decisions and laws, 1922 volume, first
part, page 148

So._____Southern Reporter (United States)
S. Rept._____Senate Report (United States)
26 Stat. 209_____Statutes at Large of the United States of America, volume 26, page 209
Supp._____Supplement
Sup. Ct._____Supreme Court (United States)
S.W._____Southwestern Reporter (United States)
Tenn. _____Tennessee
Tex._____Texas
TGWU_____Transport and General Workers' Union (United Kingdom)
T.U.C._____Trades Union Congress (United Kingdom)
United Kingdom__United Kingdom of Great Britain and Northern Ireland
U.S.C._____United States Code
323 U.S. 248_____Decision of the United States Supreme Court, published in the United States series, volume 323, page 248

Introduction

This volume contains some of the results of a more comprehensive study of public policies on rights and duties of organized labor groups in the United States and selected European countries, chiefly France, Germany, Sweden, and the United Kingdom. It deals with one right of labor, namely, the right to organize. This right is a fundamental one. The nature and scope of nearly all specific rights of organized labor such as, for example, the right to bargain collectively and the right to strike, have been determined in the light of prevailing opinion on the character and limits of the right to organize.

It is believed that comparative inquiries into labor problems and efforts to solve them, such as undertaken in this study, serve a useful purpose. Though economic, social, and political conditions of one country differ more or less from those of any other, labor relations and their problems are not so different that useful lessons could not be drawn in any country from experience in others. Apart from that, postwar plans for close co-operation of the democracies to overcome the effects of the war and to preserve the democratic way of life are relying in no small measure upon the support of labor movements of the various countries in both the domestic and the international scenes. Wholehearted and effective collaboration of the various movements, however, obviously presupposes knowledge and respect of each other's basic principles and peculiarities.

Our government and leading labor organizations are taking an active interest in European and international unionism. This course can yield the desired results only if we take careful notice of the views and traditions of foreign governments, unions, and managements concerned, which differ in various respects from those of our own.

As to controversial problems of our domestic policies, it goes without saying that we have to solve them in our own way. But, despite fundamental differences in the economic, political, and social conditions on the two sides of the Atlantic, consideration of European in addition to domestic experience might be helpful in our efforts to seek generally satisfactory solutions to problems arising continuously from industrial relations in general and from union activities in particular. A number of European governments have dealt for a long time with problems with which American governments are occupied at present or are likely to concern themselves in the near future. Their experience may throw additional light at crucial points and also may be useful to avoid contemplating measures which have already proved unwise somewhere else. Since the study attempts to give equal attention to American and foreign scenes, it is hoped that it may be useful not only to familiarize Americans with conditions in Europe but also Europeans with the American situation.

In the preparation of the study two major questions of approach and organization had to be decided by the author. The first was whether the treatment should be primarily descriptive or basically critical and evaluative. The purpose was to give the American reader an objective report on domestic and foreign practice in the field which will enable him to judge for himself whether foreign attempts to solve a given problem could or should be considered in efforts to settle comparable issues in the United States. The same thought with necessary modifications would seem to apply to a foreign reader. These objectives, it seemed, would be far better served by the descriptive method with a minimum of criticism and evaluation.

The second question was whether the arrangement should be by subjects or by countries. The primary purpose of the inquiry is to examine individual issues of a more or less universal character and to describe the broad concepts applied in efforts to settle them. This purpose would be better served through an arrangement by subjects than by a lengthy description of the labor policy established in each of the several countries. Each chapter thus deals with a specific issue. Within this framework individual countries are discussed separately only so far as is necessary to show that the specific policy toward a problem has been a result of historical, industrial, political, or social conditions peculiar to the country concerned. For those who are interested in gaining a more coherent picture of the labor policy of any specific country, it is hoped that the index will be of help.

To find the English equivalent for some of the foreign terms has not always been easy. In some instances the very concepts involved may be alien to American readers. Terms in the field of labor law, moreover, do not necessarily have a uniform meaning even throughout the English-speaking countries. The term "trade union" is a good illustration. In American everyday usage it is generally applied to an organization established by workers for the protection and promotion of their occupational and related interests. But in England, officially at least, the term not only embraces organizations of workers as in the United States, but it is also applied to employers' associations. In discussing the American scene the customary terms such as union security and closed shop are used in order to avoid making the complicated language problems still more difficult. The terms customary in the United States have also been used in discussing concepts, procedures, and institutions which exist in the same or similar forms in both the United States and foreign countries.

But where American and foreign concepts are entirely different, European or coined expressions are used. Although they may sound unfamiliar, they appear nevertheless to be best suited to produce the intended and correct image in the mind of the reader. Thus the various kinds of collective agreements made in different countries, which exclude certain types of workers from employment opportunities—called union security agreements in the United States—have been classified, for the purposes of comparative examination, as "exclusive agreements," since this is their chief common trait in all countries despite differences in nomenclature. To give one more example, foreign legislators have tended to give both unions and employers' associations (in the strictly technical meaning of the term), the same legal status with the same rights and duties, because considerable functional and structural analogies exist in both types of organization. Where the significance of this fact has to be brought out in this study, they are grouped together under the name of "occupational associations" or "occupational organizations."

To present a complete glossary appears unnecessary, since it is hoped that most of the terms used are self-explanatory. Where it seems advisable, their intended meaning is defined in the text or footnotes. For the sake of brevity, the term "America" is used in this study to mean the United States of America, and the term "Europe" refers to the chief European countries used for comparison, namely, France, the defunct German Republic, Sweden, and the United Kingdom.

The reader must always keep in mind that this study is not focused on the United States or any one other country. Unless it is explicitly stated that a statement applies to the United States or another particular nation, it relates to the situation prevailing in the field covered by the inquiry as a whole. If conditions, say, in the American sector of this field at present do not tally with certain phases of the prevailing picture, this would not make the statement incorrect. Nor would it lessen its significance for the purposes of the study, which is in a large measure concerned with comparison of diverse situations and the question whether concepts and practices developed abroad may be utilized in the domestic scene.

PART I

FREEDOM TO ORGANIZE

CHAPTER I

Evolution of the Right to Organize

The rise of the capitalist entrepreneur and the industrial revolution initiated profound changes in the economic and social status of those who work for wages. Rapid expansion of the factory system, growing use of machines, and other economic developments enhanced capital requirements in such a degree that in the majority of countries most wage earners could no longer expect to become employers themselves after working for some time in a dependent position. Moreover, progressive mechanization and division of the manufacturing process into relatively simple operations gradually increased the number of those who could, and did, take over parts of it. More and more semi-skilled and unskilled workers, women, and children began to work in the factories. Apart from that, in the words of Justice Frankfurter, "The coming of the machine age . . . turned men and women into 'hands'."[1] A new type of wage-earning class thus came into existence. It was confronted with a trend toward oversupply of labor and the danger of unemployment even in expanding economies—serious problems that are still with us.

The new industrial era began about the time when progressive forces embarked on vigorous campaigns for removal of the last vestiges of the medieval structure of society and for establishment of full political, economic, and social freedom of the individual. Where this movement prevailed, the wage earner was relieved from restrictions to which governments, guilds, and custom had subjected him. He attained the right to work at any place where he could find employment. He gained freedom of contract, which permitted him to negotiate the conditions of his employ-

[1] *A. F. of L.* v. *American Sash Co.,* 335 U. S. 538, 542 (1949).

7

ment directly with the employer. He became entitled to demand such terms as he deemed proper and to reject conditions which he did not like.

An ever-growing number of workers, however, came to realize that their position under the changed industrial situation, more often than not, prevented them from putting their new rights to practical use. Since supply of labor in industry as a whole ordinarily had a tendency to exceed demand, bargaining between individual job applicants and the employer tended to work in favor of management. Increasing concentration of economic power in combines of entrepreneurs made the position of employers still stronger. In the long run, Adam Smith pointed out, the worker is as necessary to the employer as the employer is to him; but the average employer, because of his better economic position, ordinarily can hold out for favorable contract terms much longer than the average individual worker.[2] It thus is not surprising that prevailing economic theory held for a considerable time that workers in the long run are unlikely to receive more than subsistence wages.

This prospect was not very satisfactory for the members of the wage-earning class. As more and more workers became convinced that individual freedom without power or the material requisites for its exercise was not of much use to them, they sought to gain the freedom of contract in reality which statute books had granted them on paper. To reach this goal, in their opinion they would have to minimize, if not eliminate, the power differential between management and labor. The best way of making their strength commensurate with that of the employers, they held, was to use the same strategy which entrepreneurs used to strengthen their economic position—namely, combination. The existence of large numbers of workers, they were convinced, meant weakness if each of them operated singly, but strength if they acted in concert.

2 *The Wealth of Nations*, Edwin Cannan, ed. (1922), Bk. 1, Chap. 8.

FUNDAMENTAL DIFFERENCES IN
AMERICAN AND EUROPEAN UNION THOUGHT

Owing to fundamental economic, political, and social differences between the two continents, the American and European labor movements have not pursued the same course. They have in many respects been going different ways, at least since the turn of the century when organizations of workers began to become stable in the United States. This, in the course of time, has given rise to more divergences in the general development on the two sides of the Atlantic. Since the differences in both the general conditions and union policies have been responsible for differences in the determination of the rights and duties of organized labor, it seems necessary to discuss them briefly at this juncture.

European unions have been affiliated
with certain political parties.

In Europe the labor movement did not and could not have a purely economic character. It was not a drive merely for recognition of the right to form and join unions and to bargain collectively. Neither its ultimate objectives nor the measures taken to achieve them were confined to the labor market. It was and continued to be part of the common man's struggle against the privileged for equal political, economic, and social opportunity. Even where as in France political equality of all citizens had been established, labor realized very soon that improvements in its economic conditions, in general, and freedom to act in concert, in particular, could not be attained without vigorous political action. But in most European countries equal rights and freedoms of all citizens did not materialize until many decades after the French Revolution, and until numerous workers and nonworkers had shed their blood in the streets. In these countries permanent improvement in the living conditions of the workers seemed impossible without profound changes in the political and social setup. Historical experience, as well as the close interrelation between economics and the social question on the one hand and politics on the other, has prevented the European labor movements from assuming the character of mere business unionism even after the fight for freedom to organize and bargain collectively was won.

Owing to differences in the political and economic history of the various European countries, workers' organization did not develop at the same time or along the same lines in every individual nation. In many countries several movements with divergent philosophies sprang up and have continued to function. As a rule the first organizational step undertaken by laborers to provide for mutual aid and to press their demands was the formation of unions. Political parties, such as labor, social, or social-democratic, were established when and where workers gained the full right to vote and the opportunity of forming a parliamentary representation of their own. The socialist unions—the largest in all European countries—are closely connected with such parties, either directly or indirectly. Other union movements, such as the democratic (nonsocialist) or Christian (Roman Catholic),[3] maintain close relations with those political parties which represent their political, economic, and social ideology. In recent years, unions also have co-operated with communist parties in a substantial number of European countries. Co-operatives, established especially by socialist unions, may be considered the third branch of European labor movements. These three branches—unions, political parties, and co-operatives—ordinarily pursue both political and economic objectives, though in their every-day work a certain degree of division of functions is maintained.

[3] They function in the typical union manner but accept Christian principles, particularly those laid down in the Encyclical *Rerum Novarum* of Pope Leo XIII, as the basis for human society. Membership is not necessarily limited to Roman Catholics. In 1920 the Christian union movements in the single countries formed the International Federation of Christian Trade-Unions (*Confédération Internationale des Syndicats Chrétiens*, CISC).

Co-operation, particularly of the political branch of the labor movement, with other segments of the population such as the middle class is frequent.

The first labor organizations in European countries were formed by skilled workers on occupational lines. Higher wages and shorter hours were their chief objectives. Though early efforts were made to achieve these objectives through collective bargaining, vigorous opposition by both employers and public authorities frequently caused resort to fighting tactics. The necessity to overcome governmental resistance, in addition to employer counteraction, soon gave the originally socio-economic movement a marked political flavor.

Two developments brought organization on a structural and ideological basis broader than occupational solidarity: the steady increase in numbers and significance of unskilled workers and the political and economic teachings of Karl Marx. The former entailed a very strong trend toward organization on industrial rather than craft lines. The latter, spreading among the fighting workers, caused many of them to adopt class solidarity in the place of occupational and industrial solidarity as the ideological basis of their movements. To men with their experience, especially with public authorities, the doctrine that to improve their standards permanently they would have to change the existing order was very appealing.

Equally convincing appeared the concept that to achieve this radical change they would have to overthrow the traditional regime by force. The labor movement became international. Its most significant organizations considered the class war against capitalism a more effective method to attain improvement of wages, hours, and conditions of labor, employment security, and a voice in the determination of their industrial (and, not infrequently, political) destinies, than efforts to persuade management to collaborate with them. In the view of these organizations, collective bargaining within the frame-work of the existing system became only an interim device to safeguard the short-run interests of the workers until the final goal, the new order, could be reached, primarily by other means. This development, which had been largely the result of vigorously hostile public policy, in turn gave rise to even stronger countermeasures—sometimes likewise on an international scope—by those who controlled society politically, economically, or socially.

The largest European unions have rejected capitalism.

Replacement of the capitalistic system in its present form by some kind of socialism, or at least its thorough revision by expansion of public ownership of essential enterprises and introduction of public control over the private sector of the national economy, has remained one of the most important objectives of the leading European labor movements.[4] But the introduction of universal, equal, and secret

---

[4] The General Council of the British Trades Union Congress, for example, re-emphasized in its 1944 "Interim Report on Post-War Reconstruction," its previous statements of policy that its objectives—and those of other important groups of the population—can be fulfilled only within a system of public control. "The modern economic system," the Report set forth, "bears little resemblance to the *laissez faire* form of capitalism of a century ago. Before the present war it was a system subject to a considerable amount of control exercised in many cases by private individuals and organizations and not infrequently in a manner in which public responsibility was not clearly defined or accepted. Technical development and the greater complexity of economic relationships have made higher forms of business organization advantageous and, indeed, inevitable; but the concentration of economic power in private hands, which so far has been a consequence of this development, brings with it dangers of which the whole community is now acutely aware. Although the supporters of private enterprise still frequently plead their cases in the name of freedom, it is now abundantly clear that the liberty of the individual is most endangered by a system of unrestrained private enterprise. Equally fallacious is the claim that only free private enterprise can provide a rising level of industrial efficiency. . . . One of the strongest arguments for the transfer to public ownership of key industries and for the introduction of those other forms of public control which we propose is that these changes are essential for efficient industrial organisation and to ensure that industrial efficiency serves its proper purpose of improving the standard of life of the community. . . . The choice before us is not between control or no control, but, in principle, between control of public authority responsible to the community, or control by private groups and persons owing a final responsibility to themselves alone and, in detail, between degrees of control and types of control." *76th Annual Trades Union Congress* (1944), App. D., pp. 397 ff.

suffrage sooner or later opened opportunities to achieve this goal without resort to violence. Ever since, labor leaders have made great efforts to organize the huge labor vote in order to gain strong influence on or the power over the governmental machinery via the parliamentary system. In this manner they have sought to attain social and economic objectives through legislation, with the help of congenial political parties. This type of policy has rejected suppression of civil liberties, armed revolution, and abolition of the right to political opposition. In short, it has scoffed at any kind of dictatorship, including "dictatorship of the proletariat." It therefore has been called democratic socialism or social-democracy.

Social-democratic unions and parties—like "christian" and "democratic" unions and affiliated parties of the center and left of it—have been opposed to economic and political communism and its tactics. They still represent the majority of those Europeans who want to rob totalitarian communism of its ammunition by satisfying the strong European longing for a new order without destroying the fundamentals of liberal democracy. These efforts have, over a long period, met with considerable success as regards both the introduction of reforms and restraint of Soviet Russian influence. It was not until the political power situation in Europe underwent radical changes in the period following the Second World War that Soviet Russian influence became so strong that in many countries violence has again been used on a large scale to change the existing order—in quite a number of instances successfully.

Most American unions accept
the capitalistic system.

American workers began to form and join unions when they encountered difficulties in the labor market similar to those that confronted labor in European countries. There were, at times, strong trends to deal with these diffi-

culties in the same manner as in Europe. Socialist and syn-
dicalist organizations sprang up, labor parties were formed
to represent the laboring class in legislative bodies, and
American workers co-operated and affiliated with socialist
"internationals."

Policies and tactics of American unions still may resemble those of European organized labor so far as problems
are concerned that have arisen in the same manner and
setting on both sides of the Atlantic. Economic, political,
and social conditions in Europe and the United States,
however, have differed so frequently and in such a measure that American unionists, very often, have operated in
a quite diverse atmosphere. Marked divergences in union
thought and strategy thus have developed between the two
continents. As unionism grew up in the United States, the
majority of labor leaders, including many European born
persons, sooner or later adopted the view that, as contrasted
with the situation in European countries, there was nothing
wrong with the fundamental principles on which the order
of American society was founded. Accordingly, these leaders have held that, while European workers may have to
strive for radical changes in the institutional framework
of their society, Americans should be satisfied with working toward a better application of those basically sound
economic and political principles.

Prevailing union policy in the United States, by and
large, thus accepts the basic principles of the American
capitalistic, private enterprise system. Under the conditions that prevailed in the United States, private capitalism
offered sufficient opportunities for workers to advance and
to set up in business to prevent the class-war philosophy
from spreading in the United States as it has spread in
Europe. The trend toward combination, inherent in any
system of free enterprise, has led to concentration of economic power in private hands on this side of the Atlantic as
well. But in contrast to prevailing European public policies, the federal and state governments, through antitrust

laws, have sought for many decades to keep this trend within bounds and to prevent it from restricting competition in a manner regarded as prejudicial to the public interest.

The vast majority of American labor leaders believe that public control of the economy should not go beyond such measures. They do not work toward socialization or nationalization, but want the American type of private enterprise preserved in a form in which the employees have such influence upon the determination of their economic and social status as, in their opinion, is commensurate with their contribution to the successful operation of the system. Most unions do not doubt that free private enterprise can provide a rising level of both industrial efficiency and living standards. Therefore they do not conceive of collective bargaining as a temporary expedient to be used until an entirely different economic system can be put into operation or as a means to establish such a system. They regard it rather as a permanent device to restrict competition based on wage differences and to secure for the workers what they consider a fair share in the achievements of the private enterprise system, of which they are an important part.[5]

American unions by and large are
politically nonpartisan.

Since American unionism developed under constitutions guaranteeing political freedom and equality, it did not have to fight for political emancipation of the workers, as was necessary in so many European countries. This is another factor which has greatly contributed to the devel-

[5] William H. Davis, when chairman of the National War Labor Board, stated that "of all the major drives being made by the common men throughout the world today, the drive for extension of collective bargaining is the only one which accepts private ownership, the wage system, and the profit motive as the best means of producing goods. In genuine collective bargaining, management's function is acknowledged as a vital, productive part of the free enterprise system." Speech before the Ohio Chamber of Commerce, Nov. 29, 1944, National War Labor Board Release B—1855.

opment of characteristic differences between ideology and strategy of American and European labor movements. The American labor movement is concentrated almost exclusively in the unions. In the course of their historical development, unions have changed their position with respect to political activities again and again. There have been times when most of them held it not advisable to seek to attain their objectives through political, in addition to economic, action. However, the necessity to defend the interests of themselves and their members against public policies deemed hostile to concerted labor action or against court practices regarded as obstructing the free exercise of the right to organize, and the desire "to secure legislation covering those conditions and provisions of life not subject to collective bargaining with employers," or to prevent legislative action supposedly prejudicial to the interest of the employees, ultimately caused American unions to take an active interest not only in economic but also in political issues. In recent decades, direct political union activities have steadily increased. Yet, as preceding discussion has shown, they were bound to differ with regard to scope, character, and objectives from those undertaken for similar reasons by labor organizations in Europe.

The majority of American unions are not engaged in socialist or communist policies; nor have they used revolutionary tactics. Labor, socialist, and communist party organizations, which did or do exist in the United States, have not played a role in the American labor movement comparable to that performed by European political parties of the same names. "The organization of a political Labor Party," said President Gompers of the American Federation of Labor, "would simply mean the dividing of the activities and allegiance of the men and women of labor between two bodies, such as would often come in conflict."[6]

---

[6] American Federation of Labor, *Report of the Proceedings of the Thirty-Ninth Annual Convention, 1919*, p. 105.

As contrasted with Europe, the vast majority of American unions are not affiliated with specific political parties. Nor under the traditional American system do the leading political parties act for certain economic, social, religious, or similar groups. They rather represent cross-sections of the whole population, including both employers and employees, persons connected with industry and with agriculture, rural and urban populations, rich and poor, and adherents of diverse ideologies. The unions have not permanently endorsed either of the two leading parties. It has become the traditional policy of American unions "to encourage the workers in the exercise of their political suffrage so as to favor helpful legislation and promote to public office and authority aspirants who are known to be friendly and helpful to labor regardless of their political affiliations."[7]

While European big labor organizations influence legislation and public administration by co-operating permanently with specific political parties and by acting directly as pressure groups, the primary method used by American labor organizations is exercising pressure on both governments and political parties. Every large union movement in the United States now has a "political arm" which, without being a political party, is the instrument through which it carries through important phases of its political program. The Congress of Industrial Organizations established in 1943 the "Political Action Committee" as its political agency. The American Federation of Labor followed in 1947 with its "Labor's Educational and Political League." "Railway Labor's Political League," established in the same year, is the political branch of the railroad unions.

CHANGES IN PUBLIC POLICY TOWARD UNION ORGANIZATION

In the initial period of the labor movement, efforts of workers to form and join organizations of their own ran

[7] The same, p. 374.

afoul of prevailing social, political, and economic tenets of
the time. This applied to absolute states as well as liberal
and democratic countries, and to organizations for the purpose of extending financial aid to their members in case of
need as well as to organizations for the purpose of reducing
the power differential between management and labor.
Objections came from all directions. Private and official
measures, based on them, sought to prevent workers from
combining and acting in concert or, where they had combined, to prevent their organizations from performing
characteristic functions. A discussion of these objections is
more than merely a survey of a closed chapter of historical
development, since a number of them have not by any means
been completely forgotten and some, such as the fear that
unions may become compulsory organizations of the type
which was characteristic of the corporate state, still occupy
the thoughts of people concerned with industrial relations
in no small measure. Employers naturally wished to preserve their favorable position in the labor market which
allowed them largely to determine terms of employment
and working conditions. They were convinced that interference with the free play of the economic forces and
restriction of their existing freedom to direct and operate
their businesses as they saw fit would be prejudicial to the
national economy and hence contrary to the public interest.

Economic theory, chiefly occupied with the wage problem and paying relatively little attention to the question
of hours and working conditions, tended to consider the
labor movement a hopeless and undesirable undertaking.
The majority of leading economists held, in the words of
the Webbs, that

. . . the way of the Trade Unionists was blocked in all directions.
They could not gain any immediate bettering of the condition of
the whole wage-earning class, because the amount of the wage-fund
at any given time was predetermined. They could not permanently
secure better terms even for a particular section, because this would
cause capital immediately to begin to desert that particular trade or
town. They could not make any real progress in the near future,

because they would thereby check the accumulation of capital. And finally, even if they could persuade a benevolent body of capitalists to augment wages by voluntarily sharing profits, the "principle of population" lay in wait to render nugatory any such new form of "out-door relief." . . . If it [unionism] fails, at once, in forcing higher terms on the employers of labor, the whole cost of the organisation, in money and exertion, is simply thrown away. . . . If, on the contrary, it should attain, for a time, a seeming success, the ultimate result is even worse. Nature's violated laws vindicate their authority by a sure reaction. The presumptuous mortal, who dares to set his selfish will against divine ordinances, brings on his head inevitable retribution; his momentary prosperity disappears, and he pays, in prolonged suffering, the penalty of his suicidal success.[8]

Union efforts to protect the interests of sellers of labor through restrictive measures and regulation of competition in the labor market also were condemned as irreconcilable with the dogma of free competition, the whole philosophy of *laissez faire,* and other libertarian principles. John Stuart Mill's opinion that "associations of labourers, of a nature similar to trade unions, far from being a hindrance to a free market for labour, are the necessary instrumentality of that free market; the indispensable means of enabling the sellers of labour to take care of their own interests under a system of competition"[9] was not by any means shared by many economists.

The absolute states considered the labor movement inimical to the existing divine order of society and therefore unlawful. And liberal governments were disinclined to depart in the case of unionism from the doctrine that no organization should stand between the state and its citizens and detract from the allegiance which the latter owe to the former. Le Chapelier, addressing the French Constituent Assembly during the great revolution, stated:

It should not be permissible for citizens in certain occupations to meet together in defense of their pretended common interests. There must be no more guilds in the State, but only the individual interest of each citizen and the general interest. No one should be allowed to arouse in any citizen any kind of intermediate interest and to

8 Sidney and Beatrice Webb, *Industrial Democracy* (1920), pp. 615-16.
9 John Stuart Mill, *Principles of Political Economy, New Impression* (1929), p. 937.

separate him from the public weal through the medium of corporate interests.[10]

Democratic and liberal regimes rejected unionism because they viewed it as a danger to individual freedom and because they were apprehensive that unions might develop into a new type of compulsory, occupational organization such as had restricted personal liberty in the corporate state. In those European countries in which the right of association was not yet recognized as a fundamental right of all citizens, nobody could form an association without express authorization. In view of the prevailing public policies here discussed, workers had no prospect to attain permission to form a union. When the denial of freedom of employees to organize called forth worker hostility to governmental policies and activities, governmental opposition to labor organizations increased. As contrasted with employers' associations, the governments did not expect any support from organized labor. The rise of socialist and revolutionary tendencies among the workers certainly did not make the authorities more inclined to recognize or even protect the labor movement.

Apart from systems in which the law was positively opposed to free formation of associations in general, it was in many countries at least doubtful whether, in the absence of legislative enactments or binding contracts establishing expressly the right of workers to form and belong to organizations of their own, a right to organize really existed. In other countries it may have been read into the context of provisions declaring the rights of citizens in the written or unwritten constitution. But even where the existence of freedom to organize was legally not seriously questioned, it was doubtful whether it constituted a right with a remedy in court. The judiciary, largely influenced by the attitude of economists, businessmen, and politicians, displayed little if any inclination to give it effective protection. Many of

10 *Moniteur*, June 15, 1791. See International Labour Office, *Freedom of Association*, Vol. 2 (1927), p. 89.

the typical union activities were contrary to existing statutes or could be construed as illegal and even criminal acts under civil or penal law. Under Anglo-Saxon common law most of the customary concerted labor actions were considered to constitute unreasonable restraint of trade or civil or criminal conspiracies, and the organizations which carried them through accordingly were regarded as illegal. Most activities of management to prevent unionization of workers, on the other hand, were legal under traditional law.

In the beginning of the nineteenth century, when the guilds as well as many of the regulations restricting freedom of industry and commerce were gradually abolished in the German states, existing prohibitions of combinations of workers remained in force and were made stronger. The Prussian Industrial Code of 1845—like industrial codes of other states—still provided for harsh punishment of union activities by journeymen and factory workers. These restrictions severely hampered, yet did not completely prevent, the formation of unions and other concerted labor activities. A temporary change in public policies, caused by the revolution of 1848, gave new impetus to the labor movement and led to the establishment of several large, national organizations. But legislative bodies and administrative authorities, with the backing of the employers, soon resumed the old course. This caused vigorous opposition on the part of labor, which sometimes took the form of acts contrary to existing law and led to clashes with the police. Labor leaders also secured the support of political parties left of center. All this further increased the hostility of the conservative governments to the labor movement. While the activities of organized management were not seriously interfered with, the Prussian Act of 1854 extended the prohibition of concerted labor action to virtually all agricultural and nonagricultural workers.

In France, where the act of March 2-17, 1791 had abrogated "the offices . . . of the associations of masters and guilds and all their professional privileges," the Constituent Assembly, alarmed by an increasing trend among masters and journeymen to form associations, took action designed to defend the recently established individual freedom and to forestall conspiracies against the new constitution under the guise of occupational organization. The Law Le Chapelier of June 14-17, 1791 outlawed the re-establishment of any type of corporate body of citizens in the same occupation under whatever pretext or in whatever form. It also virtually prohibited persons of the same occupation and workers in any art or craft from organizing in the form of an association for the protection of "what they call their common interests." To prevent the formation of such organizations under the guise of legitimate societies, Articles 291-94 of the Napoleonic Penal Code subsequently made the legality of any association of more than twenty members dependent upon previous governmental authorization. Under the July monarchy the law of April 10, 1840 reinforced this legislation by providing for more severe punishment of noncompliance and by prohibiting expressly the dividing of associations with more than twenty members into sections comprised of fewer than twenty persons.

As in other countries statutory prohibitions did not prevent the existence in France of labor and employer organizations and *de facto* toleration of the latter. Labor organizations, however, were vigorously prosecuted. Only mutual benefit societies, which workers established from the 1840's on, received better treatment. The revolution of 1848 brought a temporary change in public policy regarding association. The decree of February 25-29, 1848 recognized freedom of association, and Article 8 of the Constitution of November 4, 1848 gave it the character of a constitutional right. This led to a rapid growth of the labor movement. But only one year later the right to organize was suspended by the Assembly, and it was subsequently abolished by the decree of March 25, 1852. As a consequence, secret belligerent societies came into existence which made extensive use of the strike weapon. As more and more of the mutual benefit societies expanded their activities into the field of wages and other conditions of employment and, not infrequently, used the same methods as employed by belligerent societies, the government became equally hostile to any type of labor organization.

In Britain unions were treated as unlawful associations at common law, since most of their typical activities were considered unreasonable restraint of trade. When the labor movement made headway at the end of the eighteenth century, the Combination Acts of 1799 and 1800 declared unions criminal associations. After having received the report of a parliamentary committee of inquiry on the living conditions of the workers, the legislators repealed these acts in 1824.[11] This resulted in a marked growth of unionism and demands for better conditions of employment, accompanied by belligerent activities. Consequently, management demanded reintroduction of restrictions. In 1825 Parliament repealed the act of 1824 and introduced the offense of molestation and obstruction.[12] Though courts did not apply the act in a manner which would have made the existence of unions impossible, the new statute and traditional common law doctrines of conspiracy rendered strikes and other typical union activities precarious. They continued to be legally risky after the Molestation of Workmen Act softened the provisions concerning "molestation and obstruction" in 1859. Despite these legal obstacles, strikes, sometimes accompanied by violence, were not infrequent.

Following essentially British common law concepts, courts in the United States likewise rejected unionism. According to prevailing judicial opinion, union wage and other policies and practices were irreconcilable with freedom of industry and commerce. Union activities, it was said, expose commerce to inconveniences, if not ruin, and

---

[11] Combination Laws Repeal Act.
[12] Combination Laws Repeal Act Amendment Act, sec. III.

hence undermine the public welfare. Subjection to union discipline, judges further held, deprived workers of their individual freedom and, therefore, were repugnant to basic constitutional principles. Even acts which an individual worker might do in his own interest without violating the law, it was said, many combined might not do with impunity."A combination of workmen to raise their wages," stated one court, "may be considered in a twofold point of view: one is to benefit themselves . . . the other is to injure those who do not join their society. The rule of law condemns both."[13] Only occasionally judges held that acts for a lawful purpose, which were legal if done by an individual worker, were equally legal if done in concert, provided the means were not criminal.[14] The majority of courts at least up to the middle of the eighteenth century, considered the typical union activities to constitute criminal conspiracies. However, as in other countries, this policy did not prevent workers from forming unions and undertaking concerted actions when they believed their strategic position favorable.

A period of toleration followed the period of
attempted suppression of the labor movement.

The continual growth in the economic and political strength of the labor movement in the face of vigorous private and official counteraction—in a number of countries together with an increasing trend to modernize basic earlier concepts—sooner or later caused governments, and sporadically also employers, to modify their policies with respect to the demand of workers for freedom to organize. A period thus began in which the mere establishment of labor organizations was no longer considered an illegal or even criminal act, and in which individual workers could combine with-

13 Philadelphia Cordwainers, *Commonwealth* v. *Pullis*, Mayor's Court, Philadelphia (1806) in John R. Commons and Associates, ed., *A Documentary History of American Industrial Society*, Vol. 3 (1910), pp. 59 ff., 233.

14 See, for example, *Commonwealth* v. *Moore et al*, Mayor's Court, Philadelphia (1827), the same, Vol. 4, pp. 99 ff., 255.

out being prosecuted for doing so. But there was still great reluctance on the part of the judiciary to treat freedom to organize as a right with a remedy in court. The law, now as before, did not protect workers against employer discrimination on account of political or union activities or membership in a political organization or union. Antiunion activities of employers, such as refusal to employ unionists or workers who did not promise that they would not join a union and would not otherwise participate in concerted actions, were not unlawful. Nor did labor organizations enjoy the same protection as did other associations. Courts and administrative agencies tended to apply and interpret old and new law in a manner which rendered the exercise of freedom to organize and the functioning of unions difficult.[15]

The change from the policy of suppression to the policy of toleration began in the German area, when in 1861 and 1863, respectively, the Industrial Codes of the Kingdom of Saxony and the Grand-Duchy of Saxe-Weimar permitted employers and employees to combine to protect their economic interests. Within a short time numerous new local and central labor organizations sprang up, especially in the highly industrialized Kingdom of Saxony. These organizations, however, had no legal personality. The new law provided for special protection of persons willing to work during a strike but not for protection against interference with the exercise of the freedom to combine.

In Prussia several bills proposing repeal of the prohibitions of alliances for joint action did not pass—among them one submitted by the government. Though these prohibitions were frequently disregarded, prosecution under the penal provisions of the Industrial Code gradually ceased.

---

[15] Justice Frankfurter of the United States Supreme Court, concurring in *A. F. of L.* v. *American Sash Co.*, 335 U. S. 538 (1949) appraised the legal situation in the period, here discussed, in these words: "Unionization encountered the shibboleths of a pre-machine age and these were reflected in juridical assumptions that survived the facts on which they were based. . . . The result was that economic views of confined validity were treated by lawyers and judges as though the Framers had enshrined them in the Constitution."

The ban of the code on occupational combinations was lifted in 1869, when the Reichstag of the North-German Confederation passed a new code, which was taken over by the German Reich in 1872. This new Industrial Code repealed the provisions under which industrial and commercial entrepreneurs, industrial and commercial employees, journeymen, or factory workers were liable to be punished for entering into agreements and combinations for the purpose of securing favorable wages and conditions of employment, especially by means of work stoppages or discharge of workers. But in contrast to general, especially contract, law participants were declared free to resign from such combinations and to cancel such agreements at will. Moreover, it was stated that the latter were not enforceable in the courts. The legal status of labor organizations thus was inferior to that of other associations. In addition, courts and administrative agencies including the police remained unfriendly to unionization and concerted labor activities. Finally, the statutory bans on combinations by employees not coming under the Industrial Code were not affected by the new legislation and remained in force up to the November Revolution of 1918.

Public authorities of all kinds became even more unfriendly to unions under the Law Against Socialists, which was in force from 1878 to 1890. Though this statute did not apply to unions as such, the close alliance beween the dominant "free unions" and the Social-Democratic Party offered opportunities to strike against these unions as well. The other unions, too, all of which were connected with parties of the center or left of it, were seriously affected. After the repeal of the Law Against Socialists, administrative agencies still were inclined to apply to unions the restrictions to which the law subjected political organizations. In addition, it was not at all infrequent that strikers were in difficulties with the police and criminal courts. Though the unions continued to grow in numbers and significance, a real change in public policy did not occur until the First World War.

French unions participated in the formation of the First International in 1864. Two years earlier a delegation of French workers had visited the international exhibition at London at the personal suggestion of Emperor Napoleon III. After the delegation returned, it reported on the British labor movement and its progress and demanded anew the repeal of section 414 of the Penal Code,[16] according to which combinations of employers to secure lower wages or of workers to compel work stoppages were as such punishable by imprisonment. The legislators softened the law by providing that work stoppages to force wages up or down or to impair the freedom of industry or work should be punishable only if they were accompanied by violence, assault, intimidation, or fraudulent action.[17] The International Exhibition at Paris in 1867 offered another opportunity for labor leaders of different countries to discuss the problem of freedom to organize. Subsequently, a committee of French workers undertook a study of social problems and unionism. It recommended the formation of union organizations in all occupations. On March 30, 1868 the government declared that it would not interfere with the activities of occupational organizations, unless they sought to impair the free exercise of trade and industry, and that the associations of employers and employees would enjoy equal toleration.

This meant for all practical purposes the factual recognition of freedom of employers and employees to organize. It called forth a spectacular growth of unionism. But severe setbacks followed. The Franco-Prussian War, the subsequent disorders under the regime of the Commune, and the state of siege (martial law), which existed until 1876, delayed the further progress of the labor movement.

[16] In the wording given to it in 1849.
[17] See p. 261.

Moreover, affiliation with the International was prohibited by the law of March 14, 1872.

In Britain complaints by employers that unions fomented strikes and acted against the law, together with serious disorders in Sheffield, during which a can of gunpowder exploded in the home of a worker, caused in 1867 the appointment of a Royal Commission to make a thorough investigation of the whole union problem. The majority of the members of the commission recommended in 1869 that unions be granted a limited legal status; the minority suggested that unions should be legally recognized and should no longer be considered illegal because they acted in restraint of trade. The government submitted two bills to the parliament: the Trade Union Act, 1871, and the Criminal Law Amendment Act, 1871. As a result of extension of the suffrage to new large portions of the working class, this was the first parliament in the election of which workers had played a significant role. Making use of their increased political influence, unionists exerted strong pressure on the legislators to change the existing law. Both government bills were passed.

The Trade Union Act, 1871, which is still one of the basic statutes governing the union law, provides that the purposes of a trade union are not unlawful under criminal or civil law merely because they are in restraint of trade, so as to render members liable to criminal prosecution for conspiracy or otherwise, or to render void or voidable any agreement or trust. But the customary internal trade union agreements regulating rights and obligations arising out of membership, as well as agreements between trade unions, are not directly enforceable in court.[18]

The Criminal Law Amendment Act, 1871, repealed the acts of 1825 and 1859. It provided among other things for imprisonment of every person who, with a view to coercing another for trade purposes, should "molest or obstruct"

18 Secs. 2-4. The term "trade union" covers employers' as well as labor organizations.

by persistently following anyone about from place to place, by hiding his tools, clothes or other property, by watching or besetting his house, or following him along any street or road with two or more other persons in a disorderly manner. This act did not contain the proviso of the repealed 1859 act that no one was to be held guilty of molestation or obstruction by reason merely of endeavoring peaceably and in a reasonable manner to persuade others to cease or abstain from work. Organized labor, therefore, interpreted the statute as making any kind of picketing illegal. Labor leaders demanded its repeal, since they felt, in the words of the Webbs, that "it seemed of little use to declare the existence of trade societies to be legal if the criminal law was so stretched as to include the ordinary peaceful methods by which these societies attained their ends."[19]

The protests of labor against the Criminal Law Amendment Act and its application by the courts led to the appointment of another Royal Commission. As a result of its work the Conspiracy and Protection of Property Act was passed in 1875. This act repealed the Criminal Law Amendment Act, 1871, and declared inapplicable to labor disputes the common law doctrine that an act which an individual may do with impunity may be criminal if done by a combination. Section 3 of the act provides that an agreement or combination by two or more persons to do or cause to be done any act in contemplation or furtherance of a trade dispute shall not be indictable as a conspiracy if such act committed by one person would not be punishable as a crime. The same is stated with respect to acts done in pursuance of an agreement or combination. The act still includes penal provisions dealing with intimidation or annoyance likely to occur in labor disputes. Such acts as were criminal under the Criminal Law Amendment Act are punishable if committed wrongfully and without legal authority with a view to compel another person to do or to

[19] Sidney and Beatrice Webb, *The History of Trade Unionism* (1894), p. 263.

abstain from doing things which he has a legal right to do or to abstain from doing.[20]

In Sweden the existence of general freedom of association has never been seriously questioned. Freedom of association has, at all times and in all its aspects, been considered a corollary of personal liberty. Combinations of workers as such were never treated as contrary to law, though provisions of the Penal Code and police regulations were for some time used to render union and other concerted labor activities precarious. Like employers in other countries, Swedish employers made vigorous efforts to prevent the formation and functioning of unions. The Master and Servants Act, though not proscribing labor organizations, in fact made combination difficult up to the beginning of this century, at least in agriculture. Opposition of agricultural employers to concerted labor activities was so strong and effective that until recently an organized worker would hardly have been able to find employment on a farm. This retarded the rise of unionism, since Sweden until late in the last century was primarily an agricultural country. But with increasing industrialization a strong labor movement came into existence, which grew so fast that Sweden now is considered the country with the largest relative union membership. The economic and political strength of the labor movement is correspondingly great.

Most of the unions which were formed in the nineteenth century sought to overcome employer opposition by fighting tactics, especially strikes. Their ideology became Marxist by the 1880's, and close co-operation between unions and the Social-Democratic party became the fundamental policy of the labor movement. The Confederation of Trade Unions—still representing the vast majority of Swedish unions and organized workers—was established under the influence

[20] Organized labor was so satisfied with the new legal situation that at the Trade Union Congress at Glasgow in October 1875, the Home Secretary and the Conservative Party received so much praise, that someone proposed an amendment deprecating such "fulsome recognition of the action of the Conservative Party." Henry Strauss, *Trade Unions and the Law* (1946), p. 8.

of the Congress of the Social-Democratic party in 1898. For some time all members of the Confederation had to belong to the party, and the bylaws of member unions still may and usually do provide that their members have to enlist automatically and collectively with the exception of those who reserve the right not to do so.

The growing size and power of the labor movement caused Swedish employers to organize likewise. In 1902, only three years after the establishment of the Swedish Confederation of Trade Unions, they formed the Federation of Swedish Employers—a central organization to which the great majority of important employers belong. The employers associations opposed the strong socialist influence upon the unions as well as alleged lack of discipline in strikes. But like the government most of them did not directly question the freedom of workers to form and join unions, though they would have preferred that the employees did not exercise it. Rather soon the struggle between organized management and labor became one about the limits rather than the existence of the workers' freedom to organize.

The Federation of Swedish Employers before long became convinced that under the given circumstances recognition of unionism and regulation of wages, hours, and other conditions of employment through collective bargaining was the desirable policy. In 1906 the two central organizations of management and labor entered into an agreement in which they undertook to respect each other's right of association and simultaneously determined its limits.[21] The so-called "1906 compromise" laid down provisions to be embodied in the collective contracts made between the members of both organizations—a technique employed in subsequent master agreements regulating conditions in the labor market. The provisions state that the

[21] As will be seen throughout this study, both Swedish unions and management have sought to forestall governmental intervention in industrial relations by adjusting controversial issues, which in other countries had to be settled by legislative action, in direct negotiations and basic agreements.

right of association of either side must not be interfered with; that the employer has the right to direct and assign the work, to hire and discharge workers at his own discretion, and to employ workers regardless of whether they are organized; and that workers, who believe that they have been discharged under circumstances which may be considered an interference with the right to organize, may, before other steps are taken, demand an investigation through their organization to vindicate their rights. In Sweden freedom of employers and employees to organize thus was guaranteed by private contract before public law took over protection of it. Regulation by collective agreement proved so satisfactory that thirty years elapsed before the legislature became concerned with this matter and passed the act respecting the right of association and the right of collective bargaining.

In the United States, a new era of public policy regarding unionism was ushered in when in 1842 the Supreme Judicial Court of Massachusetts issued its decision in the *Commonwealth* v. *Hunt* case.[22] "Though men may band themselves together to effect a criminal object under the disguise of a trade union," stated Chief Justice Shaw, "such a purpose is not to be assumed without positive evidence." The court acquitted the defendants, setting forth that a union is lawful or unlawful as the means by which it attempts to reach its objectives are lawful or unlawful. This decision contributed much to dispel the dogma that unions as such were unlawful conspiracies at common law. But it still was a long time before workers and their organizations could exercise full freedom of association without governmental interference of one kind or another. Prosecutions of unionists for conspiracy subsided gradually. Moreover, a number of state statutes were enacted designed to make concerted labor actions legal. Many states by now have embodied the *Commonwealth* v. *Hunt* doctrine in their written law. In a number of states, however, legisla-

[22] 45 Mass. 111 (1842).

tion was passed to restrict collective labor activities. In addition, courts of equity frequently prevented concerted actions, now considered lawful, by issuing injunctions on the ground that the employer otherwise would suffer irreparable injury to his property without adequate remedy at law. Expanding the theretofore traditional definition of property by recognizing property rights in intangibles, such as the expectation that customers will continue to do business with one's enterprise, and declaring employers entitled to the good will of their employees, the courts felt authorized to enjoin strikes, picketing, and boycotts.

The Sherman Act of 1890[23] became another impediment to customary union activities. It was the first of the anti-trust laws, which proscribe contracts and combinations in restraint of trade and the establishment of monopolies. Whether the act applied to combinations of workers also was at first controversial. The controversy was ultimately settled by the United States Supreme Court.[24] Thirty-seven years after the British legislators had provided that the purposes of a union are not unlawful merely because they are in restraint of trade, this decision declared that the act made illegal every contract, combination, or conspiracy, *whoever may be the parties to it,* if it directly or necessarily operates in restraint of trade or commerce. Accordingly, the court interpreted the statute as prohibiting activities by combinations of workers which have the effect of restricting interstate commerce. It held further that under the act suits for damages might be brought against individual union members. The decision was very serious for labor organizations as well as their members. Unions felt that unqualified application of the Sherman Act to all concerted labor activities would render effective exercise of their functions difficult, if not impossible. In addition, the decision made the attachment of union funds possible and endangered

[23] 26 Stat. 209, amended by act of Mar. 3, 1911, 36 Stat. 1167.
[24] *Loewe* v. *Lawlor*, 208 U. S. 274 (1908); *Lawlor* v. *Loewe*, 235 U. S. 522 (1915); known as the Danbury Hatters case.

the personal assets of individual union members. The judgment of the United States Supreme Court, therefore, was vigorously attacked by organized labor. Agitation began immediately to bring about a change of the law.

In 1914 the United States Congress passed the Clayton Act.[25] This statute provides, among other things, that the labor of a human being is not a commodity or article of commerce and that the antitrust laws should not be construed to forbid the existence and operation of labor organizations, instituted for the purposes of mutual help, and not having capital stock or conducted for profit. Nor should the antitrust laws be interpreted as forbidding or restraining individual members from lawfully carrying out the legitimate objectives of such organizations. The act further states that these organizations or their members should not be held to be illegal combinations or conspiracies in restraint of trade, under the antitrust laws.

In addition, the act introduced restrictions of injunctive relief in labor disputes. It provides, in particular, that no restraining order or injunction may be granted by a federal court in cases between an employer and employees, or between employers and employees, or between employees, or between persons employed and persons seeking employment, involving a controversy concerning terms or conditions of employment, unless it is necessary to prevent irreparable injury to property, or to a property right, of the party making the application, for which there is no adequate remedy at law. But even if the statutory conditions for the issuance of a restraining order or injunction exist, it may not prohibit persons, whether singly or in concert, from doing acts such as terminating a relation of employment, ceasing to work, or persuading others by peaceful means so to do; or watching any place where such persons may lawfully be, for the purpose of peacefully obtaining or communicating information, or peacefully persuading any person to work or to abstain from working; or ceasing to

25 38 Stat. 730.

patronize or to employ any party to such a dispute, or persuading others by peaceful and lawful means so to do; or peaceably assembling in a lawful manner, and for lawful purposes. Moreover, no injunction may forbid any act which might lawfully be done in the absence of a labor dispute as mentioned by the statute. The act also rules that none of the activities specified in the provisions restricting injunctive relief may be considered a violation of any law of the United States.

These provisions were widely considered to exempt labor organizations from the antitrust laws, to make their customary fighting tactics, such as striking, picketing, and boycotting, expressly legal, and to prevent management from using the injunction as its counter-weapon in industrial warfare. The United States Supreme Court, though recognizing that under the Clayton Act a labor organization as such could not be regarded as an illegal combination or conspiracy in restraint of trade, however, held in *Duplex Printing Press Co.* v. *Deering*[26] that there was nothing in the statute "to exempt such an organization or its members from accountability where it or they depart from its normal and legitimate objects and engage in an actual combination or conspiracy in restraint of trade. And by no fair or permissible construction can it be taken as authorizing any activity otherwise unlawful, or enabling a normally lawful organization to become a cloak for an illegal combination or conspiracy in restraint of trade as defined by the antitrust laws." Moreover, the court found that the restriction upon the granting of injunctions, and also the relaxation of the provisions of the antitrust and other federal laws, were confined to dispute cases between an employer and employees and between those persons enumerated in the Clayton Act, and to controversies concerning terms or conditions of employment. Finally, in *American Steel Foundries* v. *Tri-City Central Trades Council*,[27] the same court

26 254 U. S. 443 (1921).
27 257 U. S. 184 (1921).

set forth that the Clayton Act did not legalize concerted labor activities theretofore held illegal. In short, the act was interpreted as declaratory of existing law and as not substantially changing the legal status of concerted labor activities.

Freedom of workers to organize now is
recognized and protected as a right.

The governments of the countries here discussed no longer merely tolerate certain collective labor actions. They have recognized, in one way or another, the right of individual workers to form, join, and assist labor organizations and to engage in other concerted activities for the purpose of protecting mutual interests, as well as the right of the organizations to pursue their bona fide objectives freely. Statutory provisions and judicial and administrative practices, inconsistent with the right to undertake such concerted activities, have been removed. This alone has strengthened the power of unions in such a degree that in the United Kingdom further reaching legislative measures for the protection of the right to organize apparently have not been considered necessary.

In other countries constitutions or statutes, or both, have expressly stated that workers shall have the right to form and join organizations of their own and otherwise to act in concert to safeguard and advance their legitimate, common interests. This constitutional or statutory right now enjoys legal protection at least similar to that granted to other comparable rights. In a number of countries special legislative steps have been undertaken to protect the free exercise of the right against interference, so that it can be enforced without resort to industrial warfare. Disputes about freedom to organize are no longer disputes involving merely interests but disputes about a right. Impingement of this right has been declared unlawful no matter whether it is committed by private persons or groups, or by public authorities. Job seekers as well as employed individuals have been brought under protective statutes. Traditional legal doctrines have been discarded, and measures have been taken that are unorthodox from the angle of traditional legal theory.

About the turn of the century, after a long period of depression, British unions entered into a new phase of vigorous activity. Organizing campaigns were undertaken with special emphasis upon unskilled workers. In 1900 the Labor Representative Committee was established out of which the British Labor Party developed. The Conspiracy and Protection of Property Act of 1875, which was mentioned above, had made strikes legal "in the broadest terms."[28] This did not exempt union officers and members from civil liability for unlawful acts.[29] But it was commonly supposed that a union as such could not be sued to pay damages since it was not a legal person. In the Taff Vale case,[30] however, an injunction and damages were granted not only against union officers but also against the union itself. The House of Lords emphasized that the legislature had not authorized "the creation of numerous bodies of men capable of owning great wealth and of acting by agents with absolutely no responsibility for the wrongs they may do to other persons by the use of that wealth and the employment of those agents."[31] The unions immediately began a vigorous campaign against this doctrine arguing that they could not perform their legitimate functions without occasionally causing damage to employers.

[28] Lord Coleridge, C. J., in *Gibson* v. *Lawson*, 2 Q.B. 545, 558 (1891).
[29] See, for example, *Allen* v. *Flood*, A.C. 1 (1898) and *Quinn* v. *Leathem*, A.C. 495 (1901).
[30] *Taff Vale Railway Co.* v. *Amalgamated Society of Railway Servants*, A.C. 426 (1901).
[31] The United States Supreme Court referred to the Taff Vale decision when it held in *United Mine Workers* v. *Coronado Coal Co.*, 259 U.S. 344, 390 (1922), that unincorporated unions, recognized as distinct entities by numerous acts of Congress, as well as by the laws and decisions of many states, are suable as such in the federal courts, upon process served on their principal officers, for the torts committed by them in strikes, and that their strike funds are subject to execution.

A Royal Commission was appointed to investigate the problems involved. It reported in 1906. The main report recommended most emphatically that—apart from enacting two provisions designed to safeguard proper benefit funds and to give unions an opportunity to protect themselves against liability for "unauthorised and immediately disavowed acts of branch agents"—the law contained in the Taff Vale decision should not be modified. "When Trade Unions come in contact by reason of their own actions with outsiders, and, *ex hypothesi,* wrong those outsiders, there can be no more reason that they should be beyond the reach of the law than any other individual partnership or institution."

The Trade Disputes Act, 1906, however, reversed the doctrine of the Taff Vale decision. It provides in section 1 that an act done in pursuance of an agreement or combination by two or more persons shall, if done in contemplation or furtherance of a trade dispute, not be actionable unless the act, if done without any such agreement or combination would be actionable. The Trade Disputes Act, 1906, thus exempts persons engaged in industrial disputes from liability for the civil wrong of conspiracy, just as the Conspiracy and Protection of Property Act, 1875, protects them against prosecution for criminal conspiracy. Section 2 declares lawful peaceful picketing for the purpose of obtaining or communicating information, or of persuading any person to work or abstain from working. Section 3 removes liability for an act done in contemplation or furtherance of a labor dispute on the ground only that it induces some other person to break a contract of employment, or that it is an interference with the trade, business, or employment of some other person or with the right of some other person to dispose of his capital or his labor as he wills. While these sections preclude legal suits against *persons* for *acts done in connection with labor disputes,* section 4 of the statute provides that legal actions against a *trade union,* under its own name or by representative procedure, in respect of any tortious act alleged to have been committed by or on behalf of it, shall not be entertained by any court, *no matter whether the act was done in connection with a labor dispute or not.*

Workers and unions thus attained all the immunities they had sought. The general strike of 1926, however, caused the parliament to pass the Trade Disputes and Trade Unions Act, 1927, which included some restrictions of the unions' great liberty of action. The statute declared illegal strikes and lockouts for any purpose going beyond the furtherance of a labor dispute within the trade or industry in which the strikers or employers concerned were engaged, if they were calculated to coerce the government either directly or by inflicting hardship upon the community. Persons instigating or supporting such strikes or lockouts, or inciting others to participate in them, were declared liable to criminal punishment. The law governing intimidation through picketing was made more severe. The act further made it illegal to require a member to contribute to the political fund of a trade union unless he had given written notice of his willingness to contribute. Civil servants were prohibited from joining unions which were not limited exclusively to civil servants or pursued political objectives, or were affiliated with a political party or any other organization admitting as members persons other than civil servants. Finally, local and other public authorities were forbidden to make union membership or nonmembership a condition of employment, or to make it a condition of a contract that any person to be employed by any party should or should not be a member of a trade union.

British organized labor protested strongly against the act and made repeatedly great efforts to obtain its repeal or at least amendment. Accordingly, the statute was repealed by the Trade Disputes and Trade Unions Act, 1946, soon after a new labor government had come into power. British unions have again the same legal status which they had before the Trade Disputes and Trade Unions Act of 1927 became law.

In France the labor movement resumed its upward trend from 1877 on. By 1883, 587 unions with a membership of 50,000 (and 101 employers' associations) were active in many regions of the country. The demand for express statutory recognition of the right of employers and employees to organize into occupational associations, accordingly, became more and more urgent and widespread. The pressure came not only from the Socialist but also from the new Christian Workers' movement and from the employers' associations. In 1884 the legislature passed the Waldeck-Rousseau Act.[32] It repealed the law Le Chapelier of 1791 as well as Article 416 of the Penal Code which had provided for punishment of interference with the freedom of industry or work by means of fines, prohibitions, restrictions, or interdictions, pronounced under a concerted plan. While the general right of association of all citizens was not recognized by a statute until the law of July 1, 1901 was enacted, the Waldeck-Rousseau Act introduced the principle that unions or other occupational organizations may be formed freely without governmental authorization. Occupational organizations were defined as organizations which have the sole objective to study and defend economic, industrial, commercial, or agricultural interests.

The principle of freedom to organize was not questioned again in France until after the armistice of 1940. A decree of that year dissolved the central organizations of both workers and employers. The Labor Charter, issued by the Vichy regime, eliminated freedom to organize almost completely. The bulk of the members of the dissolved unions shunned the governmentally supervised, compulsory organizations which the government attempted to set up

---

[32] J.O. No. 81, Mar. 22, 1884.

under the Charter and banded together clandestinely in the resistance movement. After the liberation the provisional government repealed the Labor Charter[33] and restored the right to organize. The unions and central organizations existing on October 3, 1939 were reinstated in the rights and duties they had at the time of their dissolution. Members of their governing bodies and officers were given back their former positions and the pre-armistice law concerning occupational organizations was re-established. The new Constitution, as adopted by the National Constituent Assembly in 1946,[34] declares in its preamble that everyone may defend his rights and interests by collective action and may join the organization of his choice.

As discussed above, employers recognized the freedom of wage earners to organize at a relatively early stage of the Swedish labor movement. But they were not inclined to grant equal recognition to, and to bargain with, unions of salaried employees which came into existence in growing numbers as progressing industrialization—especially from the First World War on—caused a considerable increase in salaried employees. Most firms opposed unionization of their nonmanual workers because they believed that their positions linked them so closely to management as to preclude intervention by unions in their relations with their employers. Salaried employees, on the other hand, felt that modern production and business methods had made their relations with the employing interest so impersonal that they were now a special wage-earning group with interests of their own which might conflict with those of the employers when their compensation, hours, and other conditions of employment were determined. They thus continued to organize into unions of salary earners and to demand the right to bargain collectively. In 1931 they

[33] Orders of July 27 and Sept. 26, 1944.
[34] J.O., Oct. 28, 1946, p. 9166.

formed a central organization of salaried private employees: The Employees' Central Organization (Daco).[35]

Hostility of many employers to unionism of salaried employees led to mounting tension. The government thus became apprehensive that the salary earners might undertake large-scale industrial warfare as the wage earners had done prior to the "1906 compromise." Accordingly, the legislators thought it desirable to pass legislation which would enable the salaried employees to enforce recognition of their freedom to organize and to bargain collectively by other means than industrial strife. The ensuing legislation, however, covered not only salaried workers but also wage earners. Protection of the latter's right to organize by orderly procedure thus is no longer dependent upon a contract. It now is also protected by statute.

The Act Respecting the Right of Association and the Right of Collective Bargaining of September 11, 1936,[36] for the reasons given above, did not create the right to organize but rather prohibits interference with it. The statute considers it to be infringed upon if measures are taken either by employers or employees to compel any employee or employer to refrain from becoming a member of or to resign from an employees' or employers' association. Pressure on an employer or an employee to abstain from exercising his rights as a member of or from working for such an association or for its formation are likewise regarded as unlawful interference. Finally, the statute prohibits actions calculated to cause prejudice to an employer or an employee on the ground that he is a member of an association protected by the act, exercises his rights as such, or works for such an association or its formation. The measures mentioned by the act constitute an infringement of the right to

[35] In 1937 a special central organization of salaried public employees was established: The Tjänstemännens Centralorganisation (TCO). In 1944 the Daco and TCO formed a joint central organization uniting all the groups of salaried employees in Sweden, the new Central Organization of Salaried Employees (TCO).

[36] Svensk Författningssamling, Sept. 22, 1936, p. 957, amended by act of May 17, 1940; the same, May 17, 1940, p. 636.

organize even if they are taken under a clause of a collective or other contract.

The German Reichstag recognized the right of unions to take care of the economic interests of employees for the first time positively and without qualification in the Auxiliary Service Act of 1916,[37] a temporary World War I statute regulating conscription of workers. To secure passage of the act and to attain the wholehearted support of organized labor, the government provided for participation of employers' and employees' representatives in the administration of the law and in the settlement of industrial disputes. On May 22, 1918 section 153 of the Industrial Code was repealed. Under this provision any person had been liable to be punished by imprisonment who compelled others by means of bodily force, intimidation, defamation, or boycott to participate in or to comply with agreements for the purpose of securing favorable wages and conditions of employment, or who prevented others by these means from withdrawing from such agreements.

On November 12, 1918, two days after the collapse of the Imperial Regime, the Council of the People's Commissars proclaimed that the right of association henceforth was not subject to any restriction and that this also applied to civil servants, government employees, agricultural workers, and domestic servants.[38] Since on the one hand the workers were in possession of the government, and since on the other hand both management and labor faced complex tasks in reconverting the economy from war to peacetime conditions under most uncertain economic and political circumstances, the German employers at that time were more inclined to come to terms with the unions than they had ever been. Before legislative measures could be taken, only three days after the proclamation of the People's Commissars, the leading unions and employers' associations

[37] RGBl. 1916, p. 1333 and RGBl. 1917, p. 87.
[38] RGBl. 1918, p. 1303. The Council of the People's Commissars, composed of Socialist workers, was the provisional German government during the revolution of 1918.

thus signed a master agreement,[39] which already contained the principles subsequently laid down in the constitution and the labor statutes of the German Republic. The unions were recognized as the proper representatives of the employees. Any restriction of the right to organize was declared inadmissible. In addition, the agreement provided that the employment conditions of all employees should be determined by collective contracts with the employers' associations and that these contracts should set up bipartite machineries for the settlement of industrial disputes. The new (Weimar) constitution[40] guaranteed freedom to organize for the purpose of protecting and advancing the conditions of employment and of the economy. This freedom was granted to everyone and to all occupations. Any agreement and action seeking to abridge or obstruct it was declared void.[41] The Works Councils Act of 1920[42] imposed the duty upon the works councils to safeguard the right to organize of the employees they represented.[43]

The principle of full freedom to organize was not attacked again until 1933 when the National Socialists took over the government. One of their first actions was to "suspend" this right "for the present" together with many other fundamental rights such as freedom of speech, personal freedom, freedom of the press, the rights to assemble peaceably and to form associations.[44] Because of their totalitarian concept of the state, the National Socialists denied the existence of any significant conflicts in interest between management and labor which would justify separate organizations of employers and employees. In accordance with totalitarian practice, however, they did not by

[39] Deutscher Reichsanzeiger No. 273, Nov. 18, 1918.

[40] RGBl. 1919, p. 1383, Art. 159.

[41] Art. 9 of the "Basic Law for the Federal Republic of Germany" (Bonn Constitution), enacted in 1949 to govern the federation of western German states (Laender) until "the day when a constitution adopted in a free decision by the German people comes into force," contains virtually the same provision.

[42] RGBl. 1920, p. 147 sec. 66 (6).

[43] See below, p. 78.

[44] Order for the Protection of People and State of Feb. 28, 1933, RGBl. I, 1933, p. 83.

any means attempt to convince management and labor of the correctness of their philosophy and to induce them, for example, to form voluntarily joint organizations. They proceeded by force, obviously because they realized that the prospects to popularize their view were slim. Moreover, a totalitarian system cannot tolerate powerful independent organizations of any kind or self-government in industry. Even more than the absolute state of the eighteenth and nineteenth century the National Socialists were bound to prohibit organized groups representing a variety of ideologies.

On May 2, 1933 the National Socialist storm troops seized the business offices of every free (socialist) union, arrested department heads, and confiscated the funds and other property of the unions. Other labor organizations for some time continued efforts to reach a compromise with the National Socialists. But they too had to dissolve "voluntarily" or were broken up. The employers' associations disappeared likewise. The government used the seized union funds to establish the German Labor Front, an organization including both employers and employees. Its official function was to safeguard industrial peace in a manner "which conforms with the National Socialist principles." In reality its purpose was National Socialist indoctrination of employers and employees, in other words of the bulk of the population. According to its constitution the Labor Front was a subsidiary organization of and supervised by the National Socialist party. Its "leader" was not elected by the members but was appointed by the leader of the party—Adolf Hitler. He also appointed and discharged the other officers as he saw fit. Though membership was officially voluntary, it was in fact compulsory. Employers and employees who would not join would have been considered politically not reliable, and the consequences might have been serious. But even this rigid system did not eliminate conflicts between employers and workers, and the

National Socialists more than once were compelled to compromise.

After the end of World War II the representatives of the powers occupying Germany decided at the Berlin (Potsdam) Conference to dissolve the National Socialist institutions and to authorize the free establishment of occupational associations subject only to the needs of military security. Measures were taken in the different zones of occupation to ensure the free formation of unions and employers' associations. In addition, new constitutions adopted in certain parts of Germany and the Bonn Constitution of 1949 expressly guarantee freedom of association in a manner similar to that under the Weimar Constitution. The German workers hastened to make use of the regained right to organize. By June 1947 about 41 per cent of the wage and salary earners belonged again to unions—a higher percentage than in the United States.[45]

Owing to the great demand for labor and favorable business conditions, antiunion activities of American employers abated temporarily during the First World War. This, together with the policy of the War Labor Board to protect unionism and collective bargaining, considerably strengthened the status of organized labor. After the war, however, numerous and powerful employers and employers' associations resumed the old course with new vigor and methods. There was much industrial unrest, and union membership fell from five millions in 1920 to less than three millions in 1933.

Campaigns to induce the United States Congress to pass legislation protecting the exercise of full freedom to organize, especially by limiting the use of the injunction in industrial disputes, resulted first in the enactment of the Federal Anti-Injunction Act (the Norris LaGuardia Act).[46] This procedural statute was the first federal law in which the

[45] See p. 183. An average of 90 per cent of the workers eligible to vote participated in the first plant elections after the war; in some instances the vote was as high as 98 per cent.
[46] Act of Mar. 23, 1932, 47 Stat. 70.

legislators formulated expressly public policy in regard to the workers' freedom to organize. They declared that:

> . . . under prevailing economic conditions, developed with the aid of governmental authority for owners of property to organize in the corporate and other forms of ownership association, the individual unorganized worker is commonly helpless to exercise actual liberty of contract and to protect his freedom of labor, and thereby to obtain acceptable terms and conditions of employment . . .

and that it is therefore

> . . . necessary that he have full freedom of association, self-organization, and designation of representatives of his own choosing, to negotiate the terms and conditions of his employment, and that he shall be free from the interference, restraint, or coercion of employers of labor, or their agents, in the designation of such representatives or in self-organization or in other concerted activities for the purpose of collective bargaining or other mutual aid or protection.

The act contains two main rules to protect these rights of labor. It defines and limits the power of the federal courts to issue injunctions in most instances of a labor dispute, and it declares unenforceable in the federal courts arrangements by which either party undertakes or promises not be become or remain a member of a labor or employers' organization or to withdraw from an employment relation in the event that he joins, or remains a member of, any such organization (yellow-dog contract). In addition, the statute provides that no officer or member of an organization, and no organization participating or interested in a labor dispute, shall be held responsible or liable in a federal court for the unlawful acts of individuals, except upon clear proof of actual participation in, or actual authorization or ratification of, such acts. A considerable number of states passed similar laws, some before, most after the federal act came into force.[47]

The fundamental philosophy laid down in the Federal Anti-Injunction Act, has guided the United States Con-

---

[47] Since 1947 the power of the courts to issue injunctions has been restored with respect to some types of industrial disputes.

gress in all subsequent legislative steps dealing exclusively or in part with the freedom to organize. Examples of defunct acts of this kind are the National Industrial Recovery Act of 1933[48] and the Bituminous Coal Conservation Act of 1935,[49] which were both declared unconstitutional by the United States Supreme Court, as well as the Bituminous Coal Act of 1937,[50] which expired on August 24, 1943. When the Railway Labor Act,[51] which covers labor relations in most of the railroad industry and air transport, was amended in 1934, an explanation of the purposes of the statute was added. Among these purposes are listed prevention of any limitation upon freedom of association of employees, preclusion of any denial, as a condition of employment or otherwise, of the right of workers to join a labor organization, and protection of complete independence of employers and employees with respect to self-organization.

To amplify and further clarify the principles laid down in the acts mentioned before and to establish machinery for their enforcement,[52] the United States Congress passed in 1935 the National Labor Relations Act (Wagner Act).[53] Section 1 of the statute states the dual objective of the legislators as: to promote industrial peace and equality of bargaining power of management and labor, both by encouraging the practice of collective bargaining and by protecting the exercise by workers of full freedom of association, self-organization, and designation of representatives of their own choosing, for the purpose of negotiating the conditions of their employment or other mutual aid or protection. Owing to the experience that "the denial by employers

---

48 Act of June 16, 1933, 48 Stat. 195.
49 Act of Aug. 30, 1935, 49 Stat. 991.
50 Act of Apr. 26, 1937, 50 Stat. 72.
51 Act of May 20, 1926, 44 Stat. 577, amended by act of June 21, 1934, 48 Stat. 1185; act of Apr. 10, 1936, 49 Stat. 1189; act of June 25, 1936, 49 Stat. 1921; and act of Aug. 13, 1940, 54 Stat. 785.
52 See *National Labor Relations Board*, H. Rept. 969, 74 Cong. 1 sess., p. 1 and S. Rept. 573, 74 Cong. 1 sess. (1935), p. 1.
53 Act of July 5, 1935, 49 Stat. 449, amended by act of June 23, 1947, 61 Stat. 136.

of the right of employees to organize and the refusal by
employers to accept the procedure of collective bargaining"
had caused strikes and other industrial strife which had
seriously interfered with the smooth functioning of the
American economy, the act was designed not only to protect
but also to encourage unionism and to make it strong
enough to overcome employer opposition.[54] Hereby the
legislators hoped to safeguard the fundamental freedom
of association of workers as well as to restore and preserve
general prosperity. For constitutional reasons the law
covers only employers and employees engaged in activities
affecting commerce among the several states forming the
United States of America, and between these states and
foreign countries. Though some classes of such employers
and employees are excluded from the coverage of the
statute, the scope of its application is very broad. Ten states
and the Territory of Hawaii have enacted similar labor
relations acts. Other states, too, have declared interference
with the right to organize unlawful. The constitutions of
some states, such as Florida, Missouri, Nebraska, New York,
and South Dakota, guarantee this right explicitly. The
National Labor Relations Act and a large number of state
laws ban "yellow dog" contracts.

The Federal Anti-Injunction Act has had the intended
effect of restricting the use of the injunction in labor disputes very considerably. The United States Supreme Court
decided that the act also prevents the issuance of injunctions in case of alleged violation of the antitrust law.[55] In

[54] A federal Circuit Court of Appeals explained the significance of the National
Labor Relations Act in these words: "The right of employees to form labor
organizations and to bargain collectively through representatives of their own
choosing with employers has long been recognized. The right is protected by
the Constitution against *governmental* infringement, as are the fundamental
rights of other individuals. But prior to the National Labor Relations Act no
federal law prevented *employers* from discharging employees for exercising
these rights or from refusing to recognize or bargain with labor organizations.
The National Labor Relations Act created rights *against employers* which did
not exist before." The court added that, since Congress granted these rights,
it also may take them away if it deems a change in policy advisable. *National
Labor Relations Board* v. *Edward G. Budd Manufacturing Co.,* 169 Fed. (2d)
571, 577 (1948).
[55] *Milk Wagon Drivers' Union* v. *Lake Valley Co.,* 311 U. S. 91 (1940).

addition, it now holds that, in the light of present public policy as formulated in the anti-injunction and other labor laws, the allowable area of union activity can no longer be restricted as it was in older decisions. Accordingly, it considers unions exempted from the antitrust laws as long as they act in their self-interest and do not combine with nonlabor groups.[56]

PUBLIC POLICY TOWARD ORGANIZED BODIES OF WORKERS OTHER THAN UNIONS

The preceding discussion indicates that present-day unions differ in many respects from the organizations which governments sought to suppress in the initial stage of the labor movement. Most of them do not by any means consider their functions limited to negotiating the employment conditions of workers in single enterprises or localities. The big central and top organizations in particular look upon themselves as representatives of whole segments of the economy and the population if not of the laboring class as such, and they engage not only in economic but also in a great variety of other activities. Modern unionism, in the typical case, then, rests upon a comprehensive community of interest arising out of such factors as work in the same industry, skill in the same line of work, common vocation, connection with the same social class, common problems, political creed, or philosophy of life, and the like. Employees of an individual firm have additional common interests resulting from employment in the same enterprise or subdivision of it.

Despite the expansion of union activities into many fields, protection of these interests through collective bargaining and otherwise still is one of the most fundamental functions of unionism. The manner in which this function is performed under present-day conditions so affects the efficiency of the individual establishments and hence of the national

---

[56] *United States* v. *Hutcheson*, 312 U.S. 219, 231, 232 (1941). See *Hunt* v. *Crumboch*, 325 U.S. 821 (1945).

economy that not only the interests of the employees immediately concerned but also those of management and the public at large are involved.

Agencies representing workers in individual enterprises have been established by collective agreement.

Many an employer has believed that more beneficial results could be achieved for everyone if he could deal with representatives of his own staff because he has considered them better informed about his business and more interested in its prosperity than officials of "outside unions." The majority of unionists have been cool toward this concept and have viewed it as an attempt to maintain the superior bargaining position of management. But to be better equipped to handle industrial relations in single enterprises, unions have established shop committee, steward, or similar systems. Apart from that, the idea has sprung up in relatively recent times that unionism and the procedure of collective bargaining about wages and other conditions of employment should, in the interest of all persons and groups concerned, be supplemented by schemes especially designed to improve and secure co-operation between individual employers and their staffs.

This idea has met with considerable opposition on the side of management as well as organized labor. Both employers and unions have feared that any such plan might interfere unduly with their respective functions. Many of the former have rejected the suggestion because, in their opinion, the proposed devices would encroach upon functions and responsibilities of management which must be preserved in the general interest. Organized labor, on the other hand, has been afraid that institutions consisting solely of staff members would operate more or less under the direct or indirect influence of their employer and might be used to impede union activities. However, employers and unions in many countries have arrived at compromises and have signed collective agreements providing for some kind of permanent machinery for staff-management co-operation, such as management, works, or joint production committees.

In several European countries workers' organization in individual enterprises is regulated by law.

A number of governments have held that the problem as to whether or how workers of individual establishments should be organized for the specific purpose of ensuring employer-employee relations which make for maximum efficiency touches the public interest in such a measure that its solution should not be left exclusively to collective bargaining. They have taken legislative action establishing uniform rules. These enactments indicate, even more than the laws protecting the right to organize into unions and to bargain collectively, how far legal and social thinking has moved away from traditional concepts. They are typical of the most recent phase of the evolution of collective bodies of workers, and hence, as will be seen, are of significance for this study. The advent of the novel collectivities has affected union rights and obligations, and they have been assigned important rights and duties of their own. Moreover, they had to be fitted into the system of freedom to organize.

All of them have a number of features in common: the task to improve industrial efficiency through better co-operation, limitation of their direct field of action to single enterprises,[57] conceptual independence of unionism, and

---

[57] Some systems have provided for councils not only on the level of the individual enterprises but also on higher levels. Art. 165 of the German (Weimar) Constitution, for example, set up a pyramidical structure of workers councils, consisting of works councils in the single establishments as the base, district labor councils organized according to economic areas, and a national labor council as the apex. As to the functions of the higher bodies the article provided that the district labor councils and the national labor council, together with the representatives of the entrepreneurs and of other interested groups, should form district economic councils and a National Economic Council. These economic councils were assigned the right and duty to deal with general economic problems and to co-operate in the execution of laws concerning socialization. The constitution further provided that the national government

statutory regulation of their formation, composition, functions, and relations to individual workers. In addition, most of them have been conceived as the desirable device to achieve what has been called "democracy in the enterprise." Apart from such similarities, marked differences exist. Since the development of the new types of organized bodies was a result of a great variety of factors, their history, character, types, and functions have not by any means been uniform.

Wartime needs were one of the factors that have given rise to public policies favoring intra-plant labor organization. The necessity to increase and accelerate output, to minimize industrial disputes, or to secure the wholehearted collaboration of the workers, caused a number of governments to promote the establishment of employee representative or similar systems at the level of the establishment during one or both world wars.

The German Auxiliary Service Act of 1916 established, for these reasons, the right of workers' committees to protect the interests of employees in individual enterprises and recognized the wage-earning staff as an entity capable of being a party to a labor dispute and settlement proceedings. The British government, in the same year, set up a Committee on the Relations between Employers and Employed under the chairmanship of J. H. Whitley, at that time the Speaker of the House of Commons. Its purpose was to make suggestions for improvements in labor relations and

---

should consult the National Economic Council before it introduced bills dealing with fundamental questions of social and economic policy. The National Economic Council was entitled to propose such bills itself. If the national government did not approve them, it had nevertheless to submit the bills to the legislature with a statement of its own viewpoint; the Council could have the bill supported before the legislature by one of its members. Finally, the constitution provided that functions of control and administration could be transferred to the labor and economic councils within the fields assigned to them. Only parts of this constitutional program were put into practice during the short life of the Republic.

The British Whitley plan similarly provides not only for joint works committees representative of the management and employees in individual establishments but also for district councils in conjunction with national councils.

to recommend means for systematic review of industrial conditions affecting these relations by those concerned, with a view to improving conditions in the future. This, accordingly, was more than a temporary war project. The Whitley Committee, taking the view that "it is not enough to secure co-operation at the centre between National Organisations—it is equally necessary to enlist the activity and support of employers and employed in the districts and in industrial establishments," recommended among other things the appointment of works committees representative of the management and the workers in individual enterprises. At the outbreak of the Second World War many such committees existed, and British war labor policy again relied heavily on them.

The United States government established in 1942 a War Production Drive Headquarters in the War Production Board to determine policies under which joint labor-management committees in war and other plants could best contribute to war production and to implement these policies by contact with such committees and the armed forces. This was merely a war measure; in contrast to the United Kingdom, only a few hundred such committees have outlasted the armed conflict.

In a number of instances systems of the type here discussed have been established or re-established as a phase of efforts to overcome economic effects of wars by maximizing production or to carry through reforms of the economic, social, or political order, or not infrequently, to do both. The law of the Control Council of April 10, 1946, authorizing again works councils in Germany,[58] as well as the act of March 28, 1947, dealing with the same subject in Austria, were due chiefly to considerations of the former kind. In this connection also the basic agreements may be mentioned through which the central organizations of

---

[58] In 1949 the Soviet Military Administration again abolished the works councils in its zone of occupation for reasons similar to those which caused their dissolution by the National-Socialist regime. It could not "switch them into line."

Swedish employers and employees introduced enterprise councils on August 30, 1946.

With respect to the French post-World War II legislation, instituting works committees,[59] the Ministry of Labor had this to say:

> It denotes the revision of capitalistic concepts of the 20th century and, discarding the notion that the worker is merely a tool, it has the purpose of permitting him to participate in the affairs of the factory as a whole, instead of performing solely the mechanical and fragmentary task which is necessarily his lot under division and mechanization of labor.

The French works committees are composed of the head of the enterprise or his representative and representatives of the employees. Their statutory function is to co-operate with the management "in the improvement of the conditions under which the employees generally work and live, and of the regulations bearing upon these matters." They are advisory bodies which have, among other things, the right and duty to investigate suggestions made by the management or employees with a view to increasing and improving the output of the establishment and, if suggestions are approved, to make recommendations for their adoption. Furthermore, they may submit suggestions relating to the general organization of the business. Consultation of the works committee on questions concerning the organization, management, and general development of the enterprise is compulsory. At least once a year the head of the undertaking must report to the committee on the activities of the firm and his plans for the next fiscal year. He also must inform the committee about the profits, and the committee may make suggestions for utilization of them. Within the scope of their functions the works committees are recognized as corporate bodies, which without special authorization and to the extent necessary for their operation may

[59] Order of Feb. 22, 1945, J.O. No. 46, Feb. 23, 1945, pp. 954-56, as amended by act of May 16, 1946, J.O. No. 115, May 17, 1946, p. 4251.

sue and be sued, undertake obligations, and acquire movable and immovable property.[60]

The recent French public policy, like the policies of other European governments, reflects the strong European movement toward what has been termed democracy in the enterprise. This movement, which has resulted largely from the impersonal character of employer-employee relations in the many large and incorporated industrial undertakings, has aimed at the establishment of "constitutional" conditions in individual enterprises. "Constitutional conditions" have been defined as employer-employee relations under which representatives of the staff participate, in one form or another, in the life of the firm as a whole.

But there have been works committee movements with much more radical objectives. They sprang up spontaneously to take control of the establishments. Their ultimate objective was control of industry generally and, finally, also of the government machinery. Workers' councils of this kind were outstanding features, for example, of the Russian revolution of 1917 and the Hungarian revolution of 1919. They also were active during the German revolution of 1918. In Hungary they were suppressed after a short time. In Russia their functions have by now been limited chiefly to assisting the government in carrying through its economic plans. The German revolutionary social-democratic government hastened to curb and regulate their activities. Experience with these spontaneous workers' councils, on the one hand, and with the older workers' committees set up under the Auxiliary Service Act of 1916, on the other hand, eventually led to the enactment of the German Works Councils Act of 1920,[61] which provided for intra-plant labor organization of the "democracy in the enterprise" type. This legislative course so enraged the radical minority within German labor that masses

---

[60] Decree of Nov. 2, 1945, J.O. No. 261, Nov. 6, 1945, pp. 7327-29.
[61] Act of Feb. 4, 1920, RGBl. 1920, p. 147, amended by act of Feb. 5, 1921, RGBl. 1921, p. 159, and act of Feb. 28, 1928, RGBl. I, 1928, p. 46.

of disappointed workers tried to prevent the final vote on the bill by storming the Reichstag building. It was passed while police and workers were fighting fiercely outside.

The German system rests upon the concept that certain analogies exist between the state and the enterprise. According to this concept, the organization of both types of bodies was at first absolutistic: the political ruler had the absolute control of the state and the employer had the absolute control of the enterprise. The organization of the state became constitutional when the subjects attained a voice in its administration and the respective rights and duties of the political head and of the citizens were fixed. In passing the works councils laws the German legislators intended to achieve something similar in the field of employer-employee relations. But their action was limited to this field. There was no intention to carry the analogous application of principles of political government any further and to change the status of the owner of the business in other respects. Free private enterprise was upheld as a principle and, hence, managerial freedom of enterprisers.

To put the constitutional principle into practice, legislators recognized that the staff of each enterprise is composed of two distinct groups which they granted the status of corporate entities: the wage-earning employees' unit, represented by the workers' council, and the salary-earning employees' unit, represented by the salaried employees' council. These units together, that is the whole staff, form the employees' unit represented by the works council.[62] This unit, too, was recognized as an entity.[63] The act provided that the workers' council and the salaried employees' council should consist of the wage-earning and salaried members of the works council, respectively. The statutory

[62] In American parlance this unit would be called the employer unit or plant unit.

[63] The Works Councils Act of 1920 also provided for a works assembly, composed of all the employees in the establishment. The chairman of the works council was entitled to convoke it and had the duty to do so at the request of the employer or of one fourth of the employees.

recognition of the units as entities made them "partial legal personalities." That means they became capable of taking in their own name such legal steps as are necessary to perform their statutory functions. The act thus granted them the right, subject to the terms of existing collective agreements, to agree with the employer on general work rules, to be a party in proceedings before the Conciliation Service, and to sue and be sued in labor courts in cases concerning protests against discharges as well as in a number of other cases.

While the German workers' council and the salaried employees' council take care of the special interests of those groups which they represent, the works council protects the common economic interests of all employees in relation to their employer. The act of 1920, however, gave it the important additional function of assisting the employer in attaining the objectives of the enterprise. The numerous single rights and duties, which were assigned to the works councils to perform these two tasks were partly of an advisory partly of a controlling nature. As to the advisory function the works council was entitled to submit recommendations, but it was not entitled to interfere with freedom of decision of management. The management had the duty to investigate the council's suggestions, but it was under no statutory obligation to accept them.

The supervisory functions of the German works council are of much greater significance. To carry them through, the original act gave it the right to be kept informed about transactions affecting the employment or activities of the employees; to receive quarterly reports on the situation of the business and of the industry, as well as the annual balance sheets and profits and loss statements with an explanation of their contents; and to be represented on the board of directors. It was further provided that employers, who did not fulfull their corresponding statutory obligations in due time, should be liable to fines or detention.

*American workers too have sought to gain the right
to participate in the affairs of their enterprises.*

The European public policies, discussed in the preceding paragraphs, have had the purpose of organizing the
employees, or groups of employees, within the individual
establishment in order to improve and secure co-operation
between its management and staff. A number of American
employers likewise have felt that relations with their
employees and the latter's productivity are improved if
they are given the opportunity to co-operate with management beyond, as the French Minister of Labor put it, "performing solely the mechanical and fragmentary task which
is necessarily their lot under division and mechanization
of labor." As stated by an American business leader:

> . . . Men wish to be consulted about the policies they must exe-
> cute. Consultation does not necessarily mean that management give
> up its authority. A business firm is not a debating society. Manage-
> ment does have the advantage of wider perspective and expert
> advice in making decisions. Yet it overlooks a golden opportunity
> if it fails to include its workers among its consultants.[64]

Where this concept has been recognized, it has caused
changes in basic employment policies, but it has not
resulted in any significant trend to recognize works councils of the European type.

American, like European, organized workers have engaged in campaigns for "industrial democracy."[65] However,
there has been little pressure to establish statutory works
councils of the European brand. Workers in the United
States rather have sought to attain their objective through

[64] Robert Wood Johnson, "Human Relations in Modern Business," *Harvard
Business Review,* September 1949, p. 531.

[65] Application of the principles of political democracy to employer-employee
relations, however, has been held impossible in a competitive-price system,
such as governs the American economy, especially on the ground that in such
a system considerations of price-cost relationships compel the employer to act
autocratically, whether he likes it or not. "And in a price system the employer
must go further to insist as a matter of principle upon a valid but outrageous
proposition, really true and false at the same time, that what he does is not the
concern of his employees." Charles E. Linblom, *Unions and Capitalism* (1949),
pp. 13-14.

collective bargaining. They have demanded contractual provisions giving them the right to participate in the affairs of the plant as a whole, not infrequently beyond the role merely of consultants. Two American students of the subject stated:

> Collective bargaining has two essential elements, the first political and the second economic.
> . . . There is a political settlement between the union and management over the division of authority. This involves the extent to which the union will participate in making decisions and the areas over which it will have control. A bargain is comparable to a treaty between nations marking the frontier between them and serving to keep peace.[66]

Owing largely to the fact that the authorities have excluded very few subjects from the area of the duty to bargain collectively, as established by the National Labor Relations Act, American unions frequently have been able to compel employers to enter into agreements providing for their participation in, or control of, matters which under the traditional concept of private property and enterprise have been generally considered to fall into the sphere of the exclusive functions of management. In this manner, a number of unions in the United States have obtained a contractual right to participate in managerial matters, which has given them the same, if not a more influential, role in solving managerial problems as European works councils and the like generally have had under public law. Apart from that, efforts have been made on the part of American labor to achieve the objective, sought by European statutes providing for a duty of the employer to inform the workers about the situation of the enterprise or for membership of workers' representatives on boards of directors, by buying stock in companies with which contractual relations exist. The president of one of the largest unions, for example, stated that

> . . . We bought one share of stock in every company under contract with our Union, so that our Research Department could sit in

[66] Edgar L. Warren and Irving Bernstein, *Collective Bargaining* (1949), p. 4.

on every Board of Directors' meeting, and see if we could not peep behind the Iron Curtain.[67]

American statutes have assigned important functions to groups of employees in individual enterprises.

As to public policy in the United States, it was mentioned above that federal war labor policy during both world wars included promotion of intra-plant labor organization for the purpose of maximizing efficiency and minimizing industrial disputes. But the federal and a number of state governments also have taken steps of a permanent nature. They too have enacted laws assigning important functions to units of employees at the level of individual enterprises. The character of these units, however, differs profoundly from that of the European units discussed previously. Moreover, unlike the European governments mentioned above, American legislators have not been satisfied with supplementing collective bargaining in its traditional form, leaving untouched the right of every union to represent the interests of its members. They rather have made the units the basic element in a novel system of collective bargaining, intended to reduce strikes and other forms of industrial strife or unrest.

Under the National Labor Relations Act, the most comprehensive federal statute dealing with the subject, and the state labor relations acts, modeled on the federal law, workers now are represented in collective negotiations by agents "designated or selected for the purposes of collective bargaining by the majority of the employees in a unit appropriate for such purposes." These agents are the exclusive representatives of all the employees in the unit. The act does not provide that only unions can be bargaining representatives. Any "individual or labor organization" can be chosen. In addition, "labor organization," in the language of the act, is not identical with "union." The

[67] United Automobile Aircraft and Agricultural Implement Workers of America (UAW-CIO), *Proceedings Twelfth Constitutional Convention* (1949), p. 13.

statute defines the term to mean "any organization of any kind, or any agency or employee representation committee or plan, in which employees participate and which exists for the purpose, in whole or in part, of dealing with employers concerning grievances, labor disputes, wages, rates of pay, hours of employment, or conditions of work."

Under this system then, there can be no collective bargaining until a "bargaining representative" has been chosen, and there can be no choice of such representatives unless units are first determined which are entitled to designate them and which they will subsequently represent. The majority of the legislators held that "employees themselves cannot choose these units, because the units must be determined before it can be known what employees are eligible to participate in a choice of any kind."[68] Consequently, the National Labor Relations Board, the governmental agency administering the act, has been given the power to determine appropriate units. The law states that this board "shall decide in each case whether . . the unit appropriate for the purposes of collective bargaining shall be the employer unit, craft unit, plant unit, or subdivision thereof."[69] These units are in the typical case coherent groups of workers within an enterprise. The plant unit includes all the workers in one plant. Inclusion of employees of several firms in one and the same bargaining unit has been exceptional. Membership in a bargaining unit is not contingent upon membership in a union. Members of various unions as well as unorganized workers may belong to the same unit. Nor does the law prescribe that the bargaining representative must be a union. There is nothing in the law which would prevent the making of a

[68] *National Labor Relations Board,* S. Rept. 573, 74 Cong. 1 sess. (1935), p. 14.
[69] See p. 231n.
American state labor relations acts, covering industrial relations in intrastate commerce, generally use the same principle. The state of Delaware recently departed from it and defined the collective bargaining unit as "an organization selected by secret ballot by a majority vote of the employees of one employer employed within the state who vote at an election specially called for the selection of such unit." L. 1947, H.B. 212, sec. 1 (k). This statute was repealed in 1949 by act H.B.1.

collective agreement with a bargaining unit composed of nonunion workers and represented by a duly chosen unorganized employee. American legislators generally have refrained from determining expressly the legal nature of the bargaining unit. There are no statutory provisions comparable, for example, to those which have defined the status of the (different) intra-plant units recognized by the German labor law.

Unions everywhere control the organization of employees at the level of the individual enterprise.

Governmental policies of the kind here discussed have produced various types of representation plans and collective bodies. Joint committees, including both representatives of management and the staff, as well as employee committees, composed exclusively of workers' representatives, have been established. Novel concepts of the nature of "the establishment" and of "the staff" have arisen, and groups of workers have been given collective rights and duties which do not tally with conservative thought. Sometimes the initiative was with the government, sometimes the stimulus was supplied by the workers. In the latter case, the movement occasionally was directed against orthodox unionism, but more often it was an outgrowth of unionist philosophy.

Although permanent institutions, which statutes have established in the course of the development, could theoretically operate without union participation, liberal governments have not by any means conceived of them as substitutes for the unions. On the contrary, there has been a marked tendency to grant the latter a strong influence upon the formation and activities of the new bodies. The opinion has prevailed that without the existence and cooperation of the unions the systems could not function effectively. Labor leaders in a number of countries have considered the statutory employee representation plans a challenge to traditional unionism in that they too combine workers into organic structures designed to deal with industrial relations, but not on customary unionist lines. After much opposition, they have, however, accepted the challenge, have regarded the plans as a new field for union activities, and have controlled them in a very high degree, no matter whether the statutes provided expressly for their direct participation.[70]

[70] Under the French law the employee members of the works committee are elected by the wage and salary-earning employees of the individual enterprises from lists of candidates drawn up by the most representative unions for each class of employees. Moreover, the basic order provides that it should not be construed as preventing the operation of any provisions respecting the activities or powers of works committees which are derived from collective agreements. The German Works Councils Act similarly emphasized that it was not intended to affect the right of unions to represent the interests of *their members,* especially by bargaining collectively for them. The act further provided that the wage-earning members should be elected by the wage earners and the salary-earning members by the salary earners of the enterprise, each from among their own ranks. Both types of representatives should be elected from lists of candidates by a direct and secret vote on the principles of proportional representation. In these elections unions competing in the individual establishments have played a similar role as competing parties play in political elections; they have submitted lists of their candidates and campaigned for them. The British Whitley Committee was appointed at a time when the authority of the legitimate union leadership was seriously threatened by the militant Shop Stewards' Movement, which worked toward transfer of authority to labor organized on the level of the work shop and toward the establishment of workers' control over the shops and industry in general. The unions have exercised a paramount influence upon the systems established on the recommendations of the Whitley Committee. In the United States unions have been designated as bargaining representatives in the vast majority of selections.

CHAPTER II

Nature and Protection of the
Freedom to Organize

When and where governments recognized the right to organize, differences of opinion as to its meaning and scope were accentuated. In the present stage of development frictions between governments and labor, governments and employers, or management and labor have been often due to conflicting views on the limits of the right. It is for this reason that efforts to define the nature of the right to organize will be discussed in this chapter and that policies with respect to its legitimate scope will be the subject of large parts of this volume.

The summary of the evolution of the right to organize, presented in the preceding chapter, is believed to facilitate an understanding of the various positions taken by governments, employers, and labor organizations with respect to its compass. The story of its development confirms the view that determining rights and duties of organized labor means, in the last analysis, defining the right to organize; or, to state it differently, that rights and duties of organized labor are constituent parts of the right to organize. In addition, our brief historical examination sheds light upon the factors which have gradually shaped contemporary government, management, and union policies with respect to freedom of association in general and the rights and obligations of organized labor in particular.

The following analysis of the nature of the freedom to organize will show that present views and regulations clearly mirror past experience.

NATURE OF THE FREEDOM TO ORGANIZE

Section 1 of the National Labor Relations Act declares, among other things, that it is the policy of the United States to protect the exercise by workers of full freedom of association. This programmatic statement is implemented by sections 7 and 8. Section 7 includes the provision that employees shall have the right of self-organization, to form, join, or assist labor organizations, and to engage in concerted activities, for the purpose of collective bargaining or other mutual aid or protection. Section 8 regulates the protection of these rights. In American everyday usage these rights of workers, taken together, are commonly called the "right to organize." This right, then, is considered to be one phase of the more comprehensive freedom of association. It is construed as the right of workers to make full use of this freedom by organizing into unions or engaging in other concerted activities for the purpose of mutual aid or protection.

*Frequently, freedom to organize also refers
to the right of employers to combine.*

In many countries pertinent enactments define right of association or right to organize as the right of *employers and employees* to form, join, or assist associations composed of employers or employees, respectively, to defend their specific interests in the labor market or, more generally, in the economic field. The convention concerning freedom of association and protection of the right to organize adopted by the International Labour Conference at its thirty-first session in San Francisco in 1948[1] defines freedom of occupational association of individuals as the right of workers and employers, without distinction, to establish and, subject only to the rules of the organization concerned, to join organizations of their own choosing without previous authorization.

[1] Art. 2; 127 countries voted for the convention, none against it, 11 abstained from voting.

In the United States, too, both employers and employees have the right of self-organization. But although the amended National Labor Relations Act includes some provisions designed to prevent infringements of the right of employers to associate, labor relations statutes in the United States generally do not mention this right explicitly, apparently, because it has never been questioned or seriously interfered with. Within the purview of the American antitrust and anti-injunction acts, however, employers engaged in concerted activities are subject to restrictions which are not imposed upon analogous activities on the side of labor.

In contrast, numerous foreign governments do not draw any distinction, as regards exercise of freedom to organize in the field of industrial relations, between employers and employees. Emphasizing the marked structural and functional analogies between unions and employers' associations, legal systems abroad have given them the same duties and the same rights. It is true, the legislators in foreign countries, as in the United States, have been primarily concerned with the protection of the exercise by workers of full freedom to organize, since the exercise of this freedom by *employers* has been interfered with less frequently and vigorously. Yet, they have believed that, in view of the principle of equality before the law, it should be explicitly provided that workers and employers have the same rights and duties both in the exercise of their right to organize and in operating their organizations.[2] Although this study is focused on the rights and duties of organized *labor* rather than *management,* it should be kept in mind that statements respecting the exercise, for example, by French,

2 The policy of the International Labour Organisation has been governed by the same principle. In submitting a proposed resolution on freedom of association to the General Conference, held at Geneva in 1947, the ILO moreover emphasized that "the experience which the world has had of totalitarian systems in the interval between the two wars has proved that the suppression or domestication of workers' organisations was followed very shortly by the suppression or domestication of employers' organisations." International Labour Office, *Freedom of Association and Industrial Relations,* Report VII (1947), p. 108.

German, and Swedish workers, of full freedom to organize also apply in principle to the exercise of this freedom by French, German, and Swedish employers.

Freedom to organize frequently has not been considered merely a phase of the freedom of association.

The right of employers and employees to organize for the purpose of protecting their respective common interests in the field of labor relations, with relatively few exceptions, has not been considered merely a component part of the fundamental rights to assemble peaceably or to form associations. It has been indicated in legislative enactments and otherwise that workers on the one hand, and employers on the other, may act in concert without assembling or establishing associations. Moreover, legal guarantee of the basic right of assembly and of association has been interpreted as a protection against interference by public authorities, while provisions guaranteeing specifically the right to organize of employers and employees have been drafted in such a manner as not only to preclude restrictive measures by governmental authorities but to prevent interference by private groups or persons. The legislative intent has been to shield the right from infringement by political and also by social forces. If the right to form and join occupational associations is embodied in the constitution, it is protected to a certain extent even against legislative measures. Finally, the fundamental freedom of association entitles individuals to combine for any lawful purpose. But there has been a certain tendency to define the objectives which unions or individual workers acting in concert may pursue if they want to come under the special protection of freedom to organize in the field of industrial relations.

Differences in the interpretation of the general right of association and the right to form and join occupational associations may explain in part why legislators and courts at times have considered it justifiable to recognize the one but not the other. It was mentioned above that in the United States, as in other countries, union activities for decades were treated as unlawful, although freedom of association was firmly established; and that, conversely, French workers attained the right to organize about seventeen years before full freedom of all citizens to associate was expressly recognized by statute.

Freedom of individuals to combine is a fundamental component of the freedom to organize.

A considerable number of rights have been considered essential elements of freedom to organize. One of the most fundamental of them is the freedom of workers to form and join occupational organizations. This freedom usually is protected by provisions in statutes or agreements prohibiting discrimination against job applicants or employees with regard to hiring, tenure or conditions of employment, discharge, promotions, demotions, transfers, etc., on the ground of union activities or membership.

In almost all liberal countries the opinion prevails that recognition of the right of workers to organize does not compel any employee to make use of it. Otherwise, according to common view, freedom to organize would not be a freedom but a duty. It is widely held that, in recognizing this freedom, the legislators primarily intended to expand the individual worker's freedom of action rather than to abridge it. Hence, employees may still exercise their freedom of will and choose not to organize. This freedom, which antedates the formal recognition of the right to organize, has been called negative freedom of association, as contrasted with the right to engage in concerted activities, which has been called positive freedom of association.

Complete freedom of every individual to choose his union, if he wishes to join one, has in many countries been considered an essential element of full freedom to organize. Occasionally, this principle also has been referred to in defense of the right to refrain from joining a union. If the worker is free to choose the union to which he wishes to belong, it has been said, he is also free to choose not to belong to any union.

Though the right to form and join unions is a very significant, if not the most significant, phase of the individual worker's right to organize, the latter also covers other types of concerted activities. Employees may establish organized bodies other than unions, and they may combine permanently or temporarily for a variety of purposes. This study mentions a number of labor groups, formed to bargain collectively or for other purposes, which are conceptually unrelated to unionism, and the establishment and operation of which are protected by industrial relations laws. In some cases the existence of such groups has been held so desirable that their establishment has been required by law, either directly or indirectly. The bargaining unit, which legally may be formed by unorganized workers and be represented by an individual, is an American example of a protected organized labor group conceptually unconnected with unionism. The National Labor Relations Act in the United States, further, defines the term "labor organization" to mean any organization of any kind, or any agency or employee representation committee or plan, in which employees participate and which exists for the purpose, in whole or in part, of dealing with employers concerning grievances, labor disputes, wages, rates of pay, hours of employment, or conditions of work.[3]

Prior to the development of large, stable labor organizations, it was not uncommon that nonunion workers com-

---

[3] Act of July 5, 1935, 49 Stat. 449, sec. 2 (5). The National Labor Relations Board held, for example, that a group of ten individual employees, seeking to procure a wage increase, constituted a labor organization entitled to protection under the National Labor Relations Act. *Gullett Gin Co., Inc.*, 83 NLRB No. 1 (1949).

bined temporarily to achieve certain objectives especially through picketing, work stoppages, or other militant actions. The origin of not a few of the present labor organizations can be traced back to such spontaneous undertakings. Unionism once firmly established, actions of that kind will tend to decrease. Yet, they still occur. Even unionists may engage in concerted activities in which their union is not involved, for example, in unofficial work stoppages. Agreements to act temporarily in concert generally come under the legal protection of freedom to organize, while the legality of the methods used in carrying through the actions—as in the case of permanent combinations—depends upon the general law. At any rate, the guarantee of freedom to organize of individual workers has not been construed as covering only freedom to act collectively through the medium of a union. The freedom to combine for the purpose of undertaking strikes or other drastic steps, for instance, has not been interpreted as applying only to strikes under union leadership. To give another example, the French Labor Code, prior to 1946, treated contracts made with occasional groups of employees as protected collective agreements.

In the United States, as mentioned above, an agreement regulating terms of employment, entered into with an appropriate bargaining unit composed of, and duly represented by nonunion workers, similarly, would be a valid collective agreement in the meaning of the labor relations laws. The principle that concerted activities of employees which bear a reasonable relation to their conditions of employment come under the protection of freedom to organize, even if no collective bargaining be contemplated or no union activity be involved, has been emphasized in the American National Labor Relations Act. Section 7 states in this respect that employees shall have not only the right to form, join, or assist labor organizations but also to engage in *other* concerted activities for the purpose of collective bargaining as well as *other mutual aid or protection.*[4] Finally, it may be mentioned that the British trade union law considers a trade union *any combination, whether temporary or permanent,* which is engaged principally in certain activities enumerated in the Trade Union Act, 1913.[5]

The right of organizations to operate freely is another fundamental element of freedom to organize.

Experience, as discussed in the preceding chapter, has shown that recognition of the freedom of workers to organize without protection of its actual exercise aggravates rather than reduces industrial unrest. This applies not only to efforts by individuals to combine and act in concert but also to efforts by labor organizations to perform their characteristic functions. If the right to organize is recognized, but the operation of the organizations is obstructed, they tend to resort to drastic action, for

> It is the development of the *right of action in combination* which makes it possible for a strong and organised body to take the place of the individual, necessarily weak and isolated. If the right of *action* in combination is not granted, the right of combination is merely delusive.[6]

Accordingly, it is now generally accepted that freedom of association in the field of industrial relations includes not only the right of individual employees (and employers) to band together, but also the right of their organizations to formulate and carry through their programs free from restrictive interference by public authorities or private individuals, as long as they act in conformity with the law of the land.

The convention concerning freedom of association and protection of the right to organize, adopted by the Inter-

---

[4] See *NLRB* v. *Phoenix Mutual Life Insurance Company,* 167 Fed. (2d) 983 (1948); cert. den., 335 U. S. 845 (1948). This doctrine was stated in the original text of the act; its statement was made still stronger when the Labor Management Relations Act, 1947, inserted the word "other" in front of the words "concerted activities."

[5] Sec. 1 (2).

[6] International Labour Office, *Freedom of Association,* Vol. I (1927), p. 66.

national Labour Conference at its San Francisco session in 1948, defines freedom of association of workers' and employers' organizations as the right to draw up their own constitutions and rules, to elect their representatives in full freedom, to organize their administration and activities and to formulate their programs, adding that public authorities shall refrain from any interference which would restrict this right or impede its lawful exercise. The United States government, in its reply to a questionnaire circulated by the International Labour Office in preparing the Conference, stated that these rights

> . . . seem inherent aspects of the right freely to associate. Unless the members of associations can decide for themselves the basis for their association and can determine democratically how their association shall be constituted and how it shall function, any right of free association would seem an empty theory, of little substantive import or practical value.[7]

The statement proposed to write expressly into the convention that public authorities which would impede organizations in their actual operation would violate the principle that governments must refrain from a negation of these rights.

Freedom to organize must not lead to infringement of the public law or interest.

It is self-evident that, in exercising the rights involved in freedom to organize, workers and employers, as well as their respective organizations, like other persons and organized bodies, must respect the law of the land.[8] The legislators, of course, are free to define "freedom to organize" and to restrict it, as they deem proper; but they will have to observe the rules governing amendment of the constitution where the latter positively protects the freedom against restriction. However, there is general agreement

[7] International Labour Office, *Freedom of Association and Protection of the Right to Organise*, Report VII (1948), pp. 30-31.
[8] So stated in Art. 8 of the international convention concerning freedom of association and protection of the right to organise, adopted by the International Labour Conference at its San Francisco session in 1948.

that legislative, judicial, or administrative measures impairing freedom to organize are incompatible with its recognition as a fundamental principle.[9] According to common
view, governments which accept the doctrine of freedom to
organize should ensure to workers as well as employers
maximum freedom to combine and to act in concert. In
determining the scope of this freedom they should, however, not neglect their paramount duty to maintain public
order and to protect the rights of the community as a whole.
It is generally accepted that the guarantee of freedom to
organize does not entitle organizations of labor—or employers—to pursue their objectives by unlawful means or by
means contrary to public morals, to disturb the public
order, or to endanger the security of the state.[10]

Many governments have defined the field of activity of
those workers' and employers' organizations which come
under the protection of the special law dealing with the
right to organize. The definitions in the countries primarily examined in this study have been so broad that they
have not been considered restrictive. The United States
National Labor Relations Act, which deals primarily with
the right to organize of labor, covers labor organizations
which exist for the purpose, in whole or in part, of dealing
with employers concerning grievances, labor disputes,
wages, rates of pay, hours of employment, or conditions of
work.[11] The definition of the purposes of protected
workers' and employers' organizations is: in France, study-
ing and defending economic, industrial, commercial, and
agricultural interests;[12] in Sweden, defense of the interests

---

[9] Art. 8 of the aforementioned international convention provides that "the
law of the land shall not be such as to impair, nor shall it be so applied as to
impair, the guarantees provided for in this convention."
[10] "Each side of industry is equally justified in organizing to protect its legitimate interests, and is equally unjustified in exploiting the needs of other sections
of the community for selfish or anti-social purposes, or in holding the community
to ransom for political or quasi-political objects." Political Committee of the
Constitutional Club, *Restrictive Practices; An Examination of the Effect of Restrictive Practices in Industry on Cost and Out-put* (London, 1949), p. 5.
[11] 49 Stat. 449, sec. 2 (5).
[12] Labor Code, Bk. 3, Art. 1.

of employers or employees, respectively;[13] in the United Kingdom, regulation of the relations between workers and employers, or between workers and workers, or between employers and employers, or the imposing of restrictive conditions on the conduct of any trade or business, and also the provision of benefits to members;[14] in the German Republic, it was protection and advancement of conditions of employment and of the economy.[15]

In a considerable number of countries regulations exist which associations of workers and of employers must observe to be entitled to the special privileges provided by the law protecting freedom to organize. Such regulations have laid down certain procedural rules concerning the establishment and management of the organizations, as, for example, registration and filing of financial or other reports. Like statutory definitions of workers' and employers' organizations, they have usually not been considered to restrict the right to organize or to interfere with its lawful exercise. Nor have they been regarded as subjecting the exercise of freedom of association to preliminary governmental authorization. It has been pointed out that organizations which pursue objectives other than those mentioned in statutory definitions, or which disregard the rules of procedure mentioned a few lines above may still be lawful. But they have to be satisfied with the status given voluntary, private associations by the general law.

---

[13] Act respecting the Right of Association and the Right of Collective Bargaining, dated Sept. 11, 1936, amended by Act No. 332 of May 17, 1940.
[14] Trade Union Act 1913, sec. 2 (1) and sec. 1 (2).
[15] (Weimar) Constitution, Aug. 11, 1919, Art. 159.
    Art. 10 of the convention concerning freedom of association, adopted by the International Labour Conference at its 31st session in 1948, states that, as used in the convention, the term labor organization means any organization of workers for furthering and defending their interests. This broad language and the discussion at the conference indicate that countries which ratify the convention are expected to recognize the right of employees to pursue, within the framework of the law of the land, political and any other objectives through their organizations. Proposals that the guarantee of the workers' freedom of association be limited to the relations between employers and employees or to the defense of social and economic interests, or to restrict the freedom of unions to participate in political activities, were rejected.

Lawful exercise of the freedom is protected against
interference by public authorities and private persons.

As mentioned above, it is commonly held that the law
governing freedom to organize should protect associations
against interference with their lawful activities not only by
public authorities, but also by private persons. In terms
of the right to organize of workers this means that labor
organizations should be accorded adequate protection
against employer interference with their establishment,
functioning, or administration. Agreements between the
central organizations of employers and employees, in which
the parties undertake to respect mutually the exercise of
the right of association, have been widely suggested as the
most desirable method of securing this protection. Such
basic agreements, indeed, have been made in several countries, for example, France, Germany, and the Scandinavian
area. Apart from that, many national laws prohibit employers from dominating or interfering with the formation
or conduct of labor organizations or from supporting them
financially or otherwise. In not a few countries special
protection has been provided for union officers and agents
against discharge on account of their union activities. Moreover, statutes have declared it an unlawful practice if
employers refuse to recognize the union or to negotiate with
it. Sometimes, for example in the United States, such
statutes apply only to unions which are considered truly
representative of the employees of the employer concerned.

However, employers are not the only private individuals
with whose interests labor organizations may come into conflict in exercising their freedom to carry through their
programs. Interests of labor organizations, considered legitimate by the law, may be at variance with interests of
individual employees, likewise regarded as rightful. One
of the most complex of the many problems raised by such
conflicts of interest has been that of protecting simultaneously the interest of labor organizations in bringing the

maximum of workers into the fold and the interest of individual workers in deciding freely whether they should join a union and which one. This problem will be discussed in the part dealing with compulsion to organize.

PROTECTION OF THE FREEDOM TO ORGANIZE

Various techniques are employed in the different countries to prevent and remedy infringements of the right to organize of individual workers or of labor organizations. Employees and unions may bring economic pressure on employers who interfere with their freedom of association. Governments which guarantee this freedom explicitly, however, have sought to reduce industrial warfare of this kind. Some countries have established special administrative or judicial agencies which workers or their organizations may petition for protection or redress if employers interfere with their rights. In a number of legal systems special regulations have been enacted dealing with violations of the worker's freedom of association. In many countries, however, no need has been seen for legal treatment of the effects of, and remedies for, actions imparing the right to organize, which would differ from the principles commonly governing the violation of rights. In such nations the general substantive law, possibly with the help of some special procedural rules, has been held likewise adequate to remedy infringements of the freedom to organize. Noncompliance with a contractual obligation to respect this freedom has been treated as a breach of contract, for which injured persons or organizations may demand redress under contract law.

European countries tend to protect the right to organize in the same manner as other rights.

The German (Weimar) Republic presented an example of the situation under an effective constitutional guarantee of freedom to organize. This guarantee was more than merely a declaration of public policy. It was implemented in the constitution itself by the provision that any agreement or action seeking to abridge or impair the freedom was unlawful.[16] This was interpreted as covering contractual as well as unilateral measures, and actions on the part of private persons or organizations as well as public authorities. The constitutional regulation meant that any legal transaction under private law and any measure taken by administrative agencies was by the law itself invalid if it infringed upon the freedom to organize. Everyone could simply ignore any such contractual provision or official directive without first having to take legal action to obtain a judgment declaring it null and void. Acts interfering willfully or negligently with the right to organize, moreover, gave rise to a claim for compensation for any financial damage, subject to the provisions of the civil code concerning torts or breach of contract, respectively, and injunctive relief could be sought.

Discriminatory discharges or refusals of employment because of union affiliation fell under the ban of the constitution. Employees, when given a notice of discharge, had the right to file a protest with the council of wage earning or salaried employees if suspicion existed that the notice was given on account of the worker's membership or nonmembership in a political, religious, military, or labor organization.[17] If the council considered the protest justified, it had to attempt to bring about an understanding with the employer. In case this attempt failed, the council or the employee concerned could sue at the labor court for continuation of the employment or compensation. If the labor court held the protest justified, it passed judgment against the employer either to re-employ the worker or to pay damages. The decision fixed the compensation to be paid in case re-employment was refused. Within three days after the judgment was served upon him, the employer had to

16 Art. 159.
17 Works Councils Act, secs. 84 ff., RGBl. 1920, p. 147.

notify the discharged worker whether he chose reinstatement or payment of damages. The employer had to bear the costs of the legal action no matter whether he won or lost.

In France as in Germany infringements of the right to organize may be remedied in court. In both countries most of the decisions have dealt with efforts to refuse the hiring of, or to discharge union workers. In France the yellow-dog contract has been a relatively frequent cause of complaints. Applying the principles of the civil code, decisions of French courts established the doctrine that discharges of employees merely because they are members of a union, or refusals to employ workers merely because they do not sign a binding promise that they will not join a labor organization, are unlawful if the guiding motive is animosity against the union or the desire to interfere with its operation. Such actions on the part of employers have been held to give rise to claims for damages because they constitute illegal interference with the right to organize and abuse of the right "to hire and fire."[18] Not only the individual worker concerned but also his union may claim

18 See Court of Cassation, Mar. 9, 1915, D. 1916.I.25; and Court of Cassation, Mar. 20, 1929, S.1929.I.351.

At least older decisions recognized that, under special circumstances, employers may have a legally justified interest in refusing employment of unionists or demanding a promise not to join a union. In the case decided on Mar. 9, 1915, for example, the Court of Cassation held that the municipal Casino of Nice did not act contrary to law when it refrained from hiring organized musicians or such musicians who refused to undertake the contractual obligation "to renounce temporarily their right to join a union," because it sought to protect itself against the possibility of prolonged interruption of its concerts by strikes, which would have ruined the enterprise. In view of the special circumstances of this case the behavior of the employer was considered to be motivated exclusively by the desire to safeguard important business interests rather than by antiunion bias.

American jurisprudence at the time of this French decision similarly considered employer insistence upon contracts making nonmembership in a union a condition of employment to be a lawful managerial method to prevent interruptions of production through industrial warfare or other union interferences with managerial activities. The United States Supreme Court, for example, stated: "The same liberty which enables men to form unions, and through the union to enter into agreements with employers willing to agree, entitles other men to remain independent of the union and other employers to agree with them to employ no man who owes any allegiance or obligation to the union. In the latter case, as in the former, the parties are entitled to be protected by law in the enjoyment of the benefits of any lawful agreement they may make. This

damages because its interests are affected if its members are not hired or are discharged because they belong to it. According to the French Labor Code,[19] unions may exercise all the rights of a civil plaintiff concerning acts impairing, directly or indirectly, the collective interests of the occupation or trade which they represent. Infringement of the right to organize not only of individual workers but also of unions thus can be remedied in the ordinary French courts.

In Sweden, as in the other European continental countries here discussed, the court is the public authority which has jurisdiction over disputes arising from interference with the freedom of self-organization. As in Germany, the establishment of a special court of justice for labor matters—the Labor Court—has facilitated the prevention and settlement of such disputes. In contrast to France, Germany, and Great Britain, Sweden has a special statute dealing at some length with the right to organize (and bargain collectively) and its protection. But its enforcement provisions, by and large, merely apply general legal principles to the special situation. Apart from that, the Swedish law reflects very clearly the difference between the statutory and the contractual right to organize.

The statute of 1936, as amended in 1940, declares that the freedom of association is infringed when measures are taken by employers (or by employees) for the purpose of compelling an employee (or employer, respectively) to refrain from joining an organization or to resign from it. Moreover, compulsion to prevent a person from exercising his rights as a member of an organization or from working for an organization likewise constitutes an infringement of

---

court repeatedly has held that the employer is as free to make nonmembership in a union a condition of employment, as the working man is free to join the union, and that this is a part of the constitutional rights of personal liberty and private property, not to be taken away even by legislation, unless through some proper exercise of the paramount police power." *Hitchman Coal Company* v. *Mitchell*, 245 U. S. 229, 250, 251 (1917).

19 Bk. 3, Art. 10.

freedom of association. Finally, any measure taken by employers (or employees) intended to cause prejudice to an employee (or employer, respectively) on the ground that he is a member of an organization, exercises his rights as such, or works for an organization or its establishment is contrary to law. Actions of such kind cannot be made legal by collective or individual contracts. As in the German Republic, any contract clause or other legal transaction impairing the right to organize, such as discriminatory discharge, reclassification, and the like, is null and void.

Persons who interfere with the right to organize are bound to make compensation for any loss caused by their action. If they represent an organization, the latter, too, is liable for damage. The associations on both sides, further, are under the statutory duty to prevent members, as far as possible, from impairing the right of association and to avert losses which may result from such interferences. To satisfy the statute, the organization may impose upon members any penalty provided in its rules for noncompliance with membership obligations. It even may, irrespective of its rules, suspend members for a period up to one year. If such measures are not taken, the organization is liable for any loss caused by its lack of action.

Damages for infringement of the right to organize include "compensation for personal suffering and for encroachment upon the interest of the injured party in carrying on his occupation without interference." The amount of the compensation may be reduced if this appears appropriate in view of the slight degree of culpability of the person who caused the loss, the situation of the injured person, the extent of the loss in relation to the means of the person who caused it, or other circumstances. Even complete exemption from liability may be granted. Legal actions arising out of interference with the right to organize come under the jurisdiction of the Swedish Labor Court. Such suits may be instituted by a labor (or employers') organization as representative of the members whose right of association was

violated. The members themselves are not entitled to file
the suit unless they can prove that their organization refuses
to act on their behalf.

The statute states explicitly that it applies only to relations between employers and employees. Accordingly,
labor organizations and workers who exert compulsory pressure upon fellow workers to make them become or remain
union members do not violate the act. The fact that the
organizations can file damage suits only for injured members but not for themselves, further demonstrates that the
statutory provisions protect only the right of individuals
to organize. The freedom of association of labor organizations is still regarded primarily as a right to be protected by
contract, as was also the freedom of association of individual
workers prior to the enactment of the act of 1936. In case
of violation of such a contract, unions of course can take
the appropriate legal action. This regulation obviously
differs considerably from the French law.

In Britain the law has not established special rules for
prevention or redress of interference with the right of
workers to form and join unions and the right of unions
to pursue their bona fide objectives freely. But it has
granted workers' organizations such a strong position as to
make antiunion activities risky and to enable organized
labor to protect its interests effectively. The right to organize of individuals and unions thus has been, directly or indirectly, recognized by management in numerous collective
agreements. Though such agreements cannot be directly
enforced in court, at least in the frequent instances in which
the employer party is an association, they have been generally complied with. Controversies usually have been
settled out of court.

*The United States has established special principles
for protection of the right to organize.*

Conspicuous differences exist between prevailing European and American views for prevention of interferences

with the freedom to organize and redress of prejudice caused by it. European countries have relied primarily on the general civil law concerning wrongful acts, or, possibly, breach of contract. In the United States it has been considered necessary and desirable to protect the right to organize of most workers in a different manner. As compared with Europe also a relatively strong tendency still exists to bring the criminal law into play. Governments on the other side of the Atlantic have seen no reason to deviate, in the case of the right to organize, from the basic principle that the courts are the place to which parties may turn if they want infringment of a right rectified. They have not gone beyond establishing special expert courts of justice and adapting civil procedure rules to the particular requirements of the adjustment of labor disputes. American legislators, on the other hand, have to a very large extent resorted to the administrative process as the means of protecting freedom to organize (and to bargain collectively) and have made almost no effort to introduce reforms in the judicial system, designed to improve its efficiency in labor litigation. Finally, it may be mentioned that European governments, in dealing with protection of the right of association, generally treat all private employees alike without regard to the segment of the economy to which they belong. In the United States, however, the individual statutes providing safeguards for the exercise by workers of freedom of self-organization, cover only parts of the national economy and do not necessarily apply to all types of workers employed even in these areas. Some classes of workers do not come under any of the protective laws.

Under the federal Railway Labor Act, as amended, which covers steam railroads and air lines engaged in interstate commerce and their subsidiary undertakings, employers are criminally liable for willful interference with the right of employees to organize. Such interference is prosecuted in the criminal courts. The penalties are a fine or imprisonment or both.[20] The statute does not mention civil remedies, but the United States Supreme Court awarded a union an injunction against interference by an employer with the right of association of his workers.[21] The Bankruptcy Act imposes the duty upon a debtor or trustee to report to the judge any agreement restricting or interfering with the right of employees to join a labor organization of their own choice or to refuse to join or remain members of a company union. The judge then will order the agreement terminated.[22] The Federal Anti-Injunction Act declares the yellow-dog contract, which was subsequently made illegal by the National Labor Relations Act, unenforceable in any court of the United States whether at law or equity. The statute defines it as a promise, made in a contract of hiring or employment, whereby either party undertakes not to join, become, or remain a member of any labor or employer organization, or to withdraw from an employment relation if he joins, becomes, or remains a member of any such organization.[23]

The most comprehensive federal law, providing for protection of employees in self-organizational activities, is the National Labor Relations Act. It includes in its scope almost all private employers engaged in interstate commerce, or whose operations affect that commerce. It covers all employees of such employers with the exception of agricultural laborers, domestic servants, individuals employed by parent or spouse, and supervisory personnel. Employers and workers subject to the Railway Labor Act do not come under its provisions.

---

20 48 Stat. 1187; sec. 2, fourth and tenth (1934).
21 *Texas & New Orleans R. R.* v. *Brotherhood of Ry. & S. S. Clerks*, 281 U. S. 548 (1930).
   In subsequent decisions the Supreme Court held that the Federal Anti-Injunction Act did not deprive federal courts of jurisdiction to compel, by injunction, compliance with positive mandates of the Railway Labor Act. *Virginian R. Co.* v. *System Federation*, 300 U. S. 515 (1937); *Graham* v. *Brotherhood of Firemen*, 338 U. S. 232 (1949).
22 52 Stat. 904, sec. 272 (1938).
23 47 Stat. 70, secs. 3 and 4 (1932).

To protect the exercise by workers of freedom to form, join, or assist labor organizations, to engage in other concerted activities for the purpose of mutual aid or protection, and to refrain from such activities, the legislators included in the list of "unfair labor practices," prohibited by the act, any interference by employers or unions with these guaranteed rights. The list outlaws, in particular, infringment of the freedom of association of unions by prohibiting employer domination of a labor organization, interference with the formation or administration of a union, and financial contributions or other support to a workers' organization by management. It also proscribes impairment of the right of association of individual workers by declaring illegal employer discrimination in regard to hiring or tenure of employment or conditions of employment for the purpose of encouraging or discouraging membership in a labor organization. This includes discharges because of union affiliation or nonaffiliation,[24] and employer demands that employees agree to a yellow dog contract.

In case of interference with the right to organize, as in other cases of violation of the National Labor Relations Act, a charge may be filed with the regional office of an administrative agency set up by the act— the National Labor Relations Board. If the case is not settled by adjustment, the regional director may, after investigation, issue a complaint and notice of hearing. The hearing is held before a trial examiner, who subsequently files an intermediate report with the Board in Washington, D. C., containing his findings, conclusions, and recommendations for the final disposition of the case. If any party files exceptions to the report, the Board will issue a decision, in which it may adopt, modify, or reject the findings and recommendations of the Trial Examiner. The decision contains detailed find-

---

[24] The employer, however, does not commit an unfair labor practice if he discourages or encourages membership in a specific labor organization in compliance with an agreement which requires new employees to join the contracting union after they were hired (union shop agreement), provided that the agreement was entered into in conformity with the relevant provisions of the act.

ings of fact, conclusions of law, the basic reasons for decision on all material issues raised, and an order either dismissing the complaint in whole or in part or requiring the respondent to cease and desist from its unlawful practices and to take appropriate affirmative action. If no exceptions are filed, and the respondent does not comply with the intermediate report, the Board will adopt the recommendations of the Trial Examiner.

If the respondent does not satisfy the order of the Board, or the Board deems it desirable to implement the order with a court decree, it may petition the appropriate federal court for enforcement. The respondent, on the other hand, may petition the circuit court of appeals to review and set aside the order of the Board. Following the decree of the court, either the government or the private party may petition the Supreme Court for review. The Board has the responsibility of obtaining compliance with the decision of the court. If it finds that the respondent has failed to live up to the terms of the decree of the court, its general counsel may, on its behalf, file a petition to hold him in contempt of court. The court may order immediate remedial action and impose heavy penalties, such as fine, imprisonment or both.

The National Labor Relations Board has virtually exclusive jurisdiction in matters of unfair labor practices, so that parties concerned cannot invoke the ordinary courts. Since the official proceedings are instituted through a complaint issued in the name of the Board, the injured person or organization is not a formal party to the administrative procedure. In further contrast to the European procedures already discussed, no private claims are adjudicated, but the government, through the medium of the Board, acts to enforce a public law. This is reflected in the nature of the affirmative actions which violators of the National Labor Relations Act have been directed to take. For example, employers have been ordered to rescind rules discriminating against union members, or to reinstate with back pay workers who were unlawfully discharged because of union membership or nonunion membership, and unions have been required to make up wages lost where they were responsible for unlawful discrimination against an employee. But the Board has not directed employers to compensate individuals otherwise for injury suffered as a consequence of wrongful interference with their freedom to organize, as European courts may do. Moreover, it stated that it has no power to hold a labor organization liable for loss of pay caused by an unfair labor practice committed by it where this loss is not due to severance, or interference with the tenure or terms, of an employment relationship; it thus refused to order a union to make up earnings lost by employees who refrained from participating in a strike but were prevented from working by illegal restraint and coercion.[25]

The states of Colorado, Connecticut, New York, Massachusetts, Michigan, Minnesota, Pennsylvania, Rhode Island, Utah, and Wisconsin have enacted state labor relations acts covering the majority of workers employed in intrastate commerce and modeled more or less on the national law. With few exceptions, those acts provide procedures for the prevention and redress of interference with the right to organize, which are similar to those of the National Labor Relations Act. Under the Michigan act such interference by employers or employees is punished as a misdemeanor.[26] Under the Minnesota act the aggrieved party may maintain a suit in the proper court to enjoin certain infringements of freedom of association of labor by employers, unions, or employees.[27]

In the state of Florida, which has no special labor relations act of the federal type, the question has come up in court as to whether the individual employee concerned or

---

[25] *United Furniture Workers* and *Colonial Hardwood Flooring Company,* 84 NLRB No. 69 (1949).
[26] State Labor Relations Act, secs. 16 and 17.
[27] State Labor Relations Act, secs. 11 (g), 12 (c), and 14.

his union is entitled to sue in case of employer interference with the right to join a labor organization. As mentioned above, in France both the individual worker and the union have been considered to have the right to do so, while in Sweden, as a rule, only the union has been regarded as the proper party. The Supreme Court of Florida held[28] that the right to work regardless of membership or nonmembership in a union, as guaranteed by the Florida constitution, is a right of individuals but not of labor organizations so that it can be enforced only by the employee who is discriminated against because he seeks to exercise it.

About half of the states have provisions on their statute books, designed to prevent or discourage the yellow dog contract by declaring it a punishable offense, void as against public policy, unenforceable in court, or an unfair labor practice. As mentioned above, some state constitutions and a number of state statutes other than state labor relations acts have, in one form or another, expressly outlawed compulsory interference with the exercise of the right to join or refrain from joining labor organizations. Some of these statutes provide for criminal punishment in case of violation of its provisions.[29] Others explicitly entitle parties whose interests were prejudiced, to take legal action for damages and injunctive relief.[30] Some statutes mention both penal and civil remedies.[31]

---

[28] *Miami Laundry Co.* v. *Laundry, Linen, Dry Cleaning Drivers, Salesmen and Helpers Local Union No. 935*, 41 So. (2d) 305 (1949).

[29] Alabama, L. 1943, no. 298, secs. 8, 18; Arkansas, L. 1947, Act. 101, secs. 2-4; Florida, L. 1943, H. B. 142, secs. 3, 14; Nebraska, L. 1947, L. B. 344, secs. 1, 3; South Carolina, Code of 1942, sec. 3237; South Dakota, L. 1945, c. 80, secs. 1-2 and L. 1947, S. B. 224, secs. 1, 3-5; Tennessee, L. 1947, c. 36, secs. 1, 2, 5.

[30] Arizona, L. 1947, c. 81, secs. 1, 4, 6, 7; New Hampshire, L. 1947, c. 195, sec. 21; North Carolina, L. 1947, H. B. 229, secs. 2-4, 6; Virginia, L. 1947, c. 3, secs. 1, 3, 4, 6.

[31] Georgia, L. 1947, c. 140, secs. 2, 3, 4, 5, 8, 9; Iowa, L. 1947, S. B. 109, secs. 2, 3, 6, 7.

CHAPTER III

Freedom to Organize of Government and Managerial Personnel

The preceding chapter indicates that governments, in recognizing the right to organize in its technical sense, have delimited the extent to which they intend to give special protection to the exercise of it. The types of employees or activities to be covered have been defined. Some rules to be observed by unions that wish to enjoy the special advantages provided by the law governing collective labor action have been established. Methods which may or may not be used in carrying through concerted activities have been determined in court decisions and statutes. The particular results of these governmental efforts will be discussed in later parts of the larger study, dealing with specific rights and duties of organizations. In this chapter we shall survey what governments have done to solve general problems that have arisen in connection with attempts of some peculiar classes of working persons to invoke the protection of the special law dealing with collective labor activities. This includes persons in the public service and managerial employees.

PUBLIC EMPLOYEES AND CIVIL SERVANTS

For the purposes of this study, two governmental functions must be distinguished: sovereign (political) functions and proprietary functions. The first include legislative, executive, and judicial activities, as well as the provision of public services of other kinds. The second function is performed where the government owns, manages, or operates commercial enterprises in a manner similar to private entrepreneurs. Most of the persons who carry out the operations involved in the performance of these functions, like employees in private industry, receive compensation for their services and have to follow directives. The character of their responsibilities, however, differs not only as in private employment according to their place in the hierarchy of the establishment but also according to whether they serve the government in its sovereign or proprietary capacity. Some schools of thought have treated employment by the government in its proprietary capacity like employment by a private employer. Others have held that any work for the government, that is, for the benefit of the community, is basically different from work for a private enterprise operated primarily for private profit. A number of persons in the public service have not been regarded as working *for* the government but have been considered, so to speak, to *be* the government.

*Two classes of persons are employed in
public services: employees and civil servants.*

Proprietary as well as sovereign governmental functions have been performed by employees in the technical meaning of the term—called government or public employees. Their economic relations to the employing agency by and large have differed little or not at all from those of private employees to private employers. Differences between the character of their relations to the employing governmental agencies and that of the relations between private employees and employers have been due in a larger measure to the differences in the nature of the employer and, frequently, in the work to be done than to differences in terms and conditions of employment. In the European countries discussed in this study such public employees have constituted the bulk of the personnel employed to carry through proprietary governmental functions. Much less frequently have they been entrusted with the performance of sovereign functions of governments. In the United States, however, government employees perform the major portion of governmental functions of both types.

For historical reasons and because of the peculiar nature of the public service another type of person—the civil servant—works for and in governments. He is not considered an employee in the technical meaning of the term. His status differs fundamentally from that of both private and public employees. In contrast to the latter, the civil servant is appointed rather than hired, does not work under a contract of employment, and cannot be discharged like private or public employees. His obligation to work is established by a specific act under public rather than private law. His remuneration and conditions of "employment" are not fixed by a contract but are regulated by statute or other authoritative rules. His relations to the "employer" differ from those of both private and public employees. Traditional German theory, for example, has considered national, state, and municipal civil servants to embody and represent the Reich, state, or municipality respectively. Under the British concept the civil servant is regarded as a servant of the Crown, which, in turn, is the embodiment of the state. Other countries have had similar concepts.

Civil servants are subject to special obligations, but also enjoy special privileges and protection. Their freedom to choose their residence may be restricted, they have to take a special oath of office, and their behavior not only on but also off duty is governed by strict disciplinary rules. Violation of duties is not merely a breach of contract but a disciplinary offense. The consequences are not simply discharge but disciplinary proceedings and punishment. On the other hand, civil servants are protected against prosecution for acts committed in the legitimate performance of their functions, they have special rights in their relations to superiors and subordinates, and titles and promotion are regulated and guaranteed. In the typical case they can be suspended or removed from office, or be placed in temporary or permanent retirement only on conditions fixed by law, primarily as punishment for serious disciplinary or criminal offenses. Disciplinary punishment, however, can be imposed only in a regular procedure, which frequently provides for tribunals that operate under rules similar to those of criminal courts and apply codes of discipline. This tends to make the appointment of civil servants virtually permanent.

As compensation for their permanent public service the government of the political community concerned ordinarily assumes the obligation to provide for their maintenance as long as they live, even if they cannot work because of sickness, old age, or the like. Under some systems the government also pays pensions to closely related survivors. The remuneration of the civil servant, therefore, occasionally has been construed as an alimony or annuity rather than a true wage or salary.

European and American public personnel
systems differ profoundly.

In European countries the sovereign governmental functions, as a rule, have been performed by civil servants. With growing expansion of governmental activities into other fields, increasing numbers of persons with civil service status have been appointed to perform economic or purely technical services. The terms "civil service" and "civil servants" also are applied to the bulk of persons working in or for American governments. There has been a marked trend to give them a high degree of job security and to make their employment conditions somewhat similar to those of European civil servants. Yet, only a very few of them can be considered civil servants in the sense in which this term is used in European countries. Most American government workers—irrespective of their functions—do not enjoy important privileges which the majority of the European civil servants discussed above ordinarily have been granted. They may, for example, be removed for reasons other than violation of disciplinary rules, and relatively little protection has been provided by courts. Nor do the governments which they serve assume, as a principle, the obligation to provide for their maintenance as long as they live. In contrast to European pension systems, the civil service retirement and similar acts provide for compulsory insurance under which the prospective beneficiaries have to pay contributions.[1] The overwhelming majority of Americans in the public service are what are commonly regarded as public employees rather than civil servants, and there are private employees who enjoy a similar or even higher degree of social security.

The question as to whether or not persons in the public service have substantial privileges and a more secure status than private employees has played a significant role in the development of public policies with respect to their freedom to organize, to bargain collectively, and to use militant tactics. It thus seems advisable to prepare the discussion of these policies[2] by clarifying the marked differences between American and European public personnel systems.

Government personnel in the United States during the first century of its history was appointed generally under the spoils or patronage system. Appointments were given preferably to supporters of the political party in power as a reward for party work, so that functional competence frequently was only a secondary consideration and substantial portions of the personnel changed when another party came into power. Use of the merit system, that is, recruitment on the basis of fitness for the position, which has prevailed in large parts of Europe for a considerable time, was not introduced in the United States until the latter part of the nineteenth century. It is now applied to the major portion of

---

[1] There are only a few noncontributory systems for special classes of persons in the public service, for example, federal judges.

[2] The discussion in this chapter deals primarily with the right of persons in the public service to form and join unions. The problems of their freedom to bargain collectively and freedom to use militant tactics will be taken up in more detail in later parts of the study, which deal with the right of organized labor to bargain collectively and freedom to strike.

positions in the national government. But it has not resulted in the same set-up of government personnel as in the
European countries of comparison.

For the purposes of this discussion three main groups of
persons working in or for the government of the United
States may be distinguished. Under the federal Constitution[3] the President nominates and, by and with the advice
and consent of the Senate, appoints ambassadors, other public ministers and consuls, and judges of the Supreme Court.
He also appoints judges in the so-called constitutional
courts of justice, and certain upper grade officers. The persons coming under the Civil Service Act,[4] which was enacted
to establish the merit system, constitute the second general
group of persons working for the national government. It
comprises the bulk of employees in the executive branch,
as distinguished from the legislative branch—Congress and
its employees—and the judicial branch—the courts and their
employees—which the act does not cover. Civil Service employees are appointed by officials of the government agencies, called "appointing officers," from a list of persons
certified by the Civil Service Commission—the agency administering the act—as having qualified for the position,
usually in an open competitive examination. The third
group of persons in the employ of the federal government
is made up of those who are neither appointed by the President nor covered by the Civil Service Act.

With the possible exception of employees belonging to
the third group, the act of appointment has been considered
to be a transaction under public rather than private law,
though no uniformity of opinion exists as to its precise
legal character. The emoluments of appointed officers of
the first group, such as federal judges, district attorneys,
and certain high administrative officers, are fixed by statutes. The salaries of employees coming under the Civil
Service Act are generally determined under the Classifica-

3 Art. 2, sec. 2.
4 22 Stat. 403 (1883).

tion Act,[5] which established a job evaluation plan for federal government service. The remuneration of other employees may be agreed upon in what has been termed a "quasi-contract," ordinarily on the basis of the prevailing wage.

Appointment of the federal judges, mentioned above, is for lifetime. The tenure of office of a number of presidential appointees is fixed by statute. No tenure provisions exist for others. Administrative officers appointed for a fixed term to the top positions in quasi-legislative and quasi-judicial agencies may be removed only for certain causes, listed in the statutes establishing these agencies. Other appointments may be revoked at will. The courts have tended to refuse to take jurisdiction in cases of such revocations, holding that appointees have no vested interest or contractual right in their offices. The large number of other persons in the employ of the government, including those coming under the Civil Service Act, likewise have no right to their positions, though the tendency prevails to minimize removals and to limit them to cases of disciplinary offenses and reductions in personnel.

The administrative authorities charged with making appointments also have the power to discharge. The act and rules issued by the Civil Service Commission regulate the procedure to be followed. Apart from certain exceptional situations the Civil Service Commission has no power to review the decision of the removing officer. Nor do the courts take jurisdiction to hear appeals from removals, unless a procedural rule, prescribed by *Congress* for the discharge of classified civil servants, was not complied with. Civil service regulations, made by the President on the advice of the civil service commissioners have been held to lack the effect and force of law and, therefore, to be unenforceable as such in the courts.[6]

Several laws provide for benefits to retired federal gov-

5 Act of Mar. 4, 1923, 42 Stat. 1488, as amended.
6 *United States* v. *Lapp,* 244 Fed. 377, 382 (1917).

ernment employees. The most comprehensive is the Civil Service Retirement Act.[7] It covers all officers and employees in or under the executive, judicial, and legislative branches who are not subject to other retirement systems for such officers and employees. The system, set up under this act, provides for benefits in case of old-age retirement (which is compulsory at a certain age and length of service), optional retirement (which is permissible at a certain age after a fixed time of service), disability retirement after a specified time of service, and death benefits. It is a contributory system, similar to insurance plans which exist in the private economy. Amounts are deducted from wages and salaries to cover part of the costs of prospective benefits.

A number of states, counties, and municipalities have established public personnel systems similar to that of the federal government, especially civil service systems. This development, however, has not been general.

As mentioned above, recent developments have tended somewhat to blur the line between civil servants and government employees in Europe also. Though the opinion has prevailed that the traditional civil service system has made for high efficiency, governments which have planned far-reaching socio-economic and political reforms have complained that the system renders the carrying through of such plans more difficult. Accordingly, certain tendencies have developed to make public personnel management more flexible, sometimes by hiring employees rather than appointing civil servants in appropriate situations. Moreover, on both sides of the Atlantic the view has spread that the public welfare requires regular and continuous service not only in the field of governmental functions but in important segments of the private economy as well. This has produced in the United States a movement to transplant some principles used in the government service to certain private employment and to introduce statutory restrictions

[7] 41 Stat. 614 (1920), as amended.

of full freedom to engage in concerted labor activities in public utilities and similar enterprises, as well as in situations in which the national health or safety would be imperiled. In Europe the need for continuous availability of essential services has contributed to the rise of the doctrine (and practice) first, that public utilities and, subsequently, also essential enterprises should be owned by the government concerned.[8] The transfer of such enterprises to public ownership, now going on in many European countries, is reducing the field of private and correspondingly widening the scope of public employer-employee relations. This development, obviously, has affected and is bound further to affect governmental and union policies respecting the rights and duties of organized labor in very important areas of labor relations. Where the employer is the whole people represented by its democratically elected government, union persistence in the dogma of the class war has been regarded as unwarrantable. The reasons for many restrictive union practices have no longer been held valid. Moreover, the unions' share in responsibility for maximum production and efficiency has been considered greatly increased.[9] The adjustment of governmental and union policies to the new situation is still in an embryonic stage, but some attention must be given to it in this study.

*Full freedom to organize has been considered
incompatible with the requirements of the public service.*

There have been strong tendencies to regard the right to organize, as defined in the preceding chapter, or at least certain phases of it, as not applying to public employees

8 In the United States some statutes have provided that the government may take over such establishments temporarily if labor disputes threaten to interrupt their operation. European systems, mentioned above, provide for permanent public ownership, in part, to forestall such situations.

9 After the Anglo-American Productivity Conference the British Trades Union Congress, for example, called a meeting in London on Nov. 18, 1948, to which the General Council submitted specific proposals for the participation of labor in British efforts to raise the level of productivity.

and civil servants. Complete or partial negation of the right
has been based chiefly on the nature of the public employer,
on the peculiar character of the public service, particularly
its function to satisfy social rather than individual private
wants, and—especially in the case of civil servants—on the
great amount of protection granted those working for the
government.

It has been said that the notion of the right to organize
and its corollaries pertain for historical and conceptual
reasons only to the private economy and that the considerations which caused labor to demand and legislators to grant
protection of the exercise of the right do not apply to the
government as employer or even to relations between the
government and its civil servants. Persons in the public
service, therefore, have been regarded as not coming under
the special provisions governing the right to organize and
related matters. It has been stated that the government,
in contrast to the private employer, protects the interests
of all people, which includes the interests of the men and
women in the public service, and that, accordingly, such
conflicting interests as are present in private labor relations
could not exist in the relations between governments and
those whom they employ. Moreover, it has been pointed
out that determination of the employment conditions in,
as well as supervision of the management of, the public
service is in the hands of the legislative bodies and that
public employees and civil servants in their capacity as
citizens participate in the formation of these bodies and
may otherwise influence their decisions. From all this it
has been concluded that those employed by a government
do not need special protection by unions.

Opponents of unionism in the public service further have
emphasized that government agencies, to perform their
duties, must insist upon the undivided allegiance of all their
workers, and must maintain a pronounced *esprit de corps*
and firm—sometimes semimilitary—discipline among all
their staff members. It would be incompatible with these

requirements of the public service, it has been argued, if
the personnel took orders from union leaders or put solidarity with members of the working class above solidarity
with the government. This would be inimical to the public
interest.

Moreover, it has been asserted that public agencies must
have the right to prohibit the members of their staffs from
belonging to any organization or participating in any meeting which has objectives that persons in the public service
cannot actively support without violating duties implied
in working for the government. Labor unions have been
considered to be such a type of association, especially because they are involved in politics and, in Europe, have
been affiliated with political parties, which sometimes have
sought to change the existing order. Public employees as
well as civil servants are as citizens free to join private associations and to vote and belong to political parties as they
like. But according to one school of thought by entering
the public service they must be considered to waive any
right to participate in unionism or to play an active role in
party politics. Otherwise, the fundamental principle of the
nontotalitarian countries would be jeopardized that the
governmental machinery must be impartial and nonpoliti-
cal in the sense of party politics. It has been feared that,
even if union or party activities did not actually influence
the behavior of public employees or civil servants while
they are on duty, members of the public might become
doubtful as to the neutrality of the governmental machinery.

Those who have held that government employees or
civil servants, or both, should not have full freedom to
organize very often have intended to exclude them from
the right to bargain collectively and the freedom to strike
rather than from the right to form and join associations.
A right of persons in the public service and a corresponding duty of governments to bargain collectively has been

considered incompatible with state sovereignty. It has been
said that nothing could be more dangerous to public welfare than to allow servants of the community to attempt
to impose upon the government the hours, the wages, and
conditions under which they will carry on essential service vital to the welfare, safety, and security of the citizens.
The liberty of action of the government, it has been argued,
must not be subjected to such restrictions as collective
bargaining has entailed for private management. Permitting private organizations to influence the scope of governmental powers has been held irreconcilable with the fundamental democratic principle that the powers of the government are determined by the whole people. Viewing the
issue from another angle, attention has been called to the
fact that the terms of employment in the public service
ordinarily are fixed by law or authoritative regulations.
For this reason there is no place in this field for collective
bargaining or organizations the primary objective of which
is to participate in the determination of the remuneration
and employment conditions of their members.

Opponents of unionism in the field of governmental activities, moreover, have asserted that the right to bargain
collectively carries the correlative right to strike, that the
latter is included at any rate in the right to organize, and
that any union, being essentially a militant organization,
operates on the principle that it must be free to wage industrial warfare if it deems it necessary to do so to achieve its
objectives. It thus has been held that permitting persons
in the public service to form and join unions inevitably
either implies that they are granted the right to strike or
causes them to pretend possessing it. This school of
thought has viewed such a situation as incompatible with
the requirements of the public service and as repugnant to
orderly democratic government. Neither public employees
nor civil servants, according to this opinion, can be allowed

to strike, whatever may happen, since the interests and welfare of the community require under all circumstances orderliness and continuity in the conduct of governmental activities.

The preceding arguments, which refer to both public employees and civil servants, have been used with particular emphasis to justify denial of a right of the latter to full freedom to organize. Civil servants have been considered not to come under the public policy concerning freedom of employees to organize because they do not work under a contract of employment and, hence, are not employees in the ordinary sense of the word. Full freedom of civil servants to form, join, or assist labor organizations, to bargain collectively, and to engage in strikes or other concerted activities for the purpose of mutual protection has been opposed for the additional reason that they enjoy maximum protection by the community which they serve. Any need for combinations to protect the interests of individuals or the occupation as such has been denied on the ground that civil servants have the greatest possible security of permanent employment and a maximum of social security in other respects. Application of union rules, such as are customary in the sphere of private employment, to the relations between civil servants and the government has been regarded as contrary to the fundamental principles of the civil service. It has been feared that such practice would disrupt discipline and impair the relations with superiors as well as the confidence of the public in the integrity and neutrality of the governmental machinery. The fact alone that civil servants are linked with the community not merely by a private contract of employment but by an appointment under public law which confers upon them special privileges and imposes upon them special correlative duties has been viewed as precluding the right to form and join labor unions, the right to bargain collectively, and the right to strike.

*Liberal governments no longer bar their employees
or civil servants from exercising the right to organize.*

In the countries covered by this study opposition to freedom to organize of persons working for governments has
declined in such a measure that present-day public policies
generally no longer seek to prevent such persons from forming and joining unions. It is now widely held that the
employment conditions of government employees do not
differ from those of private employees in such a degree as to
warrant their unqualified exclusion from the rights to self-
organization, to elect representatives of their own choosing,
and to engage in other concerted activities for the purpose
of mutual aid or protection. It has been widely conceded
that persons in the public service "tend to feel that they
have social affiliations with the working classes and to desire
to support their policies." This tendency has been recognized as existing not only among public employees but also
among civil servants, at least in the subordinate grades.[10]
In addition, supporters of unionism in the government
service have maintained that the general public and its representative bodies have been so frequently more interested
in economies than in fair remuneration for work in the
public domain and have been so often uninformed of the
actual working conditions in government agencies as to
justify the desire of public employees as well as civil servants to form and join organizations for the purpose of discussing these problems among themselves and to elect representatives of their own choosing to submit requests to
those who can act upon them.

The late President Franklin D. Roosevelt expressed an
opinion now widely followed in democratic countries with
respect to all classes of persons in the service of governments
when he declared that:

[10] See Herman Finer, "Civil Service," *Encyclopaedia of the Social Sciences,*
Vol. 3 (1930), p. 521.

. . . Organizations of Government employes have a logical place in Government affairs. The desire of Government employes for fair and adequate pay, reasonable hours of work, safe and suitable working conditions, development of opportunities for advancement, facilities for fair and impartial consideration and review of grievances, and other objectives of a proper employe relations policy, is basically no different from that of employes in private industry. Organization on their part to present their views on such matters is both natural and logical, but meticulous attention should be paid to the special relationships and obligations of public servants to the public itself and to the Government.[11]

The development of this policy has been accompanied by a marked decline in official opposition to affiliation of public employees and civil servants with the labor movement at large. Such affiliation has been sought by individuals as well as organizations, not infrequently in the belief that potential pressure by the powerful superiors could be most effectively resisted in this manner. At present the majority of organized civil servants and many organized government employees are members of special unions composed solely of persons working for the government, but a considerable number of their associations are affiliated with central organizations which include chiefly unions of private employees.

*Restriction of freedom to organize of European
public employees is widely opposed.*

Liberal governments, then, no longer prohibit their employees or civil servants from organizing. All of them, however, hold that certain concomitants of the right to organize cannot be transplanted into the field of public employment or, at least, cannot apply to this field without important qualifications. In Europe a trend has been noticeable to make some distinction in this respect between government employees and civil servants. The former have been employed primarily to perform economic and technical services. Only in relatively rare cases have they

---

[11] Letter of Aug. 16, 1937, to Mr. Luther C. Steward, President of the National Federation of Federal Employees, in Charles S. Rhyne, *Labor Unions and Municipal Employe Law* (1946), pp. 436-37.

been called upon to perform tasks in the sphere of sovereign governmental functions. But, whatever the nature of their activities, they have had to work under employment conditions similar to those of private employees. A number of European governments at various levels, therefore, have been inclined to acquiesce, within the scope of their powers, to the use by employees of union methods customary in private employer-employee relations. There has been collective bargaining.

Marked disinclination, however, has existed to settle the controversial question as to whether public employees may strike. Government agencies have made vigorous efforts to prevent them from doing so. Yet, in the absence of legislation on the subject, a tendency has existed—more distinct on the part of private writers than of high-ranking government officers—to concede that persons whom the government employs in its capacity as entrepreneur and, more generally, persons whom it grants only the status of employees rather than the privileged position of civil servants could not, in justice, be flatly denied the freedom to resort to militant tactics which other employees enjoy who work under similar conditions of employment. Supplementary considerations have been—at least in Europe—that the work of many such persons does not differ from that done by private employees and that their services are not necessarily more vital to the maintenance of public health and safety than those of workers in private enterprises. This school of thought has held that government employees could not be expected to practice as much restraint in matters of the freedom to strike as must be demanded from civil servants.[12]

12 Opponents of the tendency discussed in the text have held that public and private enterprises, even if they produce the same types of goods or services and function to satisfy individual wants, could not be placed on the same footing because the paramount purpose of any governmental activity, including the operation of industrial or commercial establishments, is protection of public rather than private interests, especially by providing continuously services essential to society. This purpose, it has been argued, might be defeated if the workers in the publicly owned undertakings had the same freedom to undertake all kinds of concerted labor activities as private employees enjoy.

Restriction of the freedom to organize of European
civil servants is generally held unavoidable.

As to the civil servants, it is generally accepted in the
European countries of comparison that the requirements of
their work make restrictions of their freedom of association imperative, and further that in view of their employment security and other privileges, such restrictions are
not unfair. Legal provisions excluding civil servants from
the application of the right to form and join unions of their
own choice have been repealed, and some systems have
granted them this right explicitly. But this has not necessarily meant that exercise of the right is governed in every
respect by the general labor law. Nor has it implied a recognition of freedom to strike or the right to bargain collectively in the manner customary and lawful in private labor
relations. The fact that as a rule the legislature rather than
the government agency concerned determines the occupational rights and duties of civil servants is generally considered to preclude the application to the civil service of
rules governing collective bargaining in other fields. But in
the sense of election of personnel representatives, collective
presentation and adjustment of grievances, or establishment
of joint machinery or advisory staff committees, or the like,
for the purpose of discussing general problems as well as
individual cases, collective bargaining would seem to have
become a regular feature of most public services. The
disposition to grant civil servants the right to discuss matters collectively with the authorities concerned, however,
has not led to the recognition of a right to use other than
peaceable tactics to attain compliance with requests. In
short, the principle prevails that unionism of civil servants,
to be legitimate, must be adapted to the paramount requirements of the public service so that conflicts with the public
interest and the will of the legislature are avoided.

The principle of the French Labor Code that unions can
be formed only by persons engaged in the same occupation

or profession, similar trades, or related occupations, caused a considerable number of courts, writers, and statesmen to hold until recently that French civil servants could not belong to organizations affiliated with the general labor movement. Moreover, it was widely believed that civil servants could not legally form unions of their own, chiefly on the ground that the Labor Code also restricts the objectives of unions to consideration and defense of economic, industrial, commercial, or agricultural interests and that civil servants have no such interests to defend. But a number of government agencies consented to negotiate with associations, formed by civil servants under general civil law rather than the Labor Code, and occasionally even with unions of civil servants, established to protect the interests of the occupation as such in the union manner. The government generally did not take action against such unions or against labor organizations including government officers in their ranks. The situation eventually was clarified by the act of October 19, 1946,[13] which regulates the general status of most state civil servants and, among other things, recognizes their right to form and join unions. Such unions come under the union provisions of the Labor Code, provided they deposit their rules and a list of their administrative officers with the authority for which the civil servants who applied for membership work. They are entitled to take legal proceedings and, in particular, can appeal against regulations affecting the conditions of the personnel and against decisions in individual cases which impair the collective interests of the civil servants.

It would seem that the statute does not prevent civil servants from belonging to organizations which include employees as well, provided the fundamental principle is observed that the members of an individual union must be engaged in the same or related occupations. On the other

[13] Act Concerning the General Status of Civil Servants, J. O. No. 246, Oct. 20, 1946, p. 8910, Art. 6.

hand, the act does not apply to civil servants of local governments, magistrates, military personnel, or the staffs of public offices, services, and establishments of an industrial or commercial nature. Commentators, however, have held that these persons, though not coming under the special provisions of the statute, have the right to form and join unions, especially since the new constitution expressly states that *everyone* may defend his rights and interests by trade union action and may join the union of his choice.

While the act states that unions which operate in the field of the public service are governed by the provisions of the Labor Code regulating the status of labor unions, it does not say that the provisions of the code respecting collective agreements also apply to them. The report of the parliamentary committee on the bill, furthermore, explained that recognition of the right to organize was not intended to imply recognition of a right to strike. It added that ways and means to avoid strikes must be found by the joint bodies established under the act, in which the representatives of both sides have the opportunity of discovering solutions to general problems of public services as well as to individual cases.

The German (Weimar) Constitution recognized the right of civil servants to form and join unions in 1919. Article 130 guaranteed to them "freedom of political opinion and freedom to organize." The same article provided for special representation plans of civil servants. In Germany, too, it was generally accepted that the recognition of these rights did not imply recognition of freedom to strike, especially because the Constitution did not even contain any provision granting such freedom to employees working under a private contract of employment. According to common view the legislators did not intend to abolish the traditional principle that civil servants who willfully stop working or refuse to perform duties commit at least a disciplinary offense.

Persons working for the government in Sweden have been considered to be included in the general freedom of association, which was implemented rather than established by the legislation of 1936 discussed above. The act of 1936, however, explicitly excepted from its scope of application persons in the service of the state or municipalities who "are subject to official responsibility." This has affected the right of such persons to bargain collectively rather than their organizational activities.[14] In 1937 the members of the national civil service, and in 1940 those of the municipal civil service, attained the official right to negotiate collectively with the government agencies for which they work. This right, however, does not extend as far as the right to bargain collectively of other persons. The authorities as a rule do not enter into collective agreements. As in Germany, provisions of the criminal and disciplinary law forestall strikes by persons having official responsibilities, though no special statute outlaws them expressly.

The British Trade Disputes and Trade Unions Act, passed in 1927 after the general strike of the year before, prohibited permanent civil servants from belonging to organizations with the primary object of influencing or affecting the remuneration and conditions of employment of their members, unless certain conditions were complied with. Membership was permissible only if the organization was confined to civil servants and in all respects independent of and not affiliated with any organization admitting other persons, and if it had no political objectives and was not directly or indirectly associated with any political party or organization. Thereupon the civil service unions were compelled to sever their connections with the British Trades Union Congress.[15] The repeal of the act in 1946 removed the restrictions of the freedom to organize of British civil servants, and civil service unions are rejoining the Trades Union Congress. The latter is considering the

14 See p. 42.
15 See p. 158.

establishment of a separate group of civil service unions within its structural framework.

The unions have the opportunity to represent the interests of their members in a National Whitley Council and in departmental councils[16] which have been established for the administrative and legal departments of the civil service. In addition, an agreement between the Treasury, which regulates the terms of established civil servants, and the staff side of the National Whitley Council set up a Civil Service Arbitration Tribunal in 1936. Its jurisdiction covers controversies concerning emoluments, hours of work, and leave of classes of civil servants, which government departments and recognized associations of civil servants could not settle directly. The Tribunal is composed of an independent chairman, one member drawn from a panel appointed by the Minister of Labor as representing the Chancellor of the Exchequer, and one member drawn from a panel similarly appointed representing the staff side of the National Whitley Council.[17] As in other European countries, no specific law gives British civil servants a right to strike, nor does any specific law deny it. But, again as in other European countries, the disciplinary penalties for a work stoppage or for any refusal to carry out orders would be so drastic that strikes by civil servants are to all intents and purposes precluded.

American government employees are subject to restrictions similar to those of European civil servants.

It has been previously mentioned that the bulk of the public personnel in the United States are what are commonly regarded as government employees rather than civil servants, no matter whether they carry out sovereign or proprietary governmental functions. American public authorities have tended to subject them to restrictions simi-

16 See pp. 53-54.
17 A similar tribunal has been set up by an agreement between the London County Council and the LCC Staff Association.

lar to those European governments have imposed upon civil servants. They are not covered by the National Labor Relations Act,[18] which does not include among the employers to which the statute applies the government of the United States, wholly owned government corporations, Federal Reserve banks, or the states and their political subdivisions. Similarly, state labor relations acts generally exclude the state governments and those of its political subdivisions from their coverage. Courts have upheld ordinances and administrative regulations prohibiting government workers from belonging to a union, on the ground that the public administration has the right to require discipline and individual loyalty to the service. The Lloyd LaFollette Act of 1912[19] limits the protection of the right to organize of postal employees to membership in organizations not affiliated with any outside organization imposing an obligation upon them to engage in any strike against the government.

However, the same statute also provides that membership in other unions should not be cause for reduction in rank or compensation, or removal from the postal service. In addition, it prohibits interference with the right of persons employed in the civil service of the United States to petition Congress either individually or collectively. In the absence of legislation guaranteeing freedom of association to government employees outside the postal service, the Lloyd LaFollette Act has been widely regarded as containing the principles guiding general public policy in this respect, at least in the *federal* public service. The United States Civil Service Commission expressed the belief:

> . . . that all plans should recognize the rights of an employee to join or to refrain from joining employee organizations or associations without interference, coercion, restraint or fears of discrimi-

18 See pp. 48-49.
19 37 Stat. 555.

nation or reprisal because of such membership or non-membership.[20]

The decision of the United States Supreme Court in *Railway Mail Association* v. *Corsy*[21] has been interpreted to imply recognition of a right of public employees to form and join unions, subject to limitations considered appropriate by the government. Union membership of local employees also has been, directly or indirectly, declared lawful.[22] In the absence of legal regulations to the contrary, then, it is commonly supposed that public employees in the United States are entitled to organize for their "mutual help and assistance."[23] Moreover, governments, more often than not, have adopted the policy of tolerating affiliation of public employees and their unions with the general labor movement.

Since governments as employers do not come under the National Labor Relations Act and generally are not covered by state labor relations acts either, they may—in contrast to private employers—restrict concerted activities of their employees. The federal criminal code[24] further prohibits persons employed by any agency of the federal government, like any other person, from organizing or affiliating with an organization which advocates the overthrow of any government in the United States by force or violence. Similarly, the "loyalty order" lists among the activities which may be considered in determining the loyalty of public employees membership in or affiliation with organizations or combinations designated by the Attorney General as totalitarian, fascist, communist, or subversive, or as having adopted a policy of advocating or approving the commission of acts of force or violence to deny other persons

20 Departmental Circular 251 (1941). Like the Lloyd LaFollette Act, this circular, however, limits its statement to membership in organizations or associations which are not affiliated with any outside organization imposing an obligation or duty to engage in any strike or proposing to render assistance in any strike against the United States.

21 326 U. S. 88 (1945).

22 See Rhyne, *Labor Unions and Municipal Employe Law*, pp. 133ff.

23 See *Hagan* v. *Picard*, 14 N. Y. Supp. (2d) 706 (1939).

24 54 Stat. 671 (1940).

their constitutional rights, or as seeking to alter the form of government by unconstitutional means.[25]

Whether unions have a right to bargain collectively in the field of American public employment is still a controversial question. There is marked tendency among government agencies to deny this right or, at least to refuse the making of regular collective contracts or the stipulation of clauses presumably incompatible with the character of the public service, such as union security or similar clauses. On the other hand, a number of agencies have negotiated with unions in the limited manner in which European governments have bargained with associations representing civil servants. The constitution of New Jersey, while guaranteeing to both private and public employees the right to organize, grants to the former the full right to bargain collectively but to the latter only the limited right to "present to and make known to the State, or any of its political subdivisions or agencies, their grievances and proposals through representatives of their own choosing."[26] Some American government agencies, however, have entered into collective contracts of types customary in the private economy, and even have agreed to union security provisions.

Though until recently only a few legal provisions of very limited scope outlawed strikes by public employees, prevailing view has condemned them at all times. Now, more statutes with broader coverage expressly declare that government employees have no freedom to strike. The federal government, in particular, has gone further than the European governments discussed above and has written a provision into the Labor Management Relations Act, 1947, prohibiting individuals employed by its agencies, including wholly owned government corporations, from participating in any strike. Persons, who violate this prohibition, must be immediately dismissed, forfeit their civil service status,

25 Executive Order 9835, Mar. 21, 1947, Federal Register, Vol. 12, p. 1935.
26 Art. I, 19.

if any, and will not be re-employed by the federal government for three years.[27] The United States Supreme Court further held that the Federal Anti-Injunction Act, which limits the use of the injunction in labor disputes in a very large measure, does not affect the jurisdiction of the courts to issue injunctions when sought by the United States government in a labor dispute with its own employees, because the court interpreted the general term "employer" or "person," used by the statute, as not including the United States.[28]

*Members of the armed forces and the police are
a special category of public servants.*

The members of the armed forces and the police probably personify the sovereign power of governments in the most manifest manner. Through them the governments perform the paramount duty of assuring the defense of the country, the enforcement of the law, and the maintenance of public order. Uninterrupted loyal and impartial service and preservation of the highest possible degree of discipline of the military and police forces thus are most essential to society. Although in several countries a right to organize of members of the police and at times even of members of the armed forces has been recognized, a number of countries

27 61 Stat. 136, sec. 305.
28 *United States* v. *United Mine Workers of America*, 330 U. S. 258 (1947).

An interchange of views on the right to organize of persons, working for a government, at the 1949 session of the International Labour Conference did not throw new light on the problem. The question came up in connection with the discussion of the convention concerning the application of the principles of the right to organize—a convention implementing the convention concerning freedom of association and protection of the right to organize, adopted at the 1948 session. The original draft submitted by the International Labour Office proposed to exclude "officials in the service of public administrations" from the application of the protective provisions of the new convention. This raised a number of complex problems. Nearly all delegates apparently agreed that, if any restrictions were to be envisaged at all, they should not apply to government employees but be limited to civil servants in the technical meaning of the term. It is, however, very difficult to define this term in an internationally intelligible form. Apart from this technical difficulty, some delegates maintained that public officials should be accorded the same rights of organization and collective bar-

have been unwilling to permit these persons to engage in union activities. At any rate, the opinion has prevailed among governments that their soldiers and police officers cannot have complete freedom to organize with all its concomitants. That everything must be avoided that might impair loyalty and discipline has been generally accepted. Many governments have felt compelled not to grant members of the armed forces and the police a kind of freedom of association under which they may, in particular, take sides in political struggles, have to choose between loyalty to unions or the government, or participate in union conflicts or even strikes.

Labor leaders, believing generally that the principles of freedom to organize must apply to all persons without distinction, have found it difficult to admit that soldiers and police officers should have no right, or only a restricted right, of association. Their difficulties have been complicated by the fact that in the numerous countries with compulsory military service, in the words of Jouhaux, the soldier of today is the worker of yesterday and of tomorrow, and wants to remain a union member. But by and large union leadership seems to have been more willing to recognize a necessity to limit freedom of association, at least with respect to the right to strike, in the case of the armed forces

---

gaining as employees; others held that governments should have the power to exercise some restriction on those rights. Some of the latter were prepared to contemplate the possibility of limitation of the right of public officials to bargain collectively, but were unable to agree to any restriction of their right to organize. Finally, a considerable number of delegates, while believing that the convention should permit governments to determine the extent to which the guarantee of freedom to organize and its corollaries should apply to public officials, took the view that any such provision would be inconsistent with the convention concerning freedom of association and the protection of the right to organize adopted in 1948, on the ground that the latter guaranteed freedom of association to "workers and employers, *without distinction whatsoever,*" excluding only the armed forces and the police. Eventually, a compromise was reached and the convention, as adopted, includes a provision to the effect that it does not deal with the position of public servants engaged in the administration of the state but shall not be construed as prejudicing their rights or status in any way. (Art. 6.)

and the police than in the case of government employees or public servants in general.[29]

The French law of September 28, 1948, regulating the status of police personnel, recognizes on the one hand that police officers are entitled to exercise the right to organize as guaranteed by the constitution and the act concerning the General Status of Civil Servants,[30] but specifies on the other hand that any concerted stoppage of service and any collective act of disobedience shall be punished by penalties over and above the usual disciplinary measures.[31] Explaining the reason for this regulation, the statute emphasizes that the particular nature of the functions and the exceptional responsibilities of the members of the police place them in a special category of the public service. As this is written, a corresponding law regulating the status of the French military personnel has not yet been enacted. Prevailing opinion holds that French soldiers are not permitted to form or join unions. Beyond that, various administrative memoranda in the interest of the preservation of discipline have limited the right of soldiers on active service and in the reserve as well as of several other types of military personnel to form associations under general civil law.

In the United Kingdom the Police Act, 1919 prohibits members of a police force on pain of disqualification from becoming a member of any trade union or other association which seeks to control or influence pay, pensions, or condi-

---

[29] After lively debate on the question as to whether the armed forces should or should not be excluded from the scope of convention no. 87 concerning freedom of association and protection of the right to organise, the International Labour Conference at San Francisco, 1948, adopted the following Art. 9 as a compromise:
"The extent to which the guarantees provided for in this Convention shall apply to the armed forces and the police shall be determined by national laws or regulations.
"In accordance with the principle set forth in paragraph 8 of Article 19 of the Constitution of the International Labour Organisation the ratification of this Convention by any Member shall not be deemed to affect any existing law, award, custom or agreement in virtue of which members of the armed forces or the police enjoy any right guaranteed by this Convention."
[30] P. 106.
[31] J. O. No. 231, Sept. 29, 1948, p. 9532.

tions of service of the police.[32] The act, however, established an organization, called the Police Federation, which must be entirely independent of and unassociated with any body or person outside the police service. Its purpose is to enable police personnel to consider and bring to the notice of the authorities concerned all the matters affecting their welfare and efficiency, except questions of discipline and promotion affecting individuals.

Widespread decentralization of police authority in the United States and other fundamental differences between prevailing European and American methods of police organization and selection of personnel have caused divergences in public policies concerning the right to organize of policemen in some areas here and abroad. Public policies with respect to this right also differ within the United States. Unionism of members of the police force and their affiliation with the organized labor movement have been regarded as jeopardizing the neutrality of the service in some localities. In other places it has been viewed as an effective and desirable deterrent to political use of safety departments.

The strike of the Boston police in 1919 and later union organizing campaigns among employees of safety departments caused a considerable number of local governments to restrict the right of police or firemen to engage in concerted activities, or to prohibit them from forming or joining unions altogether, at least if they are affiliated with outside labor organizations. Some municipalities have been satisfied with outlawing strikes by police and firemen. Other local governments, however, have explicitly recognized the right of all their employees to belong to unions, including the members of the police force. A federal law prohibits members of the Metropolitan police of the District of Columbia from joining or belonging to an organization,

---

[32] If a member of a police force belonged to a trade union before becoming a constable, he may, with the consent of the chief officer of police, continue his membership during the time of his service on the police force.

or an organization affiliated with another organization, which holds, claims, or uses the strike to enforce its demands. Violation of this statutory prohibition is punished by immediate discharge.[33]

The doctrine that public administrations, to preserve discipline and undivided allegiance, may restrict the freedom to organize of their staffs also has been applied to ordinances and regulations forbidding policemen to belong to unions or otherwise limiting their freedom to engage in concerted activities.[34] The United States Supreme Court indirectly sanctioned this doctrine when it denied a petition to review a decision upholding the dismissal of a policeman because of membership in an A. F. of L. union.[35]

MANAGERIAL EMPLOYEES

Employees may be divided into two broad classes: executive or managerial employees and the rank and file. In speaking of employees one usually thinks of the latter rather than the former. The higher the position of managerial employees the less they conceive of themselves as employees. Top executives of modern corporations rather regard themselves as the actual employers and entrepreneurs. At the bottom of the hierarchy of managerial personnel are the foremen and similar supervisors. Usually selected from the ranks, their status at some times and places has been controversial. Differences of opinion have existed as to whether they are already full-fledged members of management or still belong to the highest class of rank and file workers.

Top executives generally do not form or join unions of any type. Nor are their compensation and conditions of work fixed through collective bargaining. On other levels of the managerial personnel, however, a marked trend toward membership in unions of rank and file workers, or, more frequently, in special unions of supervisory employees

[33] 41 Stat. 364 (1919).
[34] See, for example, *CIO* v. *City of Dallas*, 198 S.W. (2d) 143 (1946).
[35] *McLeod* v. *City of Jackson*, 24 So. (2d) 319 (1945); 328 U. S. 863 (1946).

has developed. This trend has become especially noticeable in recent years. In the present stage of this development, no clear-cut line of demarcation exists between those classes of executives who consider themselves entrepreneurs and hence do not seek representation by organizations of the union type and those groups of managerial employees who do not regard unionization as incompatible with their position. In some countries persons in rather high positions have formed or joined associations of a union character; in others union activities, in the main, have been confined to the lower levels of management, especially foremen.

Application of the law concerning the right to organize to managerial employees also has been strongly opposed.

There has been strong opposition to unionization of managerial personnel on the part of employers as well as of executive and supervisory employees themselves. Members of both groups have held organization of managerial employees along union lines improper, especially because they have felt that they are closely connected with the employing interest and belong socially and occupationally to the class of the employers with whom they are in confidential, personal contact. They also have believed that they have no interests in common with the rank and file workers. Employers, in particular, have emphasized that exercise of full freedom to organize by managerial employees, whether high or low in the hierarchy, would make for bad relations between management and labor and would be incompatible with their position as part of management since it would cause conflicts of loyalty. Membership in or collaboration with an organization admitting other office or production workers further has been opposed on the ground that it would undermine the liberty of action and authority of the managerial personnel (and threaten the independence of the union). Many managerial employees have regarded themselves as not belonging to a homogeneous group with common interests and have not felt bound to the class of employees. They rather have regarded their position merely as a temporary stage through which they pass on their way to the post of top executives or to entrepreneurship. Aversion to collective action often has been caused simply by individualism.

Unionization of managerial employees has been increasing in recent years.

Despite objections inside and outside the ranks of the managerial employees, unionism has spread among them and in a number of countries has reached executives on levels of authority considerably higher than that of foremen. Emphasizing that, although acting for the employer in matters of the business, they still have interests of their own as employees which may be at times adverse to those of the employer, increasing numbers of managerial employees have been convinced that their occupational, economic, and social interests would be better served by organization than by individual competition. The fact that the growing size of the production units and especially the development of large-scale business corporations have tended to make the relations between employers and many types of managerial employees about as impersonal as industrial relations have become in general doubtless has contributed to this development. Not a few supervisors and executives in the lower and middle brackets share the opinion of the Chief Justice and some other members of the United States Supreme Court:

> . . . that the basic opposing forces in industry are not management and labor but the operating group on the one hand and the stockholder and bondholder group on the other. The industrial problem as so defined comes down to a contest over a fair division of the gross receipts of industry between these two groups. The struggle for control or power between management and labor be-

comes secondary to a growing unity in their common demands on ownership.[36]

Unionization of managerial personnel in the light of this philosophy, it has been argued, does not make for worse but for better relations between management and labor because the rank and file will feel that if those in the hierarchy above the workers are unionized they will be more sympathetic with the claims of those below them.[37] Still, many of those members of management who favor unionization believe that existing differences between their interests and those of the rank and file outweigh their common interests in such a degree as to make membership in common organizations or affiliation of both groups inadvisable. They rather think of themselves as a special group with typical interests of their own which should be represented by special associations. Apart from that, they agree that membership in organizations, including subordinate workers, would indeed tend to interfere with the efficient and unbiased performance of their functions. These considerations have led to a strong trend toward formation of unions of managerial employees, which are unaffiliated with general labor organizations.

*Only few laws restrict the statutory protection of
the freedom to organize of managerial employees.*

In none of the countries discussed in this study has opposition to unionization of management led to the exclusion of managerial employees from the right to form and join unions, and in only two countries have statutes restricted the protection of their freedom to organize. In France, for example, the legal provisions concerning the right to organize and its protection apply equally to maintenance,

---

[36] Mr. Justice Douglas, the Chief Justice, and Mr. Justice Burton, dissenting in *Packard Motor Car Co. v. National Labor Relations Board*, 330 U. S. 485 (1947).
[37] The same.

production, office, and managerial employees. Unions of managerial employees have existed since the nineties. While only a relatively small minority of members of management joined unions up to the outbreak of the last world war, the postwar period has brought a strong trend toward unionization, affecting not only foremen and engineers but also high officials. Most organized members of management belong to special unions which do not admit other employees to membership. Each of the three principal federations of French unions, the Confederation of Christian Workers, the General Confederation of Labor-Workers Force, and the communist General Confederation of Labor, includes a branch of managerial employees.[38] However, the vast majority of unionized members of management, especially those on higher levels, belong to the General Confederation of Managerial Employees (Confédération Générale des Cadres), an independent organization which tries to keep out of party politics.

The British law like the French law has not limited the right to organize of managerial employees. Though unionization of management apparently has not progressed nearly as far in the United Kingdom as in France, recent years have brought a considerable growth of unions organizing technical, supervisory, and managerial employees. Moreover, the contact between these organizations and the British Trades Union Congress, the principal federation of British unions,[39] has become closer. Industrial unions have sought to organize all wage and salary earners in the individual units from the bottom to the top and have established special sections for manual, clerical, managerial, or technical employees. There also exist special unions of managerial employees, for example, foremen, managers,

---

[38] See p. 260. It has been contended that the General Confederation of Labor stepped up its organizing campaigns among managerial employees after the war primarily because it realized that, in case of a communist revolution, it would be easier to take over the plants if great portions of their managements belonged to the communist organization.

[39] See p. 158.

and bank officers. But employers have continued to oppose collective bargaining with their executive staffs, and large numbers of managerial employees have remained unorganized.

Swedish foremen and other managerial employees have organized unions and federations of unions of their own. The organized employers, however, have insisted that there must be an upper limit to unionization and that officials on a higher level should not belong to unions. They have made it a rule not to promote an employee to a high supervisory position unless he quits his union because, in their opinion, he might otherwise be reluctant to give orders and enforce discipline adequately. To avoid preventing promotions of members, the unions generally have acquiesced in this rule. It proved difficult, however, to fix a clear-cut line of demarcation between managerial employees who may and those who may not belong to unions. Efforts to determine this line through agreement between the organizations on both sides have failed. Pursuant to section 23 of its constitution,[40] the Federation of Swedish Employers, for a long time, has insisted upon inclusion of a clause in all collective agreements, prohibiting managerial employees from belonging to unions of rank and file workers. The Act Respecting the Right of Association and the Right of Collective Bargaining[41] now states explicitly that a contractual provision, barring foremen from membership in an association which seeks to defend the interests of their subordinates against the employer, does not constitute an unlawful infringement of the right to organize.

In the United States, too, unionization of foremen has made considerable progress in recent years. Foremen have joined rank and file unions as well as the independent Foreman's Association of America. The movement also has spread to other types of managerial employees. The

40 See p. 163.
41 Sept. 11, 1936, Svensk Författningssamling, Sept. 22, 1936, p. 957, as amended by act of May 17, 1940, the same, May 17, 1940, p. 636, sec. 3, par. 5.

National Labor Relations Board, the federal agency administering the fundamental National Labor Relations Act, repeatedly changed its views and issued contradictory decisions with respect to status, bargaining rights, and protection under the act of supervisory employees. However, the federal government has not prohibited them from organizing in independent associations or in unions affiliated with the general labor movement. Nor have state legislators denied their right to form and join unions. Some efforts have been made to prevent their membership in organizations open to all types of workers. In Alabama, for example, it is unlawful for executive, administrative, professional, or supervisory employees to belong to labor organizations which admit other employees to membership or are affiliated with organizations which do so. In addition, any such organization would commit an unlawful act if it accepted an executive, administrative, professional, or supervisory employee as a member.[42]

In 1947 the federal legislators declared that, when used in the National Labor Relations Act, the term "employee" should not include "any individual employed as a supervisor." The term "supervisor" was defined to mean.

> . . . any individual having authority, in the interest of the employer, to hire, transfer, suspend, lay off, recall, promote, discharge, assign, reward, or discipline other employees, or responsibly to direct them, or to adjust their grievances, or effectively to recommend such action if in connection with the foregoing the exercise of such authority is not of a merely routine or clerical nature, but requires the use of independent judgment.[43]

Interpreting this definition, the United States Senate Committee on Labor and Public Welfare set forth that the provision made a distinction possible between employees with minor supervisory duties, who may have problems which justify their inclusion in the act, and supervisory employees vested with genuine managerial prerogatives,

42 Bradford Act. L. 1943, No. 298, sec. 16.
43 Act of July 5, 1935, 49 Stat. 449, as amended by act of June 23, 1947, 61 Stat. 136, sec. 2 (3) and (11).

who traditionally are regarded as part of management and therefore should not be treated as employees in the meaning of the act. Moreover, the committee refused to accept a proposal which would have provided for protection by the act at least of foremen "forming or organizing unions whose membership [is] confined to supervisory personnel and not affiliated with either of the major labor federations." In the opinion of the committee even such unions are not really independent and co-operate with rank and file organizations. But the legislators emphasized that the amendment to the original National Labor Relations Act did not prevent any one from organizing or prohibit any employer from voluntarily recognizing a union of foremen.[44] Section 14 of the statute, accordingly declared that nothing prohibits any individual employed as a supervisor from becoming or remaining a member of a labor organization, but that no employer subject to the act is *compelled* to treat supervisors as employees for the purpose of any national or local labor law relating to collective bargaining.

From all this it follows that American supervisory employees cannot avail themselves of the statutory provisions and procedures for the protection of their freedom to form, join, and assist unions, to bargain collectively and to engage in other concerted activities. Employers may, for example, discharge them for joining a union, otherwise interfere with their organizational activities, and refuse to bargain collectively, without violating the law. However, exclusion from the act also has strengthened the position of foremen, in that their organizations may with impunity undertake such concerted actions as would constitute unfair labor practices or give rise to a suit in a federal district court for contract violation[45] if done by a union covered by the statute.

44 *Federal Labor Relations Act of 1947*, S. Rept. 105, 80 Cong. 1 sess. (1947), pp. 4, 5.
45 Under sec. 301 of the Labor Management Relations Act, 1947.

PART II

COMPULSION TO ORGANIZE

CHAPTER IV

Union Problems and Policies: Pressure in Recruitment and Unorganized Workers

To avoid misunderstanding, it should be noted that the term "compulsion" is used in this study in its everyday meaning; namely, subjection of a person to high pressure to do, or to refrain from doing, an act which he would not do (or would do) in the absence of such pressure. This definition is broader than the technical legal definition, under which commission or omission of the act must be due to forcible inducement. Compulsion in the legal sense is in general unlawful, and acts done or not done under such compulsion as a rule are not binding upon a party. This survey examines to a large extent the zone in which views have differed as to whether organizing methods of unions are already or not yet compulsory in the legal sense. It deals with the "plus" in what may be called union policy of "persuasion plus." Following general custom, the terms compulsion, coercion, and constraint are applied interchangeably.

From this definition of the term "compulsion" it follows that, as used in this study, it by no means necessarily carries with it the connotation of unethical or unlawful action. A purpose of the inquiry, on the contrary, is to examine under what circumstances and for what reasons compulsion in organizational matters has been considered proper, and under what circumstances or for what reasons it has been held improper. It covers both lawful and unlawful compulsion, including statutory provisions making the establishment of, or membership in collective labor bodies mandatory.

The way in which the term is applied to union actions tallies with official usage. The International Labour Office, for example, preparing the text of a "Resolution Concerning Freedom of Association and Industrial Relations" for the thirtieth session of the International Labour Conference, analyzed collective agreements, making membership in a certain trade union a condition of employment, as providing for "compulsory membership." Yet, the Office took the view that "such a union security clause, provided that it is freely agreed upon between the parties, constitutes the soundest guarantee against discriminatory acts of an anti-trade union nature." The Conference adopted a resolution recognizing the possibility of agreeing upon such a clause.[1] Similarly, federal legislators in the United States, when the Labor Management Relations Act of 1947 was written, characterized all union security contracts as "compulsory-membership agreements" or "compulsory unionism;" yet they preserved, with qualifications, the legality of the union shop. Finally, a number of union leaders, who have advocated closed-shop and similar contracts as legitimate devices, have readily admitted that they provide for "compulsory union membership." Their position on this question will be discussed later.

DIFFERENCES IN GOVERNMENT AND UNION APPROACH

The vast majority of liberal governments have not enacted laws forcing workers to form or join unions.[2] As

---

[1] International Labour Conference, *Freedom of Association and Industrial Relations*, Report VII (1947), p. 114; the same, *Record of Proceedings, Thirtieth Session*, Geneva, 1947 (1948) pp. 329, 589.

[2] Under sec. 18 of the New Zealand *Act to Amend the Industrial Conciliation and Arbitration Act, 1925*. (1 Edward VIII, No. 6, assented to 8th June 1936) every industrial agreement is presumed to include a provision to the effect that "it shall not be lawful for any employer bound thereby to employ or to continue to employ in the industry to which the agreement relates any adult person who is not for the time being a member of a . . . union of workers bound by that agreement." Every award made by the Court of Arbitration must include a provision to the same effect. Nonunionists may be employed only if no member of a union bound by the agreement or award is ready and willing to perform the particular work required to be done.

In explaining the reasons for the introduction of compulsory unionism, it has been emphasized that New Zealand has a thinly scattered population. This fact—so runs the argument—has prevented a large number of unskilled as well as skilled workers from building up efficient union organization. The government, however, has considered the existence of strong unions desirable to secure ade-

mentioned above,[3] some countries have statutory provisions under which employees are automatically members of, or can be incorporated into certain collective labor bodies *other than unions.* This alone, however, does not mean that they are compelled to join *a union.*

Unions, on the other hand, depend for their lives on members. No labor movement can expect to achieve its objectives unless it is supported by a maximum of workers. Labor organizations thus have striven for "100 per cent membership" and have sought to organize all employees in a craft, class, or industry: industrial workers, agricultural workers, managerial employees, government employees and officials, hand and brain workers, and even self-employed persons and owners of small establishments.

As soon as self-organization began—with or without governmental sanction—tendencies rose within organized labor to exert strong pressure upon employees who were unwilling to join up voluntarily. As governments recognized freedom to organize as a fundamental right of labor, not a few organized workers came to believe that this included the right to use methods more vigorous than mere persuasion and to force fellow workers to join a union, sometimes even a specific one. This belief was strengthened in several countries by the repeal of statutes declaring compulsion to organize an unlawful act and by the increasing recognition of unions as quasi-official representatives of particular occupations or the working class.

---

quate protection of the economic interests of the workers and to improve industrial relations. Accordingly it has sought to call unions into being and to preserve their strength by suitable legislative measures. Under the present statutory regulation it has become relatively easy for a union to enroll and to keep enrolled the whole of the workers in the trade covered by the award or agreement. (See E. J. Riches, "The Restoration of Compulsory Arbitration in New Zealand," *International Labour Review,* December 1936, pp. 733 ff., and A. E. C. Hare, *Report on Industrial Relations in New Zealand* (1946), especially Chap. 7.) The law of several Australian provinces, likewise, provides for compulsory union membership.

[3] Pp. 52 ff.

*Unions have developed a pattern of
devices to compel unionization.*

Putting together experience in various countries, we gain
a systematic picture of devices for making unwilling
workers join unions or maintain membership. Before discussing union, management, and public policies pertaining
to propriety and legality of the individual devices, it seems
advisable to describe first the tactics which have been applied most frequently.

Compulsion may be used to bring workers into a union
and to preserve its strength. Devices preventing withdrawals of members have been used for the latter purpose.
The pressure may be exerted by the union as such or by
members. It may be directed against unorganized or
organized workers. In the former case the object is to make
nonunionists join up; in the latter case, to make unionists
change their affiliation. The methods used to attain these
ends are preventing the hiring of unorganized workers or
members of other unions or, if such outsiders are employed,
making them quit or causing their discharge.

The list of techniques used to prevent or put a stop to
the employment of organized or unorganized outsiders
includes special clauses in collective agreements and direct
concerted pressure on employers. Contractual clauses may
provide that only organized workers are eligible for work,
regardless of the union to which they belong. Or they may
prohibit employment of workers who are not members of
the contracting union or do not join it after they are hired.
The latter clauses exclude also organized workers who belong to another union. Instead of demanding that organized or unorganized outsiders not be hired or be discharged,
unions have insisted on agreements under which nonunion
workers or members of other unions have to work under
less favorable conditions than are enjoyed by the members
of the contracting organization. Contract clauses of all the
types here discussed have the purpose of making the situa-

tion of organized or unorganized outsiders so unpleasant and even untenable as to compel them to join a union of their choice or, if so provided, the specific contracting organization.

Unionized workers or unions, seeking to enforce exclusion from employment or discharge of organized or unorganized outsiders, not infrequently have attempted to achieve their purpose through militant tactics rather than collective bargaining. Workers have served notice that all of them will quit simultaneously or go on strike or undertake other acts of industrial warfare unless the employer accepts their demands. Through such threats or actual hostile actions, they have induced unwilling employers to refuse or to terminate the employment of outsiders rather than to suffer serious losses. The primary purpose of such labor tactics likewise has been to compel unwilling fellow workers to join a union or a specific union.

Collective agreements excluding unorganized workers or nonmembers of the contracting union from employment also prevent members from quitting the union at least so long as they wish to keep their jobs. In addition, union rules have precluded the members from resigning at will, for example, by requiring advanced notice of the intent to withdraw. Provisions of this kind not infrequently have been regarded as necessary to proper management of the union. At least in case of voluntary membership they have not been considered unduly coercive in a number of countries.

Efforts to compel union membership affect
many sectors of the population.

Involuntary unionism affects both organized and unorganized workers. In addition, important interests of other sectors of the population, especially management, and of the public in general may be involved. In so far as groups concerned have been adequately organized, they have sought to handle the matter as they have thought best for their respective purposes. Other groups—among them unorganized labor—have had to rely for protection of their interests largely upon the public authorities. Governments, as the protectors of the common weal, have taken steps to shield these groups from effects of organizing efforts of unions, which they have considered unduly injurious. Apart from that, they have endeavored to safeguard the interests of the nation as a whole, when tactics used to enroll union members have appeared to conflict with needs of the public or basic constitutional principles. The larger portion of this inquiry deals with governmental actions of that kind. Before discussing them, it seems advisable to take, at the risk of some overgeneralization, a bird's-eye view of American and European union and management policies on the subject. This preliminary analysis will shed some light on the situations with which governments have been concerned when interfering with methods of recruiting union members, and thus will explain to some extent differences in governmental attitude.

HOW MUCH PRESSURE?

The objective of those unions which have demanded that membership in any of the existing bona fide labor organizations, no matter which one, should be a condition of employment has been primarily to maintain and increase the strength of unionism. That exclusion of nonunionists tends to improve the employment opportunities of unionists has been regarded by these unions as a very welcome, additional effect of such arrangements. Labor organizations, which have gone further and have demanded that, as a condition of employment, workers have to be, become, or remain *their* members, have sought to keep out not only nonunion labor but also members of competing unions and thus to secure for themselves exclusive positions. A union, which holds a closed- or union-shop contract excluding all nonmembers from work coming under its jurisdiction, saves much of the trouble and costs ordinarily involved in efforts to recruit members and to maintain memberships; it obtains and keeps its membership in a large measure almost automatically. Moreover, job opportunities and job security of its members are considerably improved. Union demands for exclusive agreements of the first as well as the second type have been strongly motivated by the desire to obtain protection against the possibility that employers may undermine union strength by discriminating in favor of outsiders or by other hostile measures.[4]

There have been organized workers everywhere who have not had the least doubt that even the most coercive means of recruitment are justified because they feel that the outsider is asked to join their ranks merely for his own benefit. They also have believed that no worker has a moral right to enjoy the advantages coming from unionism unless he contributes to its costs by taking up membership and, in addition, actively accepts all the burdens, obligations, and responsibilities involved in union activities.

Labor leaders in many countries, though sharing the opinion that for practical and moral reasons every worker should join a union, have, however, been unwilling to sanction gross interference with the individual's freedom to organize. Many of them also have held involuntary union membership contrary to basic union ideology. Apart from such general and axiomatic reflections, union leaders have concerned themselves with the practical problem as to how high-pressure recruiting methods may affect the morale

[4] It is not possible to trace accurately the extent to which the introduction of statutory protection against such discriminatory actions of employers has influenced union policies. The general impression appears to have been that such legislation as yet has had but little, if any, effect on the tactics of unions which believe in exclusive arrangements. In the United States, according to the Secretary of Labor, the number of closed-shop, union-shop, and similar contracts even has considerably increased after the enactment of the National Labor Relations Act, which outlaws employer discrimination. This may demonstrate that unions have not thought it expedient to rely on protective legislation alone or to abandon all efforts to attain other benefits which they may derive from exclusive agreements.

of the memberships. Union policies which have resulted from the various considerations here discussed have considerable significance for the purpose of this study, for the philosophies on which they have been based have been reflected in rules regulating rights and duties of organized labor.

Profound differences in basic union ideology and in the historical development of the right and opportunity to organize have given rise to striking divergences in European and American approaches. By and large, official policies of both European governments and unions have tended to define the area of justifiable pressure narrower than have the bulk of American unions and, at least until quite recently, of American governments. Exclusion of *organized* workers from employment opportunities, in particular, has been deemed improper by most European governments as well as unions. To be sure, European courts have deviated from this general philosophy of moderation in several instances. Also, local union leaders and, even more so, union members have not always been able to check their ardor to promote the cause of unionism or of their specific organization and have compelled other workers to become or remain members. European top union leaderships as well as governments, however, have tended to preserve the voluntary character of unionism in a higher degree than union leaders and governments generally have done in the United States.

American unions have used strong pressure of various kinds.

In establishing policies with respect to recruitment of members, as well as preservation and expansion of membership and bargaining power, union leaders and members on both sides of the Atlantic have had to make up their minds as to what amount and kinds of pressure they consider justified and necessary to attain their ends.

Labor organizations in the United States, besides employing direct and indirect concerted pressure, have developed a considerable number of contractual devices suitable to make unwilling workers join unions or maintain membership. Most frequently used have been contract clauses establishing the exclusive bargaining shop, the union shop, or the closed shop, or arrangements providing for check-off of union dues and fines, preferential treatment of members of the contracting union, maintenance of union membership, and discipline of antiunion activity. Organized labor in the United States has called such clauses "union security" agreements, thus indicating that it considers them necessary for the security of the unions.[5]

Among the techniques of union security, the union- and closed-shop clauses have been the most stringent. These devices are similar in that they bind the employer to offer job applicants or employees only one of two choices namely, either to join the contracting union or not to get or to lose the job.

A closed-shop agreement requires that new employees belong to the contracting union at the time of being hired, while under a union-shop clause they must join it immedi-

[5] The demand for the closed shop is about as old as American unionism. It is said that as early as 1794 the shoemakers of Philadelphia compelled employers to hire only union members. Samuel Gompers, founder and long-time president of the American Federation of Labor, said in 1903: "It is absurd to consent to or give assent to the organization of labor and deny the logical result—the union shop." (*American Federationist*, April 1905, p. 221.) William Green, the present president of the A. F. of L., declared in 1947 that "proposals, outlawing the union security principle throughout American industry, are not only bitterly reactionary but flout over 100 years of traditional industrial practice and return organized labor to the same status it occupied at the very beginning of its struggles for recognition. They portray a profound ignorance of economics and economic philosophy and a deep misunderstanding of the purposes and functions of the union security principles. . . . We deny that any person is denied his right to work when his failure to obtain employment in a union shop is due only to his own voluntary act in refusing to become or remain a union member, although membership is open to him under reasonable terms." (*Amendments to the National Labor Relations Act*, Hearings before the House Committee on Education and Labor, 80 Cong. 1 sess., pp. 1631, 1632.) Philip Murray, president of the Congress of Industrial Organizations, testifying in the same year, likewise opposed statutory restriction of the right to make closed shop and similar agreements, calling any such measure an attempt to weaken labor unions. *Labor Relations Program*, Hearings before the Senate Committee on Labor and Public Welfare, 80 Cong. 1 sess., p. 1138.

ately or within a fixed period after they are hired. In both cases they must remain members as a condition of employment for the duration of the contract.

The effect of the closed shop on employers, employees, and unions differs from that of the union shop in several respects. In a closed shop the right of the employer to hire is limited to the hiring of members of the contracting union. Not infrequently, it has been further restricted by arrangements under which the hiring is done through or even by the union. In a union shop, however, the employer can still make relatively free use of his right to hire. The position of job applicants, not members of the union, also may be less restricted under a union-shop agreement since their qualification for the job may be left to the judgment of the employer and may not be subject to union rules, such as, for example, rules concerning appenticeship. Moreover, it is improbable that union regulations restricting admission of new members[6] will preclude their employment. This implies that in a union shop the contracting union, for all practical purposes, may have less influence upon the number and selection of new members than it has in a closed shop. It will not have the opportunities of regulating the labor supply to employers under contract which it has under a closed-shop agreement. As to pressure on workers to join the union, the two types of exclusive contract differ but little, since membership is a condition of employment under the one, and of employment beyond the short period granted to the newly hired workers to become a member under the other, and further since suspension from the union may entail discharge under both.[7]

It is of great importance for the purpose of this inquiry to note that the customary American closed or union shop is not, as popularly understood, a place of employment closed to unorganized but open to organized workers. This definition holds true with respect to most of the relatively

[6] See p. 274.
[7] But see p. 295.

rare instances of closed or union shops in the European countries discussed in this study. It does not, however, apply to the American situation in which it is not true that every qualified unionized worker has had an opportunity to be employed in a closed or union shop. Only members of *one specific* organization, namely, the contracting one, have the possibility to get or keep a job in the establishment or segment of the enterprise covered by the agreement.[8] All other unionized employees—like nonunion workers—are excluded unless they join the union holding the contract.

Under a maintenance-of-membership clause the employer has the obligation to discharge at the request of the contracting union any member who does not maintain his standing.[9] In this respect the liberty of action of management is as limited under this as under the closed- and union-shop agreement. But the employer's freedom of choice in hiring his working force is preserved. Any worker, then, who joins the union[10] is bound, as a condition of continued employment, to remain a member for the duration of the collective agreement. While closed- or union-shop clauses make membership in the contracting union a condition of employment with respect to all employees in the area covered, the maintenance-of-membership clause does so only with respect to those employees who joined though they could have retained their jobs without becoming members.[11]

The check-off agreement is a special device to secure performance of one important duty of members, namely, payment of dues. It imposes the obligation upon the employer

[8] Beyond that, an American union which, in its capacity as bargaining agent, entered into a closed- or union-shop contract, construes such a contract as giving it "a claim to the work in question." That means giving it the right to prevent the employer from assigning work tasks, ordinarily performed by its members, to anyone else. See p. 172 n. Though under different conditions, British unions too have defined the range of the work which "belongs" to its members (demarcation).

[9] Within the purview of the Labor Management Relations Act, 1947, he has this duty (and right) only when membership in the union has been terminated because of nonpayment of periodic dues.

[10] Or having been a member fails to resign during the "escape period."

[11] Preferential shop agreements do not compel workers to join a union or to remain a member in good standing. But they encourage continued membership in the contracting union by placing a definite handicap on nonmembers.

to deduct union dues, fines, and other assessments from the pay of the worker and to transmit them to the union. Through a check-off agreement unions avoid the considerable difficulties, which are otherwise involved in dues collection. They have maintained that withholding dues and turning them over to a union officer cause no, or only negligible, trouble and expense to the employer. Under the so-called general or automatic check-off clause, deductions from the pay check are made irrespective of the consent of the employees affected. Under the voluntary check-off agreement, however, the employer may withhold union dues only from the wages of those workers who authorized him individually to do so. Approximately six million workers (41 per cent of all under union agreements) were covered by some form of check-off provision in 1946. A little over half of these provisions established automatic deduction.[12]

A purpose similar to that of the check-off agreement is served by the maintenance-of-dues clause, which was written into a number of postwar agreements as a compromise solution to the controversies about the maintenance-of-membership clause. This arrangement, in its typical form, provides for the check-off of union dues and other union levies, even after employees withdraw or are expelled from the organization. In contrast to the maintenance-of-membership clause, it does not compel the employer to discipline or discharge workers who lose their good standing in the union. But it enforces payment of dues also from employees who no longer belong to the contracting union. In this respect it goes farther than the check-off agreement. As contrasted with other types of union security agreements, neither the check-off nor the maintenance-of-dues clause makes membership in the contracting union a condition of employment.

As will be discussed in a later chapter, a number of states

12 U. S. Bureau of Labor Statistics, *Extent of Collective Bargaining and Union Recognition 1946*, Bulletin 909 (1947), p. 8.

have prohibited closed-shop, union-shop, and maintenance-of-membership agreements. The National Labor Relations Act as amended in 1947 no longer considers a closed-shop agreement an excuse for refusing the hiring of a nonmember of the contracting union. The reaction up to now of many of the 60,000 to 70,000 American labor organizations to these new federal and state policies tends to show that American union thought with respect to union security agreements has not changed appreciably. They have made great efforts to replace outlawed clauses by arrangements preserving as much of former exclusive positions as is possible in the new circumstances, and they have tried to devise means of getting around the new provisions as well as they believe they can.

Some unions have sought to compel employers to sign union security agreements without regard to legal restrictions or prohibitions, occasionally with success. After decades of vigorous efforts to attain the statutory right to bargain collectively, its exercise now has been refused in some instances, in an attempt to maintain thereby existing closed shops, though refusal by unions to bargain with an employer is an unfair labor practice under the amended National Labor Relations Act. Moreover, organized labor has been trying hard to bring about the repeal of all statutory provisions restricting or eliminating their previous freedom to enter into union security agreements. Apart from that, a large number of petitions for referenda on union shop authorization, as provided by the National Labor Relations Act,[13] have been filed. In only 2.8 per cent of all referenda held from the time when the provision concerning such referenda became operative to December 1949 did the unions concerned fail to obtain the authorization of the employees to bargain for a union shop; only 7.6 per cent of the valid votes were cast against such authorization. (See table on page 140.)

13 See p. 295.

RESULTS OF UNION-SHOP AUTHORIZATION ELECTIONS[a]
AUGUST 22, 1947—DECEMBER 31, 1949

Period	Total Elections	No union authorized Number	Per cent	Eligible Voters	Total Valid Votes	Votes cast against authorization Number	Per cent
1947							
Aug. 22-Dec. 31	689	4	.6	103,072	93,691	7,258	7.7
1948							
Jan. 1-Mar. 31	5,279	89[b]	1.7	582,772	518,177	27,300	5.3
Apr. 1-June 30	11,822	251[c]	2.1	1,150,000	1,002,464	58,726	5.9
July 1-Sept. 30	8,209	277[d]	3.4	150,271	132,305	35,958	27.2
Oct. 1-Dec. 31	4,341	142[e]	3.3	457,702	392,805	24,185	6.2
1949							
Jan. 1-Mar. 31	1,295	53[f]	4.1	129,753	107,212	9,947	9.3
Apr. 1-June 30	1,137	39[g]	3.4	162,288	137,022	10,523	7.7
July 1-Sept. 30	1,231	65[h]	5.3	213,266	178,077	15,264	8.6
Oct. 1-Dec. 31	1,309	65[i]	5.0	188,106	156,933	16,416	10.5
Whole period	35,312	985	2.8		2,718,686	205,577	7.6

[a] National Labor Relations Board, *Quarterly Series of Statistics.* It should be noted that these figures mirror only the views of the relatively small number of workers who voted in these referenda and further that the percentage of elections in which authorization of the union shop was refused, has been growing over the whole period.

[b] Indeterminate: 1.	[f] Indeterminate: 2.
[c] Indeterminate: 3.	[g] Indeterminate: 1.
[d] Indeterminate: 3.	[h] Indeterminate: 3.
[e] Indeterminate: 5.	[i] Indeterminate: 4.

The check-off agreement is the only union security device which has been occasionally repudiated by American unions as contrary to proper union policy. It was opposed, for example, because dues collection was held "the union's responsibility and no affair of the company,"[14] or because direct payment was regarded as better suited "to maintain the band of friendliness with the members."[15]

A number of unions, it is true, have not used the closed-shop device. Such policy, however, appears to have been motivated by reasons of expediency rather than by ideological considerations. Unions which have refrained from demanding the closed or union shop ordinarily have done so because they have considered such request unnecessary, inadvisable, or futile in the given situation rather than because they oppose exclusive arrangements on principle.

[14] See Hamilton Watch case, N.W.L.B. release B-2219, Sept. 8, 1945.
[15] See Diamond Magnesium case, N.W.L.B. release B-1707, Aug. 20, 1944.

American unions maintain that none of their traditional security devices exerts undue pressure on nonmembers. Their stock argument is that no union security arrangement forces employees to become or remain members of the contracting union since nobody is compelled to accept work in, or to stay with, a firm operating under a security scheme not to his liking. A number of objections, however, have been raised to this kind of reasoning. It has been doubted that a union policy can be considered proper through which qualified fellow workers—even organized workers— are deprived of the opportunity to work for an employer of their choice who, without union pressure to the contrary, would be willing to employ them. Moreover, it has been pointed out that, for personal or financial reasons, considerable numbers of workers may not be able to accept, or even to look for, employment in an establishment or area other than the one covered by the closed- or union-shop agreement and thus may be compelled to join the particular union holding the contract whether they like it or not. Finally, attention has been called to the fact that union security schemes cover such a large and significant segment of American industry and commerce that job opportunities for workers, who would refuse to submit to them, have become very limited. In recent years such a large number of unions have taken to demanding the closed or union shop wherever they are selected as bargaining representatives that many unorganized as well as organized workers would find it very difficult to obtain employment and to keep their jobs without being willing to become members of a particular union because it happens to have an exclusive contract with the employer of their choice.[16] The only alternative frequently would be work at a place less desired by them or sometimes even no work at all in

[16] According to the *Report of the Governor's Labor-Management Committee* in Massachusetts (House No. 1865, 1947, p. 26) nearly one third of the non-executive and nonprofessional jobs in American industry could be held in 1945 only by persons who were members in good standing of *particular* unions.
In 1946 approximately 4.8 million workers were covered by closed- and

their chosen trade, at least in the area in which they live.

Not only the number of union security agreements increased, but figures computed by the United States Bureau of Labor Statistics also indicate that there was a marked

CHANGES IN UNION RECOGNITION IN THE UNITED STATES, 1941-46[a]

Item	1941	1942	1943	1944	1945	1946
Eligible for union-agreement coverage:						
Number (in millions)	35 [b]	31	31	30.25	29	31.2
Percentage under agreement	30	40	45	47	48	48
		Percentage Distribution[c]				
Workers under agreements providing for:						
Closed shop	} 40	45	30	28	30	33
Union shop			20	18	15	17
Maintenance of membership	d	15	20	27	29	25
Preferential hiring	d	5	2	2	3	3
Other [e]	d	35	28	25	23	22
Total		100	100	100	100	100

a U. S. Bureau of Labor Statistics, *Monthly Labor Review*, May 1947, p. 767.

b This figure is not comparable with the number listed as eligible for other years since it includes all salaried workers and all government employees. The figure which would be comparable is 31 millions.

c Percentages not strictly comparable, year by year, because of slight changes in volume of employment during the period.

d No data.

e No membership or hiring requirements are mentioned in these agreements, which have clauses specifying sole bargaining, maintenance of union dues, and bargaining for members only.

postwar trend away from the maintenance-of-membership shop, and to the more stringent union or closed shop. This is brought out by the 1946 figures in the table above.

union-shop clauses and 3.6 millions by maintenance-of-membership agreements. (*Monthly Labor Review*, May 1947, pp. 766-67.)

"Until the beginning of the war only a relatively small minority of employees (less than 20 per cent) were affected by contracts containing any compulsory features. According to the Secretary of Labor, however, within the last 5 years over 75 per cent now contain some form of compulsion." (*Federal Labor Relations Act of 1947*, S. Rept. No. 105, 80 Cong. 1 sess, p. 6.) President Truman, in his message to Congress vetoing the Labor Management Relations Bill on June 20, 1947, said that "today over 11,000,000 workers are employed under some type of union security contract."

However, American unions generally have not regarded this situation as unfair or as interfering with any freedom guaranteed by constitution or statute. They have pointed out that they have to maintain a majority status because labor laws require an employer to bargain with a union only if it has the majority in the bargaining unit. They have further maintained that they cannot carry out obligations undertaken in collective agreements unless they have disciplinary powers over all the workers who are covered.[17] Labor leaders have referred to the general trend in American labor law to grant unions, duly chosen as bargaining agents by a majority of workers, the exclusive right to represent *all* workers in the appropriate unit. Multiplicity of unions, they have said, would be incompatible with the rights and duties conferred upon them under this trend. A union duly chosen as the bargaining representative under American labor relations law has not only the *right* but also the *duty* to represent all workers in the bargaining unit, and this charges it with the responsibility of protecting the interests of both members and nonmembers with the same fairness.[18] Although statutes thus require unions to work for nonmembers,[19] they have not imposed a corresponding duty on outsiders to remunerate them for their work and expenditures. Accordingly, unions are expected to render services without compensation for nonmembers, while mem-

---

17 "To be able through union-security contracts to inflict upon wage-earners the supreme penalty of loss of employment for . . . disobedience is what gives the unions their true power over the workers: the power to make them do what the unions want them to do and to keep them from doing what the unions do not want them to do; for what greater threat is there to a wage-earner than the loss of his livelihood?" John V. Spielman, "Union Security and the Right to Work," *The Journal of Political Economy*, December 1949, p. 541.

18 See, for example, *Steel* v. *Louisville and Nashville Ry. Co.*, 323 U. S. 192 (1944); *Wallace Corporation* v. *National Labor Relations Board*, 323 U. S. 248 (1944); *Graham* v. *Southern Ry. Co.*, 74 Fed. Supp. 663 (1947); *Firemen and Engineers* v. *Tunstal*, 163 Fed. (2d) 289 (1947), cert. den. 332 U. S. 841 (1947).

19 The National Labor Relations Board rejected the plea of a union not to include in the bargaining unit a shop the workers of which were not subject to its jurisdiction and hence had not been covered by its organizational activities. The board held that neither the union's jurisdictional limitations nor the extent of its organizational activities were proper determinants of a bargaining unit. *Oliver G. Kelly* and *Local 651, Int. Brotherhood of Boilermakers*, 78 NLRB 1166 (1948).

bers have to pay for them. This dilemma is an effect of the dual position of American unions, which labor relations laws treat simultaneously as voluntary private associations and as statutory bargaining agents under public law—positions of very different character.[20] The unions consider union security agreements the best way out of this quandary.

Organized labor in the United States as in other countries, furthermore, has argued that a union which has organized the workers and established certain standards of employment in one enterprise has a legitimate interest in introducing and maintaining the same standards in all establishments in the industry and that it can achieve this goal only by securing the largest possible number of members among the workers in this branch of the economy. When efforts to organize the maximum of eligible workers clash with a desire of unorganized or organized individuals not to join the union concerned, then American union policy generally holds individual wishes must yield to union interest. This demand is justified, labor leaders have contended, especially because the union interest is identical with the well-considered interest of the individuals themselves. The latter, according to the unions, have no alternative except submission to the authority of a union or to the rule of the employer; they should choose the first since they have a voice in the determination of union but not of management policies.

Leading American unionists thus have not denied that under union security agreements workers may be forced, irrespective of their personal desires, to join the contracting union and to remain members. "Of course, it's coercion," an authoritative representative of the opinion of organized labor once said. "That's what all the argument is about: the right to force someone to do something against his

---

[20] The Kansas Supreme Court held that a union duly chosen as bargaining agent under the Railway Labor Act has the character of a government agency. *Betts* v. *Easley*, 169 P (2d) 831 (1946).

will."[21] But it has been added that the admittedly compulsory nature of exclusive agreements does not justify opposition to the closed or union shop. As we have seen, labor leaders have contended that coercion exercised by workers against other workers in the latter's own interest cannot be objectionable. In addition, the argument runs, "coercion is the fundamental basis of organized society. In fact, civilization can be said to have attained maturity when men became intelligent enough to order their affairs and compel the recalcitrant man, the ignorant man, to submit to certain compulsory rules for the common good of all men."[22]

Moreover, American labor leaders have most vigorously contended against statements by employers that their objections to closed and similar shops were predicated upon a sincere concern for the freedom of the individual worker to refrain from union membership or for his right to work.[23] They have asserted that management ordinarily has shown little, if any, interest in anyone's right to work and that the only right the worker has had in practice has been "the right to go from employer to employer in search of work. His right to work depends entirely upon his ability to find someone who has the means and inclination to hire him, and no matter how willing or anxious he cannot force himself upon an employer, but he may be denied this inalienable right upon any reason or pretext no matter what."[24] Accordingly, it has been asserted that "the alleged inalienable right to work is a myth" and that it is not one "of the precious few inalienable rights workers enjoy." On these grounds union leaders have declared the use by employers "of this false doctrine" to be "ironic and, of course, insin-

21 Clinton S. Golden and Harold J. Ruttenberg, The Dynamics of Industrial Democracy (1942), p. 217.
22 The same.
23 See pp. 186-87.
24 Golden and Ruttenberg, The Dynamics of Industrial Democracy, p. 195, quoting Clarence S. Darrow, The Open Shop.

cere." Organized labor, on the other hand, unionists have
stated, has given substance to the right to work; but it has
not established it as a pure right, because in modern society
it is always conditioned upon an employer providing work.
Consequently, compulsory union membership does not
deny workers their "inalienable right to work"—because
they enjoy no such right and, therefore, cannot be denied
something that they already do not possess.[25]

In addition, American unions have maintained that
"the right of a nonunionist to work is in no way equivalent
to or the parallel of the right to work as a union member."
They have asserted that there exists no constitutional right
to work as a nonunionist, while the right to maintain employment free from discrimination because of union membership is constitutionally protected.[26]

Since opportunity to accept or continue employment in enterprises covered by closed-shop contracts is denied only to those who
voluntarily choose to refuse to join the union, it cannot be said
that these contracts impinge upon the right to work in any absolute
sense. Where the enjoyment of rights is conditioned upon compliance with reasonable conditions, individuals who voluntarily refuse
to comply with such conditions are not being deprived of those
rights.[27]

The condition imposed upon employment in particular enterprises by closed-shop contracts, namely union membership, so runs the argument, is, however, not unreasonable
as such. "If the right to work be conceded its full meaning,
the right to work at a fair wage and under conditions attained through joint action of workers, then the closed shop
serves to advance that right and not violate it."[28]

25 The same, pp. 193-94, 199, 200.
26 *Lincoln Union v. Northwestern*, 335 U. S. 525 (1949).
27 Brief for Appellants *In re A. F. of L. v. American Sash Co.*, 335 U. S. 538
(1949); *Lincoln Union v. Northwestern* and *Whitaker v. North Carolina*, 335
U. S. 525 (1949), p. 65.
28 *The Closed Shop and Union Security*, Economic Brief of the American
Federation of Labor, 1947, p. 97, filed for the appellants in the same cases.

Most American unions contend that union security agreements also blend with the principle of freedom from employer interference with organizational activities of workers. The purpose of this principle, it is explained, is to prevent management from dominating employee organization. This purpose, the majority of American union leaders hold, is promoted rather than defeated if the employer, who entered into a closed- or union-shop agreement, requires as a condition of employment membership in the duly chosen union over which he has no control. Conclusion and execution of security contracts with such bargaining representatives, unions say, cannot be regarded as undue interference with freedom of the workers or as improper discrimination. In complying with the contract, the employer merely carries through the wishes of the union. Whatever pressure and discrimination may be involved, so runs the argument, is in the last analysis exerted by the union rather than by management, and the union acts in the interest of those whom it was chosen to represent.

As to the check-off, labor leaders in the United States have asserted that it is not only a convenient method of collecting dues and other union levies, but also a fair and efficient device to avert industrial disputes. Unions have emphasized that it is beneficial for employers because it forestalls discharge of workers employed in closed, union, or maintenance-of-membership shops merely for failure to pay union dues or other union assessments, and because it prevents interference with production by direct collection.

The persistence with which American labor leaders have insisted upon the right to make workers become and remain union members by means of exclusive union security agreements, has been largely due to the desire to checkmate potential moves by management which may weaken the position of unions. But an important contributing factor doubt-

less has been the historical experience that strong individualism among American workers again and again made
their unionization and maintenance of union stability a
very difficult task. It has sometimes been so difficult that
unions used the technique of seeking to obtain exclusive
contracts from employers instead of attempting first to
unionize their workers by means of persuasion.

Significant differences between economic, social, and
political conditions on the two sides of the Atlantic have
been responsible for the fact that group cohesiveness has
tended to be less strong among the bulk of American than
of European workers. In contrast to the latter, the former
have enjoyed political equality in the period of development of the labor movement. The social status of most
American workers, likewise, has been higher than that of
the major portion of European wage earners. It also has
been more flexible. Employees in the United States have
had greater opportunity to advance to high managerial
positions or to set up in business for themselves. Moreover,
Americans longer than Europeans have had a chance to
escape difficulties in the labor market by remaining in
agriculture or by moving to frontier areas. All this has prevented American wage earners from feeling frozen to a
certain locality or class—a sentiment that has been very
strong among European workers. Many of those, too, who
have come to the United States to find personal liberty and
independence have been little disposed to acquiesce in
limitation of individual freedom of action which membership in a union may call for. In addition, immigration and
ethnic differences, coupled with tendencies toward segrega-
tion and discrimination for reasons of creed, national origin, or color, have further hampered the development of
working class solidarity of the type that has prevailed on the
other side of the Atlantic. Largely for these reasons "the
over-shadowing problem of the American labor movement

has always been the problem of staying organized. No other labor movement has ever had to contend with the fragility so characteristic of American labor organizations."[29]

European unions have used less
pressure than American unions.

The fact that "union security" in the American technical meaning of the term has not been as significant an issue in European as in American union policies is borne out in part by the shorter list of devices used in Europe to make unwilling workers take up or maintain membership. In so far as unions on the other side of the Atlantic have worked toward contractual exclusion of outsiders from employment opportunities, they have tried to obtain a closed, union, or preferential hiring shop. In the aggregate, however, demands for exclusive agreements have been made relatively seldom. Above all, in militant as well as negotiatory steps unions in the European countries, here discussed, generally have been careful to distinguish between organized and unorganized nonmembers. Most of them have considered discrimination against members of any bona fide labor organization to be incompatible with proper union ideology. The closed or union shop, accordingly, has never reached the stage common in the United States. This attitude has been motivated in no small measure by the desire to avoid interunion controversies, such as have resulted from closed-shop and similar agreements in the United States.

The maintenance-of-membership clause has not been on the list of customary European union techniques. For preservation of membership the organizations have relied chiefly upon their rules, the advantages coming from continued membership, and the loyalty of their adherents.

[29] Selig Perlman and Philip Taft, "History of Labor in the United States, 1896-1932," *Labor Movements,* Vol. 4 (1935), p. 7.

Unions as well as many governments have not looked upon rules precluding withdrawals for a period of time as undue coercion where the members concerned had submitted to them by voluntary enrollment.

The check-off clause has been rarely demanded by European unions. Organizations functioning more or less under the influence of Marxian philosophy, that means a very substantial portion of European organized labor, oppose the check-off as a matter of principle. Acceptance of employer assistance in their activities, especially if consisting in measures against members, would not be in line with their concept of unionism. The idea also is alien to most unions with other philosophies. Leaders representing movements of diverse ideologies agree that collection of union dues by the employer instead of direct payment by the members is unlikely to promote union cohesion and loyalty. In addition, management as well as public opinion would react rather strongly against check-off clauses. Deduction of union dues and levies by the employer obviously offers the union a better chance to get the money than collection by union officers. Even though labor organizations in a number of European countries can sue members for dues and fines, it still is difficult to enforce judgments successfully. Prevailing abstention from using the check-off system, however, has not resulted in general or gross impairment of European union stability. Union rules providing for punishment and eventually writing off of members who are in arrears and regulating readmission have proved effective.

European labor organizations have been confronted with many of the problems which have called forth strong and numerous demands for closed-shop and similar agreements in the United States. Beyond that, seen through the eyes of American union leaders, the need for union security arrangements may appear even greater in Europe than in the United States. European labor laws generally have not conferred upon unions such legal powers as they have under our labor relations statutes. In many European countries, labor organizations, moreover, do not enjoy the same amount of statutory protection as anti-injunction acts and other recent laws have given to American unions. On the other hand, the number of rival movements is larger in many European countries than in the United States. Finally, the chances of workers to find employment at the place of their choice without joining a union, or even a specific union, often are greater than in many areas of our country.

Yet, all this has not caused European organized labor to put "union security clauses" nearly as high on the list of its demands as American unions have done. The discussion in the remainder of this chapter and in the following chapter will show, in particular, some of the reasons why closed and union shops of the type customary in America have not been common in Europe. One of the reasons probably has been that the pronounced group cohesiveness of labor in Europe has in many countries favored the development of strong and stable unions without much use of that kind of pressure upon workers that is inherent in exclusive agreements, especially of the brand common in the United States. Prevailing fundamental union ideology and the structure of the labor movement in the individual countries have been other contributing factors. As will be seen, European union leaders have been apprehensive of potential undesirable effects of involuntary unionism such as, for example, indifference of members and governmental intervention in union affairs. Finally, in a number of industries in some countries most employers have taken to giving hiring preference to union members without any contractual obligation to do so.

UNORGANIZED WORKERS

In both the United States and Europe unions have worked toward the highest possible degree of unionization and the ideal goal of each union has been to attain a membership including all the workers coming under its jurisdiction.

*The presence of unorganized workers hampers
the full attainment of union goals.*

In the absence of the American majority principle[30] the existence of nonmembers in an enterprise may hamper union activities even more in Europe than in the United States. In both areas the carrying through of obligations undertaken in collective agreements is more difficult if the union concerned has no power over a portion of the workers. The presence of outsiders also has impeded efforts of both American and European unions to stabilize standards of employment in whole regions or industries. The availability of cheaper nonunion labor may be a constant menace to the very existence of a union. Accordingly, organizations such as, for example, the British Trades Union Congress, have established the principle that "a union which has the responsibility of maintaining fair wages and working conditions, must also have the right to determine, according to the circumstances in the particular case, whether or not it is wise or safe to tolerate nonunionism and thereby permit the presence of actual or potential black-legs, in industries where union rates and conditions have been established." Furthermore, though European labor laws generally have not granted particular unions the statutory right to represent nonmembers, governments have tended to recognize central labor organizations as the representatives of the occupational interests of the working class. To discharge duties coming from this recognition, the organizations of course seek to have large and representative memberships.

30 See p. 232.

European unions also dislike "free riders," but
they are somewhat reluctant to force them to enroll.

For all these reasons European, like American, organized labor has looked askance at nonunionists. Union movements of any type have felt strongly that all employees should work together for their common goals and share all the responsibilities involved. In Europe this demand has been intensified through the widespread tenet of the class war and strong belief in working class solidarity. This philosophy, naturally, tends to produce special dislike for such members of the working class as do not join their fighting organizations. This dislike which has been entertained by most European unionists, no matter whether or not they believe in the class war, has produced not a few instances of refusal to work together with nonunion employees. Like American organized workers, European union members have tended to regard unorganized employees as a kind of parasite which benefits from union activities without contributing to the costs[31] and without taking the risks involved in working for union goals.

If unions determine that it would not be either "wise or safe to tolerate nonunionism" in an establishment, they

---

[31] Occasional efforts have been made to remove the basis for this complaint without compelling outsiders to join labor organizations. Some agreements in the United States provided that nonmembers of the union functioning as bargaining representative had to contribute to its expenses for collective bargaining. Under such arrangements the employer had to deduct from the wages of *nonunion* workers amounts equal to the union dues or other fixed sums, to defray the expenditures of the union. The NLRB held a provision of this kind a valid union security agreement. *Public Service Company of Colorado* and *Charles G. Smith,* 89 NLRB No. 51 (1950). A number of state statutes, however, have declared it unlawful to require a nonunion worker, as a condition of employment, to make periodic payments to a labor organization. (Ala., Bradford Act, General Laws No. 298, sec. 15 (1943); Ga., H.B. 72, sec. 11 (1947); Ia., S.B. 109, sec. 4 (1947); Mass., Chap. 149, sec. 150a (1943); N. H., Chap. 212, sec. 21 (1947); N. C., H.B. 229, sec. 5 (1947); Tenn., S.B. 367, sec. 3 (1947); Tex., H.B. 100, sec. 8a (1943); Va., H.B. 23, sec. 5 (1947).

The Federal Labor Management Relations Act, 1947, now prohibits employers from paying any money to a union, representing any of his employees. This prohibition does not apply to the check-off of membership dues, if authorized by each worker concerned. Since nonmembers of the contracting union do not have to pay membership dues, agreements of the kind discussed in the preceding paragraph can no longer be made within the purview of the new act. The latter, however, does not deal with deduction of money which is not earmarked for the union. Employers therefore have agreed to deduct an amount equal to the

may seek to unionize outsiders through coercive tactics or through persuasion stopping short of compulsion. Use of the former method may not seem basically improper to adherents of the dogma that maintenance of class solidarity is an imperative duty of every worker. On the other hand the concept of class solidarity simultaneously tends to cause aversion to measures by which workers would complicate the struggle for a living of members of their own class. A number of European unions have been somewhat relieved of this dilemma because in some countries, such as Britain and Sweden, unorganized workers are no longer hired in certain industries, though their employment is not forbid-

---

union dues from the wages of nonunion employees and to turn it over, for example, to local charity. Such employers have made this arrangement a condition of employment for nonmembers of the contracting union. Agreements of this type differ from the contracts discussed before because they do not provide for contributions to the costs of collective bargaining. But they are suitable to achieve the other end sought by unions making such contracts, namely, to discourage refusal to join them.

In foreign countries unions do not represent directly nonmembers in collective bargaining. Wage rates and other conditions of employment agreed upon in the collective contract, however, may apply also to nonunion workers in the enterprise or area concerned. Under sec. 31 of the French Act Respecting Collective Agreements of Dec. 23, 1946, for example, the provisions of approved agreements entered into by the most representative organizations of employers and employees ordinarily apply to all the workers in the occupations and areas within their scope. The Swedish Labor Court held that an employer, who is bound by a collective agreement, must observe its terms with respect to members as well as nonmembers of the contracting union, unless the agreement explicitly provides otherwise. (AD dom 95/1932 and AD dom 75/1933). In Belgium, Britain, Hungary, Ireland, Luxembourg, the Netherlands, Poland, Portugal, and Switzerland, statutory provisions exist to make a collective agreement applicable to employers and employees who are not directly bound by it, primarily if it has gained great significance in a region or industry. In case of such extension of an agreement nonunion workers, too, obtain the benefits of the contract. Besides, the existence of collective agreements may improve the conditions of unorganized workers even though they are not formally covered, because union contracts tend to establish a pattern with respect to wages and other conditions of employment not only for unionized but also for nonunionized employees.

The arbitration award of Jan. 29, 1946, settling a dispute in the Canadian automobile industry, took cognizance of this situation and ordered the compulsory deduction by the employer of union dues from the wages of all employees covered by the award, whether or not they are members of the union. See "A New Union Security Principle in Canada," *International Labour Review*, March-April 1946, p. 224.

Such arrangements as discussed in this footnote, however, have been exceptional. Nonunion workers usually do not contribute to the costs of making and carrying through collective agreements.

den by collective agreements.[32] In the many geographical or industrial areas, in which such custom does not prevail, union leaders, although doing their best to organize non-union employees, have developed considerable reluctance to use compulsion.

They have done so for many and various reasons. Sympathy with nonunionists has not been among their motives. Nor have they shown a strong desire to facilitate the exercise of a right to refrain from joining labor organizations.[33] But European unions generally tend to attach special importance to quality of members. As typical may be quoted this statement of the leader of a large federation, made in rejecting a move that all employers should be asked to hire only organized workers:

Our gain in quantity would be our loss in quality. The strength of our federation does not rest merely on the number of members. It also depends very largely on their spirit. A big mass of members who do not belong to us voluntarily would present ballast which will pull us down to the bottom.

In this vein European unions may prefer a smaller number of voluntary adherents to a larger membership includ-

[32] The reports of two American government commissions which studied industrial relations in Europe corroborated this fact. The President's Commission on Industrial Relations in Great Britain reported that "closed-shop agreements are exceptional and do not appear to be seriously sought for. Nevertheless we were told by both union and employer representatives that in some industries there is virtually a closed shop in practice, as distinguished from one by contract, the employers preferring to engage union men and in some instances, at the request of the union, suggesting to particular individuals that they should join. The check-off is very exceptional, and several union representatives stated their opposition to it." *Report of the Commission on Industrial Relations in Great Britain* (1938), p. 23. Similarly the President's Commission on Industrial Relations in Sweden stated that it did not find instances of the check-off or of closed-shop contracts either with members of the Employers' Federation or with employers not members of the Federation. "The closed shop is not a significant issue in Sweden," the Commission said, "because of the very large proportion of workers who are union members and because the employers no longer try to break down union organization, preferring to deal with their workers through strong trade-unions. On the other hand, the employers are not asked by the unions to exercise, and they do not exercise, pressure upon their employees to make them join the unions." *Report of the Commission on Industrial Relations in Sweden* (1938), p. 4.

[33] The position taken by organized labor with respect to protection of the exercise by workers of full freedom to refrain from joining a union will, for the sake of greater clearness, be discussed in the section on "The Right to Refrain from Joining a Union." pp. 197 ff. below.

ing a high percentage of involuntary members. The objective is to maintain thereby a membership willing to work for the organization. Since European unions ordinarily have functioned without encouragement by special statutes, such as the labor relations acts in the United States, their success has depended largely upon active co-operation of their members beyond payment of dues. Labor leaders thus have emphasized that expanding and improving organizations imply more than the mere enrollment of workers. They have stressed that it means encouraging members "to become active constituents of their organization, taking their part in its work and promoting its aims and objects." Basic American union philosophy has likewise recognized that a union draws its strength from the voluntary loyalty of its membership. But many European, in contrast to virtually all American, top union leaders have not expected much loyalty and discipline from workers who join merely under the pressure of arrangements making membership in a specific union a condition of employment. Where organizations include many members of that kind, they have feared "unionism will lose its momentum which springs from voluntary adherence and free choice by its members." Without this momentum, apprehension has been expressed, unions may become "inert bodies in the hands of bosses who are either dictators or inefficient bureaucrats," especially if the union be maintained automatically on the basis of the check-off system.

To sum up, European unionists have exerted strong pressure on unorganized workers. Moreover, the zeal to increase the number of members sometimes has proved stronger than considerations of the kind discussed in the preceding paragraphs. But a tendency to avoid gross impairment of voluntariness, both in enrollment of members and in legislative policies, still prevails. Under this trend unions have sought to eliminate injury to their interests, which may result from the presence of nonunionists, by

bringing a maximum of them into the fold through persuasion and through offering attractive services. If organizations have wished to close an establishment to unorganized workers they have ordinarily not worked toward a
closed- or union-shop agreement but have rather attempted
to attain a number of voluntary members large enough to
enable unionists to refuse to work with nonunionists. Even
where unions have practiced a policy of more intensive and
direct pressure, they have ordinarily not demanded exclusive agreements of the type customary in the United States,
providing that the management must employ only workers
who belong to *one specific* union. Such agreements, as will
be presently discussed, have been exceptional in Europe.[34]

[34] In at least one instance an American union, the International Typographi-
cal Union, recently proposed to write into the agreement that its members may
refuse to work with nonunion workers. The reason was that after the 1947
amendment to the National Labor Relations Act the union could no longer lawfully demand the closed shop which it had prior to the new legislation. This
proposal may have had the purpose to preserve actually the hitherto existing
situation. Its language, however, presented a change from the American type of
closed-shop policy, which is directed indiscriminately against organized and unorganized outsiders, to that type of closed-shop policy directed against unorganized workers only as has been practiced by some European unions.

CHAPTER V

Union Problems and Policies: Competition Among Unions and Government Intervention

In all industrial countries a multitude of unions compete with each other for members and in other respects. There is hardly a country in which all employees or all unions belong to one central federation. In some countries, however, most of the important unions are affiliated with one principal organization, such as, for example the British Trades Union Congress or the Swedish Confederation of Trade Unions.[1] This may be called singularism. In other countries the labor movement is split in several organized factions which are represented by a corresponding number of central organizations. This may be called pluralism. Such pluralism may be caused by a variety of factors rang-

---

[1] The purpose of the Trades Union Congress, which was formed in the 1860's, has been to co-ordinate the British labor movement rather than to centralize it. It is essentially a loose federation of autonomous organizations, to which nearly all eligible unions of importance belong. Unions operating in Scotland have established the *Scottish Trades Union Congress.* The vast majority of its members belong to unions which operate also outside Scotland and are affiliated with the British Trades Union Congress. Two other central organizations, the Irish Trades Union Congress and the Congress of Irish Unions, are active in Eire and Ulster. A number of their member organizations likewise are members of the British Trades Union Congress.

The Swedish Confederation of Trades Unions was established in 1898. Like the British Trades Union Congress, it comprises the vast majority of unions and unionists in the country. A relatively small number of manual workers belong to various minor independent organizations, among them the *Swedish Workers' Central Organization,* a syndicalistic association with 20,000 to 25,000 members. In addition, salary earners have organized unions of their own which formed the *Central Organization of Salaried Employees.* The latter has about 240,000 members, employed by private employers, municipalities, and the state. The *Central Organization* is not affiliated with the Swedish Confederation of Trades Unions, but it co-operates with it in matters of mutual interest. The members of the Confederation have been little disposed to yield much of their autonomy to the top organization. But the Confederation has exercised increasing influence upon general labor and wage policy. In 1941 its authority to do so was formally expanded by certain amendments to its by laws. Member organizations now must submit to the Confederation for approval certain decisions of great importance—for example, the calling of major strikes.

ing from diversity of political, social, or other ideologies to structural differences, such as craft and industrial unionism. Basic differences of the former type have been chiefly responsible for pluralism in European countries. In the United States disagreement in respect to structural questions has largely—though not exclusively— caused a split in the labor movement and the formation of a new central federation of unions—the Congress of Industrial Organizations—in addition to the older American Federation of Labor.[2]

COMPETITION AMONG UNIONS

The problem of rival unionism is equally significant under singularism and pluralism. Under both systems competitive strategies of unions may affect not only the workers but also management and the general public. We are here concerned merely with the rights which unions claim in competition for members.

[2] Many workers, as well as a number of employers, have held a unified labor movement more beneficial than plurality of organizations. To prove their point they have called attention to successes achieved under singularism with respect to industrial relations and social protection in countries such as Australia, Britain, the Scandinavian sector of Europe, and New Zealand. Moreover, it has been pointed out that a unified labor movement is better equipped to prevent and settle interunion disputes.

Beyond that, it has been proposed that there should be only one union movement in order to prevent ideological conflicts and disunity in the working class. This suggestion has been made by members of the latter for the purpose of strengthening solidarity of labor. But it has also been predicated upon the public interest. One school of thought has demanded, for example in France, that the establishment of only a single organization should be permitted in each group representing a community of interests. This suggestion, however, has been rejected as smacking of authoritarianism.

Others have considered the existence of several factions in the labor movement of a country, representing different ideologies, to be a natural and healthy manifestation of the manifoldness of human relations and ambitions characteristic of democracy. Adherents of this philosophy have regarded corresponding plurality of organizations as a safeguard against the trend toward ideological and economic monopolization inherent in highly organized and concentrated group movements. According to this school of thought the manner in which unions function side by side under pluralism may well be the acid test of true democratic thinking within organized labor in the countries concerned.

*In European systems of singularism unions
ordinarily have not sought employment monopolies.*

Under both singularism and pluralism the tactics of
rival unions will be influenced a great deal by the position
they take with regard to union solidarity. Where the majority of important organizations are affiliated with one
central federation, solidarity will in a large measure mean
maintenance of the degree of discipline and good relations
indispensable among unions which belong to one and the
same organization, be it only a loose one. Unions in European countries with one big central federation generally
have not sought to make collective agreements giving them
the position of the sole bargaining agent to the exclusion
of other bona fide bodies. In case of friction among organizations competing in an individual establishment, union
machinery exists to settle questions of demarcation through
negotiation, conciliation, or arbitration. A recent statement of the British Minister of Labour, himself a member
of the labor movement, may be quoted as an example of
union policy under singularism:

> We have been asked this very vital and important question about
> the attitude that only one union should be recognized. That is not
> the Trades Union Congress attitude. It is laid down by the Trades
> Union Congress that there shall not be a complete and absolute
> right of recognition in any industry to any one union. They will
> not say this class of workers must go into this union, and this class
> into another union. The American A. F. of L. does that but the
> Trades Union Congress has its own special committee, its disputes
> committee, which settles each case on its merits, and, as a rule, to
> the complete satisfaction of the unions that bring the cases before
> them. . . .[3]

Almost twenty years earlier another prominent British
labor leader, the present Prime Minister Attlee, said in the
House of Commons: "We ought not to say, 'Here is a particular union, you must join that, and leave your own.' I

---

[3] House of Commons, 19 November 1946, Debate on Closed Shop, Official
Report, *Parliamentary Debates,* 1946-1947, Vol. 430, col. 758 ff.

have resisted that when it was tried on. That is not fair."[4]

These statements mirror the official policy of the British unions as expressed in the report of the Executive Council to the 1946 convention of the Trades Union Congress:

> The "closed shop" in the sense of an establishment in which only members of a particular union can be employed, to the exclusion of members of other unions, is alien to British trade union practice and theory. Congress has never consented to the recognition of an exclusive right to organise by one union where other unions have built up their organization side by side.

About two months before this convention, the Transport and General Workers' Union, a member of the Trades Union Congress, however, had signed a collective agreement with the London Passenger Transport Board according to which only members of this union could be employed by the Board in certain types of work. This has been widely criticized as an employment monopoly for members of one specific union that is, as a closed shop of the American type. At about the same time a few more instances occurred in which members of a union objected to the presence in an establishment of members of another union. Moreover, a number of municipal governments which are controlled by Labor majorities recently have sought to exclude from employment in public services members of any union except the one which they consider appropriate.

These events caused considerable discussion within and outside the labor movement, especially because public corporations have been involved. Admission of the closed-shop system in such corporations would not only be a significant break with tradition but also would be particularly momentous in view of the introduction of government-established boards in nationalized industries. The T.U.C. General Council has protested sharply against the application of the term "closed shop" to the situation created in the London Passenger Transport service and to similar recent hap-

---

[4] Official Report, *Parliamentary Debates*, Commons, Vol. 207, 31 May 1927, col. 260-61, Trade Disputes Bill.

penings. It pointed out that the action of the Transport and General Workers' Union did in no wise interfere with agreements of a number of other unions with the London Passenger Transport Board and that it was merely directed against a "breakaway" union, namely the National Passenger Workers' union. Formation of splinter unions by breaking away from an existing union generally has been considered contrary to official T.U.C. policy. The General Council denies recognition to, and rejects application for, affiliation from any organization formed by dissident members without the assent and good will of the union from which they seceded. In another recent case company domination was cited as the reason for objection to working together with members of a particular union. In short, official British union policy still rejects the "closed shop" in the sense that only members of a specific union can be employed, to the exclusion of members of other bona fide unions. Efforts to close a shop to members of another labor organization have, as yet, been limited to unions not considered bona fide, such as "breakaway" or "company-dominated" unions. This policy, indeed differs from union policy common in the United States.

However, the principle of refusing to recognize as bona fide any new union merely because its founders seceded from another organization and without examining the merits of the case has been criticized for various reasons. It has been said, among other things, that this policy like the closed shop presents an unjustified departure from full freedom to form and join unions of one's own choosing. The T.U.C., however, has held that "the complete recognition of the right of members to move from union to union may destroy stability of organization, undermine loyalty and lead to an undesirable extension of the number of unions concerned in negotiations with a single employer. Any union facilitating this chopping and changing would probably find that in their turn they would experience the same difficulties as the original union." We are here not concerned with the merits of this policy;[5] nor do we have to discuss the question whether the events mentioned above may lead to a trend toward the American type of the closed shop. Suffice it to state that, at present, official union policy under the British system of singularism does not favor collective agreements excluding members of other bona fide unions from employment opportunities.

Such agreements likewise are not made between members of the two principal employers' and employees' federations in Sweden—another country with prevailing singularism. The constitution of the Federation of Swedish Employers, representing the great majority of the important employers, prescribes in section 23 that any collective contract must include a clause to the effect that the employer shall have the right to hire and dismiss workers at his discretion, to direct and distribute the work, and to employ workers belonging to any union or workers who belong to no union. Organized labor objected vigorously to this provision. But in a master agreement, made as early as 1906, it recognized these rights of management in return for the assurance of management that it would continue to respect the right of labor to organize.

At present unions as a rule do not demand closed-shop agreements from, and they are not granted by, members of the Federation of Swedish Employers. Clauses to the effect that only members of a particular union may be hired have been written into agreements between unions and some of the relatively few unorganized employers. According to the Federation, the number of such contracts, however, tends to decrease, largely because unorganized employers not infrequently have become members, and closed-shop clauses thus have been abolished. Organized labor and management in Sweden agree that the closed-shop agreement is no longer a controversial issue of great significance in their country, either as a device to exclude nonunionists

[5] See p. 225.

or as a device to close the establishment to members of another labor organization.

Agreements excluding members of rival unions ordinarily have not been sought under European pluralism.

Agreements excluding members of other unions from job opportunities have been exceptional also in those European countries in which the labor movement has been directed by several competing central federations. In the United States, however, such contracts have become a customary weapon in competition among rival movements.

It requires no elaboration that the reasons which cause reluctance in European countries to force unorganized workers into unions are bound to cause even stronger disinclination to demand changes in union allegiance from organized workers. Regardless of the position taken with respect to the class-war doctrine, European unions functioning under pluralism have in most instances felt that members of any bona fide union should not be deprived of opportunities to work merely because of their union affiliations. The president of the important, non-Marxist French Confederation of Christian Workers,[6] for example, declared at the thirtieth session of the International Labour Conference that a provision in a collective agreement making membership in a certain trade union a condition of employment or continued employment—the American type of the closed and union shop—"is by its very nature absolutely contrary to freedom of association."[7] The Swiss Government delegate said on the same occasion:

> I was very much surprised to learn that the American Federation of Labor was a champion of the "closed shop," because at the beginning of the memorandum which it communicated to our Organisation it said that every human being has the right to carry on his activity in freedom and in dignity. Should we be respecting that freedom and dignity for the worker if we face him with the

[6] See p. 260.
[7] International Labour Conference, *Record of Proceedings*, Geneva 1947, (1948), pp. 302-03.

alternative of joining an association contrary to his convictions, or plunging his family in poverty? That is really the dilemma which too often results from the system of the "closed shop." In saying this, I am not speaking merely on behalf of the Government of my country, but on behalf of our whole delegation, and more particularly of the Workers' representatives.[8]

Moreover, many European central organizations have taken the position that democracy means collaboration of different groups rather than monopoly of one group to the exclusion of others.

Labor organizations in Europe generally have endeavored to reconcile in some workable manner their individual business interests as well as their natural ambition to overcome competition by rival organizations with this basic philosophy of union solidarity and democracy. This of course has not been easy to achieve. Maintenance of good relations between competing labor organizations which do not belong to the same parent body has been a complex problem, especially since ordinarily under pluralism no such comprehensive and influential union machinery for the settlement of questions of demarcation exists as can be provided under singularism. Moreover, multiplicity of union movements renders it more difficult to represent the common economic- political and social interests of the working class—a responsibility which an increasing number of governments have conferred upon central organizations. Nevertheless, though interunion fights have not been eliminated in Europe either, they have been kept down in number and significance despite the fact that the various labor movements in individual countries ordinarily are separated from each other by profound differences in general philosophy.

Such self-restraint as has existed in European interunion competition, however, has not resulted exclusively from ideological considerations. It also has been dictated by necessity. Since the general ideologies of most American

8 The same, p. 323. For similar statements by Swiss union leaders see p. 169.

unions do not differ nearly as much as those of their European counterparts, an American worker may switch from one bargaining representative to another merely for reasons of expediency. He may act like any other person who has to choose an agent to represent him in important negotiations or other proceedings, so that he may be guided solely by his opinion. Where the change of the representative does not occur voluntarily but is forced upon the worker through a union security agreement or a majority vote resulting in a selection other than his preference, he may acquiesce wholeheartedly in the result if the union proves a good bargainer.

Viewing the matter from this angle, numerous American workers maintain that it does not concern them very much whether they are connected with the American Federation of Labor or with the Congress of Industrial Organizations.[9] In many European countries, however, especially those with pluralism, switching from one union to another may involve more than it does in the United States. Where pluralism has persisted in Europe, the chief reason has been that the various factions represent so different social, economic, political, or other tenets as to make unification of the labor movement impossible.[10] In areas in which promotion of such tenets, in addition to advancement of occupational interests, is an essential part of the programs of the unions, application for membership implies a kind of confession of faith in the ideology of the organization. Accordingly, changes in union allegiance may imply changes in convictions. The impossibility of bringing about a true change

[9] "Leadership rivalry is the lifeblood of unionism in the United States. After all, the American trade union is pragmatic to the core, neutral in ideology, and weak in political purpose. In the absence of competition for the allegiance of workers, there would be little else to ensure its militance and guarantee its role as an agency of protest." Arthur M. Ross, *Trade Union Wage Policy* (1948), p. 63.

[10] A trend toward singularism has been noticeable in a considerable number of European countries since the close of World War II. But it is too early to determine whether this indicates a change of socio-political, economic, and other philosophy of the members of the working class toward real uniformity or whether organizational concentration of the labor movement has resulted chiefly from political pressure caused by external influence.

in conviction by means of compulsion explains, in part, why European unions functioning under pluralism, usually object particularly strongly to the American type of closed, union, or similar shop and do not consider it a good device to strengthen their security.

It is true that, in practice, European applicants for membership may be attracted by the services offered rather than by the ideology of the union. Opponents of this approach to unionism have labeled it contemptuously "bread and butter unionism." Moreover, European labor organizations ordinarily do not examine the convictions of applicants. Most of them do not exclude anyone unless perhaps he is personally undesirable. Also they seek to convert to their respective ideologies the mass of indifferent workers as well as adherents of other tenets. But even where they apply pressure in such efforts, they usually do not go so far as to demand that members of other movements must join them as a condition of employment in an enterprise.

Though separate labor movements in individual European countries have fought each other, they have generally been careful not to cross beyond the breaking point. In the vast majority of establishments no union has claimed the privilege of depriving other bona fide unions of the right to represent their members in collective negotiations. Moreover, for the reasons discussed above there has not existed a significant trend toward the closed, union, or similar shop in the sense that members of bona fide rival unions are excluded from working for a particular employer. Though unity of action of movements representing different ideologies has not been possible in a number of respects, affiliates of the different central bodies and the principal federations as such have found themselves compelled to co-operate in collective bargaining or for the protection of common interests of the working class. They have done so in individual establishments as well as in joint organizations and public institutions of various types and on various levels. In spite of numerous and serious frictions, they have generally sought to maintain a basis for such co-operation and—to use their own language—for fighting in one and the same battle-line.

It is obvious that minority movements and smaller unions have depended on the maintenance of general union solidarity in a higher degree than federations and individual organizations representing large majorities in an enterprise or state. Where in an establishment unionists belonging to one movement have predominated, or where in a country the strength of one labor group has outweighed that of others, the powerful organizations naturally have been tempted to refuse co-operation with the weaker ones. Although unions in a number of instances have succumbed to this temptation, top leaders have resisted it in a considerable measure. They have done so not only in deference to union solidarity. They also have wished to prevent adversaries of unionism from making capital out of union disunity. In addition, they have sought to avoid the risk that unions which they suppress in one establishment or at one time retaliate in kind in some other enterprise or at some other time.

In 1937 the powerful French General Confederation of Labor thus issued a formal denial that it favored the discharge of workers not belonging to it. The statement emphasized that the Confederation rejected such methods "because it is not the strength gained in this manner which preserves our membership."[11] Similarly, in 1919, a time in which the (social-democratic) General German Federation of Unions experienced an unprecedented growth, it signed together with all other smaller German union movements a declaration against "any coercive and spiritual terrorism no matter whether it is exerted by employers, by influential persons through threatening economic injury or using moral compulsion, or by adherents of one labor organization against adherents of another labor organization." A

[11] *Bulletin quotidien d'informations du C.P.A.S.*, Mar. 27, 1937.

joint statement of all German union movements declared in 1920:

The Freedom to organize . . . entitles the worker to join an organization which conforms with his convictions. This freedom of all workers must not lead to subjection; it must not result in compulsion which presses individuals into particular organizations. The governing bodies of all central organizations categorically reject any coercive action with respect to membership in an organization. They direct all their officers, employees, stewards and members to repel most vigorously, inside and outside the establishments, any compulsory pressure upon organized workers to quit an organization or to change from one organization to another.[12]

The president of the British Trades Union Congress, in dealing with the closed-shop issue, stated in his address at the 78th annual meeting, that "the principle of voluntary association is valid in its application to every activity of citizenship. It is the guarantee against class tyranny, government dictatorship and the servile state." He suggested settling difficulties among unaffiliated unions through interunion working agreements.[13]

In the same vein the president of the powerful Union of Transport and General Workers and at that time of the World Federation of Trade Unions said:

We believe that trade union organization is best built on the basis of conviction, by persuading people that you have something of value to offer them, some service to give to them in return for their membership. We do not want strikes to enforce this principle. We want to bring home to our people a sense of responsibility, a sense of comradeship, and by and through their conviction that trade unionism is worth while, to secure the 100 per cent organization for which we are striving.[14]

Referring to the closed shop, the editor of the Weekly Press Service of the Swiss Trade Union Federation stated in the issue of February 1947 that:

A monopoly necessarily implies suppression of a minority. A union, therefore, should not seek a monopoly position. Precisely

[12] *Korrespondenzblatt des Allgemeinen Deutschen Gewerkschaftsbundes*, July 17, 1920, p. 385.
[13] *Report of Proceedings at the 78th Annual Trades Union Congress*, (1946), p. 14.
[14] The same, p. 310.

because one has the majority, one can grant the minority freedom
of speech and opinion. A majority that prevents a minority from
expressing itself is a legalized dictatorship. Such a dictatorship,
doubtless, can ideologically be advocated. If this is done, one
should, however, abstain from twaddling about freedom and
democracy.

The Secretary of the Swiss Trade Union Federation, in
an article published on July 18, 1947, in the same Press
Service, criticized a proposed resolution submitted to the
1947 International Labour Conference, which indirectly
approved of the American type of the closed shop. He
set forth, among other things, that the Swiss Trade Union Federation would benefit from the introduction of
the closed-shop system, but that it did not approve of it because it could not possibly demand freedom to organize for
itself and base this demand on high moral principles, while
simultaneously withholding from others the same freedom
by reasons of the same principles.[15]

*American unions have made much use of exclusive
arrangements as a competitive device.*

The United States is one of the countries in which the
labor movement is split in several organized factions. The
manner in which unions compete with each other has been
affected not inconsiderably by labor legislation enacted in
recent decades. American modern labor relations law em-

_____

[15] The proposed resolution would have recognized "in conformity with numerous laws concerning the protection of association" the possibility that the parties
to a collective agreement adopt a clause providing that compulsory membership
in a certain trade union shall be made a condition precedent to employment or
a condition of continued employment. In the official analysis of the proposed
resolution it was stated that "the legislature has taken the view that such a union
security clause, provided that it is freely agreed upon between the parties, constitutes the soundest guarantee against discriminatory acts of an anti-trade union
nature."

The proposed conclusions relating to a convention concerning the application
of the principles of the right to organize and to bargain collectively, submitted
by the International Labour Office to the Thirty-First Session of the International Labour Conference in 1948, stated in Art. 5 that provisions in national
regulations requiring membership in a union as a previous condition to employment or as a condition to maintenance in employment should not be covered by
the convention. After lively discussion it was agreed "to delete this provision
without prejudice, it being understood that the question of union security, if

bodies two fundamental principles which are not, or not in this manner, applied in the European countries of comparison: namely, the concepts of the indispensability of a certain type of bargaining unit and of majority rule. Under the first principle, the governmental agencies administering the specific labor relations acts, as a rule, have the authority to determine units "appropriate for the purposes of collective bargaining." Such determination places the individual worker in the "bargaining unit" considered proper by the government agency but not necessarily by him. Under the second principle the majority of the employees in the "unit appropriate for the purposes of collective bargaining" to which the individual worker belongs select the union which will represent him in his relations

---

thought necessary, could be raised again at a subsequent session of the Conference." International Labour Conference, *Provisional Record*, Thirty-first Session, San Francisco, No. 36, p. III.

The question was, indeed, raised again at the next session in 1949. The employers' members of the Committee on Industrial Relations urged that the session should give formal sanction to the principle agreed upon at the preceding session that nothing in the proposals then adopted could deprive a worker of the inherent right not to exercise his freedom of association if he so desired. They stated further that Art. 20, Par. 2, of the Universal Declaration of Human Rights, adopted by the General Assembly of the United Nations, provided that "no one may be compelled to belong to an association," and that the Conference could not disregard this fact. Accordingly, they proposed amendments to the "Convention concerning the application of the principles of the right to organize and to bargain collectively," considered by the session, prohibiting interference with the right not to organize. The Italian government, in addition, stressed the need to protect the worker in countries with a plurality of union movements against discriminatory measures owing to his membership in a particular organization.

The workers' members of the committee opposed these amendments on the theory that the preceding session had unanimously decided not to mention expressly the right not to organize. The United States workers' member, in particular, declared that the right to work also included the right not to work. The members of unions which accepted all the responsibility for the observance of collective agreements concluded by them should have the right to refuse to work with nonunion workers who assumed no such responsibility. In many cases, recognition of the right not to organize would result in depriving them of the right to organize. A number of government members likewise opposed the amendments for various reasons. Eventually, the committee agreed to include a statement in its report, on the lines of an amendment proposed by the representative of the Union of South Africa, to the effect that the convention could in no way be interpreted as authorizing or prohibiting union security arrangements, such matters being for regulation in accordance with national practice. See International Labour Conference, *Provisional Record*, Thirty-second Session, Geneva, 1949, Nos. 27 and 39.

with his employer. Only this union can act as his bargaining agent. It has the exclusive right to represent *all* employees in the unit, including unorganized workers, members of other unions, and workers who do not wish to be
represented by this union. Since representing bargaining
units is one of the chief functions of American labor organizations, the average union naturally seeks to become the
bargaining agent of units coming under its jurisdiction in
as many establishments as possible.

This trend appears to be natural not only for competitive
reasons but also as a reaction to certain incongruities between basic aspects of the "bargaining-unit system" and of
unionism. The determination of bargaining units and their
representatives takes place on a more or less limited local
basis. The bargaining unit, in the typical case, is a group
of workers in one enterprise; occasionally, it includes
workers of several enterprises. Its members are considered
belonging together because they have a common interest
in the objects of collective bargaining with their employer.
The bargaining unit may include practically all the employees of an establishment. But usually it includes only
a portion of the employees so that several bargaining units
co-exist in one enterprise. Each of these units ordinarily
is considered a separate group to such an extent that, for
example, management may have difficulty in transferring
tasks from one of them to another.[16]

Unionism, on the other hand, generally is not grounded
in a community of interest arising out of employment in
the same or a few related enterprises or subdivisions of

[16] Laying off employees in one unit and transferring their duties to employees belonging to another unit has been held an objectionable weakening
of the bargaining unit and contract, and possibly an improper interference with
seniority provisions. The Labor Management Relations Act of 1947 made
strikes or boycotts an unfair labor practice if they have as their purpose forcing
an employer to assign work tasks to members of one union or a particular trade,
craft, or class when he assigned them to members of another union, occupation,
or class. If, however, the employer's arrangements run counter to a determination of the National Labor Relations Board fixing the representation of employees performing the work tasks, then the strike or boycott is not an unfair
labor practice. National Labor Relations Act, sec. 8 (b) (4) (D).

establishments. In the typical case union movements rest upon more comprehensive community of interest, such as skill in the same line of work, common vocation, work in the same industry, common concern in problems affecting the lives of the workers, etc. Most unions, therefore, tend to function on a broader scope than a bargaining unit or one or a few establishments. They have shown a distinct tendency to organize not only on local but also on industry-wide, nationwide, and even international bases. To harmonize the comprehensive character of unionism with the limited concept of the "bargaining-unit system," the average American labor organization has striven to become the representative of a maximum of bargaining units coming under its jurisdiction. Beyond that, many unions also have sought to protect themselves against the possibility of losing this position to rival organizations by using closed-shop and similar agreements as devices to keep workers who are not their members out of the bargaining units and to restrict free interunion competition for the post of bargaining agent.

Until the second half of the 1940's, when the United States Congress and a number of state legislatures took steps to curb this practice, unions following this course could in no small measure become independent of changes in the views of the workers as to who should represent them. All the employees represented by these unions were compelled to be members of them as a condition of employment. If they attempted to help another union to gain a majority, that is, to weaken the position of the union to which they belonged—even though membership may have been involuntary—they were liable to be expelled. Such expulsion from a union holding a closed- or union-shop agreement, however, involved loss of the job. Numerous workers were not willing to take that risk.

Only during the relatively short period when the agreement was about to expire did the National Labor Relations Board give workers a chance to suggest with impunity

that another representative should be chosen. But this possibility may have been remote. The labor relations laws
have not fixed either the period of validity of exclusive
agreements or the tenure of office of the bargaining agent.
Unions have made use of this situation and have insisted
upon long periods of contract validity, automatic renewal
clauses, and similar provisions. Besides, employees working for a change in representation at the time when the
agreement was about to expire took—and in some degree
still take—the risk of running into great difficulties,
especially in case of re-election of the old union.[17]

In the American railroad field the closed shop, by and
large, has not been a more significant issue than in European countries. Possibly demands for it were even less
insistent. Prohibition of it by the Railway Labor Act is
hardly the cause but rather an effect of this situation. To
be sure, the various brotherhoods, representing different
classes of railroad workers, differ in various respects from
most of the European unions mentioned above. Moreover,
they function in an industry of a particular nature and this,
as well as the character of the work involved, has facilitated
stable unionization of the railroad employees. Despite the
differences between the American railroad brotherhoods
and the average European union, the same factor would
seem to be largely responsible for the similarity of their
policies respecting the closed shop. Both have been compelled, though for different reasons, to maintain a high degree of interunion co-operation.

GOVERNMENT INTERVENTION

Labor organizations grew up under the policy of voluntary unionism. Compulsion in organizational matters came

---

[17] The 1947 amendments to the National Labor Relations Act prevent unions
from making a union security agreement without previous authorization by a
majority of the workers in the bargaining unit, grant employees an opportunity
to revoke this authorization, and make provision for revocation of the certification of a union as bargaining representative if it lost its majority status and at
least one year has elapsed after its election. These provisions will be discussed
in later chapters.

primarily from employers who sought to prevent unionization; but the unions could hardly force workers to become members without coming into conflict with the law. Labor in the United States as well as in Europe thus built up its organizations on a voluntary basis. This situation still prevails in the liberal democracies of Europe.

European unions generally have
favored voluntary unionism.

Unions on the other side of the Atlantic, greatly influenced by historical experience and their European economic, social, and political background, usually have sought to get and keep their members and to perform their functions without relying on special legislation. Apart from that, a large number of leading unionists have put relatively little trust in compulsory methods of recruitment. Most of them have rejected such methods, especially where they might affect members of other unions. Accordingly, they have made great efforts to preserve voluntariness as the basic principle in soliciting members, although this sometimes has caused disagreement with the rank and file as well as union officers on a lower level. This study mentions a number of instances in which these policies have made it possible to limit governmental action to application of principles developed directly and accepted by the majority of unions and managements in a country.

A number of reasons why European labor movements have favored voluntary action in such a degree were discussed above. At this juncture another important reason may be mentioned. Many labor leaders in Europe have believed that, if substantial numbers of workers could not obtain or keep jobs without joining a union, governments would regulate union activities. Such legislation, in their opinion, would cover specifically admission and expulsion of members as well as administrative set-up and rights and duties arising out of membership.[18] Unionists have feared that government intervention of this kind would restrict the freedom of action to which unions have been entitled as voluntary private associations. Policy-making union bodies also have been afraid of other potential effects of governmental regulation. In their opinion, danger would exist that legislators might grant preferential treatment to specific movements and thus destroy legal equality among workers. Statutes might be enacted determining which union should and which should not be recognized. The right to organize thus might cease to be a right of *all* workers.

The fear that this might happen has been aggravated by the experience that in some instances governments, directly or indirectly, have recognized groups as most representative and have conferred upon them certain privileges.[19] To understand fully the apprehension of European unionists, it should be remembered that most of their movements, in

[18] The American Joint Congressional Committee on Labour-Management Relations stated that in its opinion "the only alternative to prohibition of the closed shop is the definitely less desirable complete Government regulation of the internal affairs of labor organizations. If there is to be a closed shop, then we can hardly permit a closed union. The class of workers to be admitted to the union, their right to democratic election of officers, and the procedure under which they may be expelled from the union, thus losing their jobs, would have to be subject to regulation by law or by the [National Labor Relations] Board." *Labor-Management Relations*, Report of the Joint Committee on Labor-Management Relations, 80 Cong. 2 sess., Dec. 30, 1948. Committee print, p. 5.

[19] The concept of "the most representative occupational organizations of employers and employees" has gained increasing significance in the development of French public policy with respect to collective bargaining. It has been used by the French legislators to solve problems which may arise from rival unionism and from the possibility that unorganized workers or employers who are not bound by a collective agreement make employment contracts which are inconsistent with this agreement and thereby prejudice its application. The concept of the most representative organizations, as embodied in the Act Respecting Collective Agreements of Dec. 23, 1946 (J.O. No. 301, Dec. 25, 1946, p. 10,932), has been characterized as maintaining the traditional principle of freedom to organize, but sacrificing the principle of equality. (See Georges Scelle, La Notion d'organisation syndicale la plus représentative et la loi du 23 décembre 1946, *Revue Française du Travail*, June-July 1947, pp. 529 ff.)

The majority union and the bargaining representative in the sense of American labor relations laws are products of similar considerations. The relatively recent introduction of these institutions into the American legal system, however, signified marked modifications of the traditional concept of freedom to organize. This subject will be discussed below.

It seems appropriate to discuss the subject of the most representative organizations in a later part of the study dealing with the rights and duties of unions arising out of collective agreements.

addition to promoting the immediate occupational interests of their members, carry on general ideological pursuits
which under the policy of most American labor organizations do not come under the functions of unions. According to labor leaders in Europe, compulsory governmental
regulations of unions might result in widespread efforts by
individual organizations to obtain special favors from legislators. This, in turn, might cause general decline of union
morale and solidarity. Independence and status of every
union thus might be jeopardized. Finally, European union
leaders have been afraid that governments might become
able to suppress such freedom of economic and political
thought as the unions are enjoying now.

European union policies with respect to union security
have been influenced strongly by these apprehensions.
Considerations of the kind discussed here have strengthened
the belief of many European labor leaders that the development of a custom to make membership in a union or even
in a particular union a condition of employment would not
be beneficial for unionism as such and therefore would not
improve, in the long run, the security of individual unions
either.

American unions have made use of statutes and
private plans providing for involuntary organization.

Events have taken a different course in America than in
Europe. Pressure of social and economic developments
caused the Congress of the United States and many state
legislatures to enact statutes designed to encourage unionism and to protect union activities. These statutes have enabled unions to claim bargaining rights to the exclusion of
other bona fide unions, even for members of the latter.
Laws have further sanctioned and protected arrangements
under which only members of a specific organization have
the right to do any or certain work in a particular enterprise
and which thus exclude other unionized or nonunionized

workers from any employment or employment in this type
of work. American unions have utilized the opportunities
offered by this legislation to the best of their ability:

> Over a long period the policies of the American Federation of
> Labor regarding the role of government were astonishingly similar
> to those of business. Labor insisted as vociferously as business that
> the true doctrine was that of *laissez faire:* let the state leave labor
> alone; it could care for itself through organization, collective bar-
> gaining, and the strike . . . . Labor thus placed great faith in col-
> lective bargaining; it sought legislation only to deal with matters
> beyond the scope of collective bargaining. The factors that caused
> a growing demand and need for industrial unionism likewise under-
> mined the practical basis of the doctrine of *laissez faire.* Giant cor-
> porations with tens of thousands of employees replaced small con-
> cerns more susceptible to coercion by the strike. Employers de-
> veloped more effective means of combating unionism, such as the
> company union, employee representation, employee stock owner-
> ship, private armies, and like devices. Outright migration of indus-
> try or transfer of production by a company from one plant to
> another in a nonunion section could be resisted only unsuccessfully
> by collective bargaining.[20]

Though exercise of the right to exclude other unions has
led to industrial unrest and interunion warfare, use of the
right to close an enterprise to nonunionists has brought a
large number of unorganized workers into unions. Many
of the basic statutes for the protection and encouragement
of unionism were enacted in the first half of the thirties.
Depression and vigorous opposition had caused the membership of unions to fall to about 2.9 millions by 1933. It
still did not amount to more than approximately 3.7 millions in 1935, the year in which the fundamental National
Labor Relations Act became law. But only one year later
the membership rose to about 4.2 millions and reached 7.2
millions in the following year. In 1941, the last year before
the outbreak of the war, 10.5 million workers belonged to
unions. At the close of the war the figure was approximately
14.8 millions, and in 1948 total union membership was
estimated at about 15.7 millions.[21] Rising production and

[20] V. O. Key, Jr., *Politics, Parties and Pressure Groups* (1944), pp. 79, 80.
[21] Figures taken from U. S. Bureau of Labor Statistics. "Membership of Labor
Unions in the United States," LS 47-3948 and 48-1865. Mimeo.

employment as well as other factors have largely contributed to this unprecedented increase in the number of unionists from the mid-thirties on. But there can be no doubt that statutory encouragement of unionism and recognition of those types of union security clauses that have become customary in the United States have been very influential not only in bringing membership up to the present level but also in keeping the members in the unions.

Developments in the United States have not
affected prevailing European union policy.

European labor has been well aware of the rapid growth of American union memberships under the new public policy to protect and encourage union activities, to grant specific unions the right to exclusive representation and to allow them in addition to hold employment monopolies. However, developments in the United States have not shaken the faith placed in voluntariness by what is probably the vast majority of significant European union leaders. This is attributable not only to economic and political differences between the two areas. Nor can it be explained fully by dissimilarities in general union ideology and structure. There have been significant additional reasons that have kept European labor leaders from promoting a change to a course in their countries similar to that which has prevailed in the United States from the thirties on. Among them apparently has been the desire to avoid such keen interunion disputes as have frequently occurred in this country during recent years. Apart from that, American public policy in the last few decades has changed the character of unions in a manner which is more or less incompatible with the basic ideology of most European labor leaders. American unions have been transformed into bargaining representatives of members and nonmembers

by virtue of public law.[22] In addition, the new governmental labor policy, no matter whether intentionally or not,
has largely increased compulsion to join particular unions.
Finally, European top union leaders have not been unaware
of the fact that one consequence of these developments has
been a strong trend toward compulsory government regulation of union activities—the very thing they have feared
would be likely to ensue from deviations from the principle
of voluntary unionism.[23] Hence, many of them still regard
preservation of the voluntary character of unionism, possibly together with reforms in the present economic, social,
cultural, or political setup, as a better method to safeguard
the security, and to achieve the ultimate goals, of their respective movements than union security agreements of the
American type.

[22] Their status as bargaining representative, therefore, has been considered
to be similar to that of a public agency. The Supreme Court of Kansas, for
example, dealing with a case under the Railway Labor Act, set forth that "a
labor union, or other organization, in performing its functions as a bargaining
agent of employees . . . , is not to be regarded as a wholly private association
of individuals, free from all constitutional or statutory restraints to which public
agencies are subjected . . . ." *Betts* v. *Easley*, 169 P. 2d 831 (1946).

[23] This trend has become conspicuous not only in legislative activities but
also in court opinions. The exclusive rights enjoyed by unions as designated
bargaining representatives, in the words of Ludwig Teller, "come not from
self-help, but from governmental assistance, and the Courts have been developing
the viewpoint that designated unions owe obligations to the employees in the
designated units as a price for this governmental assistance, obligations which
may be enforced by the Courts." *Labor Disputes and Collective Bargaining*
(1947), Vol. 1, p. 287.

NOTE: No connection exists between European union policies with respect to voluntariness and the complete collapse of the labor organizations before the assault by the totalitarian movements. There is no reason to believe that their power and opportunity to resist would have been greater if they had accepted involuntary unionism in a larger measure. They fell—temporarily—for similar reasons as other powerful organized groups, including organizations of employers. Years of economic crises and unemployment, infiltration into the old unions of totalitarian elements from the right and left, and activities of terroristic national-socialist or fascist organizations as well as of newly formed communist labor groups which were opposed to traditional unionism, had weakened union cohesion and ability to fight. In addition, a substantial number of non-national-socialist or non-fascist unionists were unwilling to undertake active resistance, and not a few of the members had become active and even organized adherents of totalitarian movements (possibly without knowing in advance their true character).

It may be mentioned in this connection that even the German Labor Front, an organization established by the National Socialist party to replace the dissolved unions and employers' associations, did not think it wise to adopt the closed shop as official policy. But according to general totalitarian practice, unofficial pressure was exerted sufficient to compel any employer and employee to join the Front "voluntarily." This has been the only instance of official encouragement of the closed shop in Germany. In France, too, the totalitarian Vichy regime was the only government that favored compulsory organization. It went further than its German counterpart and provided expressly that all members of an occupation had to be enlisted in compulsory, government-controlled bodies of a peculiar type, introduced by the Labor Charter.

The number of union members alone is not the conclusive yardstick for measuring union strength and security. Nor do statistics on union membership explain by themselves why the number of unionists have been relatively large or small in a given country or period. Yet, it may be interesting to compare percentage unionization in countries discussed in this study, that is, the ratio of the number of union members to the number of employees.

However, various factors, too numerous to be enumerated exhaustively in this note, make it impossible to do so with the desirable degree of accuracy. Neither official statistics on union membership nor tables showing the size of national labor forces are suitable to ascertain a precise picture of percentage unionization. Official data on union membership ordinarily repeat information coming from the unions themselves. The term "union membership" is defined differently by various unions. Workers may belong to more than one union and therefore may be counted more than once in the total. On the other hand, no internationally accepted standard method exists to compute the size of the labor force. Nor is the definition of "labor force" the same in every country. Persons other than wage and salary earners commonly are included, as for example self-employed persons and even employers. Members of the armed forces may or may not be included. Moreover, opinions have varied as to whether percentage unionization should be calculated on the basis of the total labor force or only on the basis of the total number of wage and salary earners, and whether, in either case, all persons coming under the classification or only those eligible for union membership should be included. Then, too, the definition of "eligibility for union membership" for the purpose of ascertaining percentage unionization has been a controversial issue. Should all categories of persons be included who may form and join a union if they wish to do so? Or should those groups be excluded that unions have not covered in organizing campaigns or that they found "unorganizable," as for example highly paid employees, agricultural workers, and domestic servants? Where it has been held necessary to exclude certain categories of persons from the calculations, lack of detailed breakdowns in official compilations has frequently proved a great obstacle to accuracy.

For all these and additional reasons it must be strongly emphasized that the following computation of percentage unionization in different countries presents only very rough estimates which, furthermore, are not strictly comparable. It is, however, hoped that gross inaccuracies have been avoided by employing the most recent data obtainable from competent government sources, by basing the calculations as nearly as possible on the number of wage and salary earners in the individual countries, by using medium figures, and, in addition, leaving an appropriate margin for error. Despite exceptions that may still be taken to numerical accuracy and degree of comparableness of the figures found, they would seem to indicate strongly that percentage unionization in the foreign countries of comparison, with the possible exception of France, is higher, or at least not lower, than in the United States.

According to the latest general census, taken in 1940, the total number of Swedish wage and salary earners was around 2 millions. (About 2.1 millions, including all types of employees, about 2 millions, excluding executive personnel, about 1.9 million excluding executive and domestic personnel; the number of wage earners without domestic workers, was nearly 1.35 million.) Union membership has been approximately 1.2 million. It seems safe to estimate percentage unionization to be not less than about 60 per cent.

The total British civilian working population was almost 19 millions in July 1947. This figure, however, includes employers and self-employed persons. The total number of persons insured against unemployment at the same point of time was about 15.5 millions. But this figure excludes substantial groups of employees who were excepted from unemployment insurance. Union membership in Great Britain at the end of 1946 was almost 8.5 millions.

Accordingly at least 50 per cent of the British workers appear to be union members.

The United States Department of Labor estimated, on the basis of Military Government figures, that in Germany as a whole on June 30, 1947, the number of union members was roughly 8.3 millions and the number of wage and salaried workers slightly more than 20.1 millions. Estimated percentage unionization thus was slightly above 41 per cent. (*Monthly Labor Review*, April 1948, p. 382.)

The number of French wage and salary earners in 1947 was estimated to have been about 19.7 millions. Information about French union membership is at present rather vague. Owing to the recent split in the General Confederation of Labor, resulting in the establishment of the Workers' Force (see p. 260n.), and further to the formation of new unions in different fields, data on total union membership in recent years have varied between about 7 millions and 4.3 millions (and even less). Apparently total membership between the end of 1947 and the beginning of 1949 dropped from the former to approximately the latter figure. It thus is impossible to present here a reliable estimate of percentage unionization. If the first figure is used, percentage unionization would have been approximately 35.5 per cent; on the basis of the second figure, it would have amounted to about 22 per cent.

The estimated number of agricultural and nonagricultural wage and salary earners in the United States was nearly 45 millions in 1947. The size of the total civilian labor force (including self-employed persons, unpaid family workers, etc.) has been estimated at slightly more than 60 millions in the same year. Estimated total union membership in the autumn of 1947 was about 15.4 millions. According to these figures, not more than about 34.2 per cent of the American wage and salary earners were union members at the end of 1947. The figure would be about 35.6 per cent, if the approximately 1.7 million domestic workers are not counted as wage earners.

CHAPTER VI

Management Problems and Policies

In the initial stage of the labor movement entrepreneurs almost everywhere made vigorous efforts to avert its growth and, if possible, to break up existing organizations. Subsequently, employers' associations adopted the policy of trying to prevent unions from enforcing demands which management considered harmful to its interests and to those of the nation. The majority of employers who have been confronted with the issue of involuntary unionism have rejected it for both reasons.

Employers have objected to making union membership a condition of employment.

A strong trend exists among employers in all countries here discussed to consider organizing of workers the exclusive concern of the unions. It is believed that it is the business of the union to solicit members by convincing employees of the advantages of unionism and union membership, but that it is not in the interest of management or labor to compel workers to enroll by making membership in a union a condition of employment.

Employers have been disinclined to participate in the recruitment of union members for a number of other reasons. They have considered demands to exclude workers from employment because of union or nonunion status as undue interference with their traditional freedom to hire and employ whomever they think fit and to direct and distribute the work as they deem suitable. Apart from that, they have feared that the efficiency of individual establishments or national production will suffer if workers must be employed, or work tasks be distributed, on the basis of union affiliation rather than solely of qualification for the job and the needs of the business. Moreover, assisting unions in enrolling members has been held bad management policy because it means making the unions numerically stronger. It has been contended that the greater bargaining power thus gained with the help of the employer is used against him to enforce the application of union rules in place of his traditional freedom to manage his business according to his discretion. Such shift in control, managements have stated, is bound to impair production and services, and in addition is unjustified since the unions have neither investment in nor responsibility for the enterprises concerned. Apart from that, it has been said that unions exploit increased bargaining power to push wages up, shorten hours, and thus to enhance costs and reduce profits.

Employers further have pointed out that employees protected by exclusive agreements may not work as hard as they might under unrestricted competition and that such agreements may prevent the employment of the best available workers. The latter fear has been expressed especially in the United States, where the restrictive effect of union security contracts not infrequently has been intensified through provisions that the hiring of job applicants must take place through the union office.[1]

The closed- or union-shop agreement making membership in *one specific* union a condition of employment—the type which has been customary in the United States—has

[1] Sec. 22 of the (repealed) Delaware Act Regulating Labor Unions and Relations Between Employers and Employees, Members of Labor Unions, (H. 212, app. Apr. 5, 1947) prohibited labor organizations from operating "hiring halls" or other employment services to coerce, intimidate, or direct employers to employ persons recommended or approved by the organization or otherwise to interfere with the employer's right to employ persons of his own choosing.

The National Labor Relations Board declared that union demands for continuance of the "hiring hall" system as the sole source of employees violated the provisions concerning discrimination because of union or nonunion status of the National Labor Relations Act, as amended by the Labor Management Relations Act, 1947. See *National Maritime Union, et al.,* 78 NLRB 971 (1948); 82 NLRB 1365 (1949). The Board also held contracts, under which an employer hires only workers referred to him by the union, incompatible with the provisions of this act regulating union security agreements. *Daniel Hamm Drayage Co.,* 84 NLRB 56 (1949).

been opposed for additional reasons. It has been said that
it may be used—and has been used—to decrease the labor
supply to employers under contract. Unions may attempt
to limit memberships in order to secure a maximum of
steady employment for their present members. This may
incidentally compel managements to bid up wages beyond
the union level in periods of good business. In addition,
it has been argued that the type of closed- or union-shop
agreement which establishes a monopoly of employment
for the members of one specific union gives the officers of
this union so much power as to tempt them to make arbitrary and unreasonable demands. Furthermore, employers
have contended that under such an agreement discipline and
efficiency are bound to be lowered because workers tend to
regard the representatives of the union as more powerful
than the foreman. Employees may feel that they hold their
jobs and qualify for advancement through union regularity
rather than the quality of their work. This, so runs the
argument, causes workers to place their allegiance to the
union above the interests of the employer who pays them.

Moreover, it has been pointed out that agreements, requiring membership and maintenance of good standing in
a union as a condition of employment or continued employment, deprives executives of so much of their traditional and
needed power to determine personnel and other operating
policies as to interfere seriously with orderly management.
This interference, it has been indicated, is even more extensive and troublesome under agreements providing for a
monopoly position of one specific union than under contracts which make membership in any of the existing unions
a condition of employment and therefore do not exclude
any union from dealing with the employer.

The foregoing reasoning stresses chiefly the needs of
management, stockholders, and business ownership in general. But employers also have asserted that they oppose
involuntary unionism in the public interest and in the well-
considered interest of the workers. They have declared that

exclusive union agreements interfere unduly not only with the right of every person to dispose of his own capital according to his will but also with the individual's right to work. By depriving him of opportunities to work unless he joins a union, or even a particular union, members of management have pointed out, his freedom to pursue his calling as he deems fit is unjustifiably infringed upon. "Such brutal method of depriving him of his livelihood," it has been said, "is wrong from any point of view." Not a few business leaders therefore have held that an employer should reject any union demand for an exclusive shop even if he believes that its acceptance would bring more advan-tages than disadvantages for his particular enterprise. They have warned that support of involuntary unionism would be contrary to the public interest and lead only to further restrictions upon individual liberty of action in other directions.[2] A number of employers—like economists—have held that wide acceptance of exclusive arrangements would make the unions so powerful that any attempt to maintain the capitalist system and free private enterprise would become hopeless.

Moreover, employers have objected to such agreements because they have felt that they establish unjustifiable union monopolies in the labor market, which may be maintained irrespective of the desires of the employees. Neither employers, nor unions, nor governments, according to this view, have any right to compel employees to belong or not to belong to private associations.[3] In this connection, American employers in particular have pointed out that, if the law prohibits them from compelling workers

[2] See "Observations on the Closed Shop", *The Conference Board Management Record*, May 1939, pp. 73-74.
The position taken by management with respect to protection of the exercise by workers of full freedom to refrain from joining a union, in particular, for the sake of greater clearness, will be discussed in the section on "Freedom to Refrain from Joining a Union", pp. 197 ff. below.
[3] For an appraisal by American unionists of employer efforts to base opposi-tion to the closed and union shop on the interests of labor see p. 145 above.

not to join a union, they also should not be laid under the obligation to force workers to join it. The president of one of the largest American corporations thus said recently that a contract requiring membership in a union as a condition of work "is as bad on the one side as the outlawed 'yellow dog' contract would be on the other." Discussing exclusive agreements, the chairman of the National Association of Manufacturers' executive committee declared in March 1947:[4]

Compulsory unionism converts the union from an agent of the employee to a dictator over the employee. The dictatorial power of compulsory unionism multiplies a hundredfold opportunities for abuse by labor leaders. It is through the closed shop that labor leaders are able to coerce employees into taking action contrary to their best interests—action which is justified on the basis of "union strategy."

There is no valid argument in support of the closed shop. Union security is provided by those provisions of the Wagner Act which should not be disturbed.

Unions do not need the closed shop in order to live up to their collective bargaining agreements. There have been at least as many cases of violations of agreement by unions operating under closed shop agreements as under any other type of agreement.

Unions do not need the closed shop to protect themselves against the free rider. If they will do a better job for the employee, they will sell themselves to employees and will not need to compel employees to join them under penalty of an economic exile.

Considerations of the kind discussed in the preceding paragraphs have caused employers on both sides of the Atlantic to resist union demands for exclusive agreements and to defend vigorously their right "to hire and to fire" at their discretion. Where many employers were not reconciled to dealing with unions at all, such resistance tended to be part of a more comprehensive struggle against unionism. However, where the climate was less belligerent, employer opposition was intended merely to prevent unions

---

[4] *Amendments to the National Labor Relations Act,* Hearings before the House Committee on Education and Labor, 80 Cong. 1 sess. (1947), p. 2638.

from overstepping the bounds of what management considered proper. The "Open-Shop Movement" or "American Plan Movement" carried through by militant American corporations and employers' associations resulted by the end of the 1920's in an extraordinary decline of union membership in almost all industries except building construction, clothing, coal mining, and printing.[5] At that time practically no unionism existed in the important mass production industries.

European managements, on the other hand, have persisted in rejecting union demands for exclusive agreements. But in recent times they have not seriously disputed the right to organize and to bargain collectively. As mentioned above, the constitution of the dominant Federation of Swedish Employers provides that collective agreements between a member of the federation or its member associations and a union must include a clause to the effect that the employer shall have the right to hire and discharge employees at his discretion, to direct and distribute the work, and to employ workers belonging to any union or workers belonging to no union. Noncompliance with this provision makes the offending member liable for damages. In the basic (Matignon) agreement, entered into by organized French management and labor in 1936, the employers insisted upon recognition of their right to make decisions in regard to hiring, conduct and distribution of work and disciplinary measures, or discharges irrespective of union membership or nonmembership.[6] European managements could secure acceptance of their demands with relative ease because, as mentioned above, European unions by and large have had comparatively little concern for exclusive agreements and because there no longer exists serious employer opposition to unionism. Finally, the law of

[5] See p. 178.
[6] See p. 256.

some countries, for many years past, has explicitly protected workers against misuse of the employer's discretion.

Some European employers give
hiring preference to unionists.

In more recent times changes in employer policy have occurred. They have been much more significant in the United States than in Europe. In both continents they were inaugurated by outside pressure rather than employer initiative. Employers in European free enterprise systems still seldom consent to arrangements restricting their freedom to hire. But a number of them, especially in Great Britain and Sweden, have accustomed themselves more or less tacitly to giving hiring preference to unionists, that is, to workers who belong to any of the unions functioning in the field concerned. Most of them adopted this practice because they wished to avoid losses from labor unrest caused by friction between organized and unorganized employees. It is true that industrial warfare over matters regulated in collective agreements is prohibited or at least restricted under many European agreements and even some laws. However, since most European collective contracts do not deal with the issue of simultaneous employment of organized and unorganized workers, labor strife about this question is not precluded by any legal obligation "to keep peace." But even where such strife would be incompatible with legal duties, employers in several industries have found that they just do not have the actual power to compel unionists to work against their will with nonunionists. Consequently, they have thought it advisable to avoid tests of economic strength about this question by refraining from hiring unorganized workers if organized ones are available. Apart from that, a number of managements have become convinced that exclusive employment of organized workers in unionized lines makes for better harmony not only among employees but also between management and the work force, and hence for improved production and services.

*Many American employers now exclude from employment
nonmembers of the contracting union.*

A considerable number of American employers have
gone further than their European colleagues. They have
signed many exclusive agreements. Moreover, these agreements generally have closed establishments or parts of them
not only to unorganized but also to such organized workers
as do not belong to, and do not wish to join, a *specific* union,
namely the one which holds the contract. Despite the great
success of the "open-shop movement" by the late 1920's,
the number of employers who have changed from unconditional rejection to acceptance of union demands for exclusive status has grown considerably in subsequent years.

*Many American employers agree to exclusive
contracts to reduce labor trouble.*

This change in policy has been due in no small measure
to the enactment in the 1930's of statutes for the protection
and encouragement of unionism, which exempted exclusive agreements with majority unions from the general
prohibition of employer interference with the workers'
freedom to organize. Legislation of this kind so strengthened the union position that an ever-increasing number of
employers have thought it expedient to change their policy
in order to avoid costly labor trouble. As American managements came to realize that it would no longer be possible to
refuse to deal with unions altogether, some of them tried at
first to avoid collective bargaining with "outside" unions
by favoring the establishment of unions the membership
in which was confined to their own workers. In a number
of instances, employers, in addition to supporting the formation and maintenance of such company unions, also
entered into closed-shop agreements with them in order to
prevent their employees from joining any other labor
organization. In the railroad industry, as mentioned be-

low,[7] opposition to such practices lead to union requests to outlaw the closed shop. As the National Labor Relations Board barred such tactics and the new labor policy took root, a number of employers came to accept the closed shop because it has the effect of reducing competition among unions. They hoped that it would curtail jurisdictional disputes and rival unionism. In addition, many entrepreneurs have considered the making of closed- or union-shop agreements the best method to prevent strife in their enterprises among unionists and nonunionists and members and nonmembers of majority unions.

Declining opposition to exclusive union security agreements in the United States has simultaneously brought a marked increase in check-off clauses. Prior to the last war the check-off was common only in relatively few American industries. Employers were generally disinclined to assist unions by acting as their dues collectors. In relatively recent years, however, the employers' attitude has been changing, mainly because the check-off enables them to forestall demands of unions, having exclusive status, to discharge workers who do not pay their dues. Such discharges may at all times interfere with the interests of management, especially in the case of good workers. During the last war and reconversion period with its great need for efficiency and uninterrupted production and simultaneous scarcity of man power, a great number of demands for dismissals merely because of dues delinquency might have had even more serious effects. This situation contributed largely to the increase in check-off agreements. Many of them were the result of collective bargaining. But not a few were ordered by the National War Labor Board together with maintenance-of-membership clauses which had become its favorite device to satisfy demands for union security. Now a considerable number of American employers believe that the check-off clause saves them at least as much trouble and

<hr>

7 P. 282.

money as it costs them. A good many of them consider deduction of union dues from the worker's pay preferable to collection by union representatives in the plant, which may impair production and lead to violation of company rules.

Some American employers hold exclusive agreements beneficial to both management and unions.

The opinion has spread among employers in several sectors of the American economy that closed-shop and similar agreements may bring benefits to management in addition to more peaceful relations with unions. It has been stated that production and services have improved where the position of unions has been strengthened through agreements excluding from employment nonunionists and members of other unions. Once labor organizations are protected against competition and breaking away of members, some managements believe, their demands are likely to be more moderate. Such unions, according to this view, may use their enhanced disciplinary powers over members to improve shop discipline and thereby efficiency. A number of employers have felt that, in addition, the greater influence that workers have in the determination of the working conditions in closed and union shops increases their interest in their jobs and strengthens their sense of responsibility. All this, according to these employers, tends to stabilize production and wage costs and, thereby, to facilitate price policies and timing. In some highly competitive industries quite a few manufacturers have welcomed industry-wide exclusive arrangements especially because they eliminate wage cost as a competitive factor.

Some American employers, further, have denied that exclusive union security agreements necessarily restrict their managerial freedom in an unwarranted degree. In their opinion, the reverse may be true because a union that feels secure is more willing to co-operate and less suspicious of the actions of management. Accordingly, adherents of this view also favor the check-off because they believe that a union which no longer has to worry either about the maintenance of its membership or the prompt payment of dues will spend more time and effort on co-operation with management.

CHAPTER VII

Government Problems and Policies: Right to Refrain From Joining A Union; Scope of Legitimate Pressure to Organize

Preceding discussion has shown that both advocates and opponents of exclusive agreements have attached some, though not necessarily decisive, weight to their potential effects on production and costs.[1] This question has played only a minor—if any—role in the determination and explanation of pertinent public policy in the countries discussed in this study. This probably has been due, at least in part, to the fact that as yet no generally accepted theory on the subject exists, and that scarcity of data has made accurate analyses extremely difficult. Moreover, the governments covered by this survey obviously have thought it proper to base their policies respecting union membership as a condition of employment primarily on broader considerations, such as compatibility with the doctrine of maximum individual freedom, with the guiding principles of freedom to organize, and with other dogmas of fundamental national philosophy. Public authorities thus have been confronted with the complex problem of safeguarding simultaneously freedom of association and freedom from association; the right of the individual to combine with others and his right to pursue his calling without belonging to an association; individual freedom of contract and collective bargaining; the right of organizations to recruit members and the freedom of the individual from undue pressure to make him join.

Where activities of management, or unions, or both have

[1] The same apparently applies to most of the writers in the individual countries who have discussed the propriety of such agreements.

tended to impair the individual freedoms to organize and to pursue one's calling as one deems fit, governments have felt it their duty to harmonize conflicting interests in the manner supposedly most fair and appropriate for every-body—management, organized labor, unorganized workers, and all other people. In this way attempts have been made to maintain industrial peace without sacrificing fundamental civil rights of citizens. In short, governmental authorities have sought to protect what they have considered the national interest.[2] Owing to the function of government to safeguard the interests of all citizens alike, considerations have determined pertinent public policies, which for obvious reasons have not necessarily been decisive in the determination of management and union policies. Differences in governmental and private approaches explain in part why public policy and the actual situation, not infrequently, have been at variance.

All liberal governments tend to acknowledge that unions have a legitimate interest in increasing membership. They further are inclined to recognize that, to carry through recruitment and other legitimate activities, unions must have as much freedom to exert pressure on others as eco-

---

[2] The Belgian employer's delegate to the Thirtieth Session of the International Labour Conference (1947), who was Deputy Reporter of the Committee on Freedom of Association, stated, among other things: "Unfortunately freedom has no value unless it is opposed to constraint. In order to see it and appreciate its meaning, it must be placed in a frame; in the absence of certain conditions, it vanishes away like the air from a pricked balloon. Our task would be simple if it were merely to draw up texts which would guarantee complete freedom of association irrespective of any restraints. It would be simple, but it would be pointless, since the exercise of complete freedom of association can be justified only if there is respect for other equally essential freedoms. . . . It is therefore for us to define the framework within which freedom of association can be exercised without prejudicing the other essential liberties. In my opinion the best definition of democracy would be to say that it is the form of government which establishes the best balance between individual and collective freedoms. In this connection there were differences of views not only between the three groups in the Committee, but between the different countries. These divergences did not reflect any insoluble incompatibility, though they meant that we in some cases had to take what were inevitably compromise decisions. That, however, only means the establishment of that balance which is characteristic of any economic arrangement. . . . Our duty is to reconcile the three different points of view, political, economic and human. It is perfectly possible to reconcile the three and each of us is right in defending what it is our duty to defend, while respecting the just opinions of others."

nomic groups usually have in promoting the interests of their members. However, there also is general agreement that recognition of the right to organize into unions has not implied official recognition of a right of unions to compel workers to join them. Governments thus have made efforts to determine the line that separates justifiable pressure from improper compulsion. These efforts, naturally, have resulted in the establishment of different principles in various countries and periods, since the determination of proper and improper union conduct mirrors economic, social, and political trends which are far from being uniform or static. It is obvious (and not at all surprising) that the problems faced by managements and unions in determining their respective policies, and the policies which they ultimately established, also have affected the formulation of government policies and practices.

FREEDOM TO REFRAIN FROM JOINING A UNION

Legally speaking, the term "right to refrain from joining a union" may not be a logical one. One could just as well talk about a legal right to refrain from keeping and bearing arms or from participating in political elections. In the absence of a legal duty to join a union nobody, obviously, is obligated to become a union member. This would seem not to be a specific right, but to follow from the general freedom of will. Nearly all liberal governments recognize that full freedom to organize includes not only freedom to form and join unions—positive freedom of association—but also freedom to refrain from such activities—negative freedom of association. This doctrine has been widely accepted by management and labor in the various countries. Accordingly, what is meant by the term "right to refrain from joining a union," is that the right to organize, being a right and not a duty, does not make union membership compulsory. And if unionists talk about a duty to join labor organizations, they have in mind a moral or social rather than a legal duty.

*Opinions of management and unions on protection
of the negative freedom to organize have varied widely.*

While the vast majority of people concerned do not
seriously question the existence of both the freedom to
join and the freedom not to join labor organizations, the
true issue involved in controversies about the so-called
"right to refrain from joining a union" has been whether
the labor law should protect the exercise, and outlaw
factual and contractual restrictions, of either freedom in
the same extent and manner. On this question opinions
have varied widely.

Management has tended to demand that labor laws should
outlaw in plain terms any act compelling an employer or
worker to join an occupational organization against his will.
Numerous employers have held that any public policy or
legislation which would not safeguard the negative freedom
of association to the fullest extent and make illegal any kind
of involuntary unionism, would tend to suppress individual
freedom in a manner smacking of totalitarianism. Strengthening the rights of organized labor at the expense of the
freedom not to join an organization, industrial executives
have argued, means enlarging the rights of one group by
restricting equally important rights of others. A worker
ought not to be denied employment, or lose his job, merely
because he refuses to join a union or even a specific union,
and management, on the other hand, ought not to be denied
the right to protect the freedom of the worker to remain
unorganized. It has been asserted, especially abroad, that
restriction of the liberty of management in this respect
might lead to curtailment of its freedom of speech, as
demonstrated by experience with the American National
Labor Relations Act.

Employers further have declared that they do not oppose
union efforts to achieve 100 per cent unionization, provided
the organizations try to attain that objective by convincing
every worker of their usefulness. It has been emphasized

by members of management that they do not desire to act as spokesmen for nonunion labor, but that they simply wish to avoid finding themselves confronted with the alternative of either forcing a nonunionist to join a union against his wish or of discharging him or having to face a work stoppage. The right to strike, it has been argued, should not be used for the purpose of compelling an employer to obligate workers to become union members; the nonunion worker should be free to make his own decision and be protected against reprisals from whatever side. Admission of involuntary membership, it has been stated, would be a disservice to the unions themselves. They should be required to justify their existence by the value of the services provided to their members, something they do not do where membership is obligatory. A number of employers, especially in countries liberated from dictatorial rule, have stressed that experience with totalitarian systems, making membership in specified organizations virtually compulsory for everyone, should have convinced everybody that protection of the freedom not to join an organization is as essential for true freedom to organize as is protection of the right to join.[3]

Though organized labor in most liberal countries has not denied the existence of a negative freedom to organize, unionists for reasons discussed above usually have entertained a very strong and active dislike for workers who exercise it. Union leaders have been guided by the philosophy that, above all, workers must be protected against

[3] The employer members of the Committee on Freedom of Association and Industrial Relations of the Thirty-first session of the International Labour Conference in 1948 emphasized that freedom of association should be guaranteed in its negative aspect—freedom not to join—as well as in the positive aspect—freedom to establish organizations and to join them. The United States employer delegation at the Thirty-second Session in 1949, declared the international convention, as eventually adopted by the Conference, unsatisfactory because "although, quite properly, guaranteeing protection for workers who want to join unions, it gave no protection whatever to workers who wish to refrain from joining. This omission made the document out of line with the Taft-Hartley Act and general employer thinking in the United States." The delegation and a number of foreign employer and government delegates undertook to get an amendment into the proposed convention which would protect or recognize

employer efforts to compel them, directly or indirectly, to refrain from joining unions and that this is of such paramount importance that all other considerations must recede into the background. Leading unionists have pointed out that employers have often more or less forcibly interfered with the exercise of the right of the worker to join unions, but that they have hardly ever questioned his right not to do so. On the contrary—organized labor has emphasized—management has been prone to defend the employee's negative freedom of association most vigorously. Therefore, it has been said, no reason exists for legislative action to protect it. Nor by the same token can the legislative treatment of the right to organize and of the freedom not to organize be placed on a footing of equality. Any regulation stating, on the one hand, that workers might organize and, on the other hand, that they are free not to do so would only aid employers who seek to restrict union activities.

Governments have used various techniques in dealing with the negative freedom to organize.

Many countries have enacted special statutes designed to safeguard the exercise by workers (and employers) of freedom to organize. A number of these statutes have emphasized that no one may be placed under the obligation either

---

the right of workers to refrain from union membership as well as the right to join a union. "When this effort was made," the report of the United States Employer Delegation states, "the United States Government Representative on the Committee, an attorney with the Department of Labor, made an impassioned speech in which he referred to the Taft-Hartley Act as having been brought about by the forces of reaction, and said that the same forces were now trying to get a similar rule written into international law." "Our own and other employers who opposed the document as a convention," the report concludes, "were voted down and it was adopted. Our Government Delegation voted for it. Because of its almost completely one-sided character, employers will doubtless want to consider opposing it when it later comes before the Senate for ratification. As indicated above, it poses in the international field something quite similar to the old Wagner Act within the United States." *The Thirty-second International Labor Conference, Geneva, June 8 to July 2, 1949, Report of United States Employer Delegation,* pp. 3, 4, and 5. See p. 170 n. above.

to belong or not to belong to an association. In some countries and American states the legislators have been satisfied with providing for protection of the right to self-organization, without mentioning freedom to refrain from organizing. A number of governments have expressly declared that the freedom of workers not to form or join labor organizations should not be regulated by special statutes.[4]

Some of those countries which have explicitly declared it part of their public policy that no worker may be required to belong to a labor organization have treated exclusive agreements as unlawful. Laws of various kinds have given this interpretation statutory force (for example, in Belgium, France, the Netherlands, and a number of American states). Express statutory guarantee of both the positive and the negative freedom of association, however, has not always precluded formal or informal approbation of closed, union, and similar shops. In a number of instances, legal recognition of such arrangements has been limited to certain types of contracts, or to agreements entered into freely and with unions deemed truly representative of the workers immediately concerned; or their validity has been made contingent upon compliance with certain other conditions. Under these public policies the economic pressure to join a union, inherent in such contracts, apparently has not been considered so coercive as to constitute under all circumstances an impermissible infringement of the negative freedom of association. When in 1947 the United States Congress outlawed the closed but not the union shop, the Senate Committee on Labor and Public Welfare cited merely expediency as the motive for giving these similar arrangements a different legal status: it declared that it wished to "give employers and unions who feel that such [union-shop]

4 As mentioned above, the New Zealand law, beyond that, even provides that every award or collective agreement must contain a provision ruling out the employment in the industry concerned of any adult who is not a member of an industrial union bound by it. Nonmembers may be employed only if no member is available and willing to perform the particular work to be done.

agreements promoted stability by eliminating 'free riders' the right to continue such arrangements.'"[5]

Where the legislators have been content with enacting special statutes providing for protection of freedom to organize without mentioning its positive and negative aspects, controversies have arisen as to whether they cover the freedom to refrain from participating in collective activities. This issue ordinarily has come up in connection with efforts to establish closed or other exclusive shops. As the case may be, such devices exclude from employment opportunities unorganized workers or unorganized and organized nonmembers of the contracting union. Such exclusion generally is a means to an end rather than an end in itself. The ultimate objective of the American union, in the typical case, is not to segregate its members from unorganized workers and members of other unions but to increase its own membership. The European union, which demands the exclusion of nonunionists, seeks to strengthen organized labor at large rather than merely to separate unionists from nonunionists. The union, which insists upon a closed or union shop, usually hopes that the excluded workers will prefer unionizing to losing or not obtaining the jobs of their choice. Owing to this element of strong economic pressure, exclusive agreements have been widely held incompatible with the negative freedom to organize. However, constitutions or statutes, declaring merely that employees shall have full freedom of association, have given rise to doubts as to whether the legislators intended to protect the negative freedom to organize at all. Under such systems determination of the validity of exclusive agreements thus has depended upon interpretation of the law, which has been far from uniform.

Those who have regarded the negative freedom to organize as a right inherent and implicit in the positive right to organize have held that any legal guarantee of the right

[5]*Federal Labor Relations Act of 1947*, S. Rept. 105, 80 Cong. 1 sess. (1947), p. 7.

to self-organization automatically protects the freedom to refrain from organizing. Accordingly, they have deemed any type of closed, union, or other exclusive shop contrary to public policy. Others have interpreted the guarantee as not covering the freedom of workers to remain unorganized, on the ground that otherwise the legislators would have mentioned it. The supporters of this doctrine, too, have not denied the existence of such freedom. They have, however, maintained that it does not enjoy the protection of the special law dealing with the right to organize, but is safeguarded only to the extent to which provisions of the general civil and penal law can be invoked against infringements of individual freedom of action. They have therefore held that exclusive agreements or union actions to enforce exclusion of outsiders are illegal only if they violate a provision of the general law.

Many governments deem the right not to
organize adequately protected by traditional law.

A large number of governments have been disinclined to place protection of the right to organize and the freedom not to organize on the same footing. They have held that the positive right to organize must be safeguarded by special statutes, while such statutes either are not needed to avert infringements of the negative right or would tend to interfere with the exercise of full freedom to form and join unions. Public policies of this kind have resulted from a variety of socio-economic and legal considerations.

Attacks on the freedom of workers to form and join unions have been made chiefly by employers. Many governments have emphasized that the relatively favorable economic position of management enabled it to undertake such attacks with great prospect of success. Moreover, most of the actions which employers took to prevent workers from forming or joining unions—such as refusing employment of unionists or demanding a promise not to participate in concerted labor activities—were legal under traditional law. They would still be permissible had they not been expressly declared unlawful. And, according to opinion prevailing among governments, the difference between the economic power of employers and that of workers ordinarily still is so great that management could continue seriously to interfere with unionism unless its liberty to do so is restricted. Accordingly, many legislative bodies have considered it imperative to safeguard the positive right to organize through special statutory provisions designed to prevent certain antiunion activities of employers. Corresponding special legislation to protect the positive freedom of association of the worker against infringement by employees has been considered unwarranted by most governments, because workers in their countries have seldom sought to prevent fellow workers from joining a union.

Attacks on the freedom of workers to refrain from belonging to a union, have been made almost exclusively by unions or their members. It has been pointed out, for example, by the German Supreme Labor Court[6] that in such attacks unions may use their greater economic strength to force the economically weaker, unorganized individual to join up, as employers, unless restrained by law, may use their relatively favorable economic position to prevent him from doing so. However, it has been widely held that unions ordinarily cannot infringe upon the negative freedom of association of the worker without committing acts illicit under traditional civil or penal law—such as assault, intimidation, violence, breach of public peace and order, unlawful compulsion, duress, etc. Owing to this view, many governments have seen no need for amending existing law through special statutory provisions which would subject *union* interference with the *negative* freedom of association of the worker to the same legal treatment as *employer* interference with his *positive* freedom to organize.

6 See p. 217.

The great majority of governments also have refrained from passing special measures to protect the right of the worker not to join a union against infringement by *management,* because employers within their jurisdiction have hardly ever opposed the exercise of this right. In the relatively few instances in which employers have opposed it, they have been considered as doing so under union pressure. Accordingly, public policy concerning *union* interference with the negative freedom of association has been held suitable and adequate to cope with such cases.

Many governments hold the dogma of the negative right to organize unsuitable to solve the problem of compulsion.

In a great number of countries which have followed a legislative course such as that discussed in the preceding paragraphs, great efforts thus have been made to safeguard the freedom to form and join unions by special constitutional and statutory provisions, while the general civil and penal law, by and large, has been deemed to meet the requirements of adequate protection of the freedom to refrain from joining a labor organization. Legislators have tried hard to forestall employer interference with freedom of workers in organizational matters, but they have hesitated to outlaw union interference unless it violates traditional, general, especially criminal, law. The legality of efforts by organized labor to make workers join a union, therefore, has tended to depend in these countries largely upon the prevailing view as to what kind and amount of pressure may in general be applied to induce individuals to become members of an organization. Probably all governments have held that unionism cannot be protected adequately without some restriction of individual freedom not only of employers but also of workers. It has been widely held that unions cannot exist, and function effectively, without liberty to exert certain pressure upon persons who are not willing to join. To determine the limits of this liberty, various principles have been used which will be discussed in the remainder of this volume. As will be seen, the relative position of the two somewhat antithetical freedoms to join and not to join a union has been the subject of so much controversy, and the desire to avoid potential weakening of the former by emphasis on protection of the latter has been so great, that a large number of governments have been reluctant to solve the problem of compulsion to organize exclusively in the light of the dogma of full negative freedom of association.

A few examples of European and American experience may be mentioned to illustrate the problem. From the establishment of the German Empire to its last days the German Industrial Code[7] provided that anyone was punishable with imprisonment who compelled or attempted to compel others by means of bodily force, threats, defamation or boycott to participate in, or comply with, agreements for the purpose of securing favorable wages and conditions of employment. The same punishment was provided for anyone who prevented or attempted to prevent others by such means from withdrawing from such agreements. Not until the critical year of 1918 were the campaigns of organized labor for repeal of this provision successful.[8] After the revolution, the German (Weimar) Constitution of 1919 listed "freedom to organize for the purpose of protecting and advancing the conditions of employment and of the economy" as one of the "Fundamental Rights of the Germans." Article 159 specifically guaranteed this freedom "to everyone and to all occupations" and declared unlawful any "agreement and action seeking to abridge or to obstruct" it.

This language of the constitution called forth a number of disputes centering around the question as to whether freedom to remain unorganized was a fundamental right of everyone. During the whole life of the Weimar Republic

7 Sec. 153.
8 Act of May 22, RGBl. 1918, p. 423.

it was not answered unequivocally by the German judiciary. The views of jurists and political scientists were divided all the time. A considerable number of them regarded the freedom to refrain from unionizing as guaranteed. Accordingly, they held any type of exclusive agreement unconstitutional and unlawful. They also rejected the concept of a social obligation of workers to join unions, on the ground that most unions represented political as well as occupational interests so that taking up membership implied an expression of political opinion.

An equally significant group of legal and political scientists, however, maintained that, although the freedom of every individual to refrain from organizing is part of the general freedom of will, it nevertheless was not included in the constitution as one of the fundamental rights. Hence these experts concluded, the individual worker had to put up with such limitations of his freedom of will as may result from the character of labor organizations and their functions, and that the law had to recognize these limitations likewise. Since working toward greater bargaining strength through increasing the number of members is one of the legitimate functions of unions, exertion of a *certain* amount of pressure on nonunionized workers to make them join—so ran the argument—neither violated the law nor good morals. In case of controversy, the adherents of this view held, it was up to the courts to determine on the basis of the general law whether under the circumstances in the particular case the scope of justifiable pressure had been exceeded.

Swedish management recognized the right of wage earners to organize in a master agreement reached in 1906. As mentioned above, this agreement also clarified the closed-shop question. The closed shop was outlawed at least in contracts between members of the parties to the master agreement. Since these parties represented a large and significant segment of Swedish labor and management, no

need for legislation was seen for a long time.[9] Controversy about the right to organize of salaried employees,
however, resulted in the enactment of the "Law Respecting the Right of Association and the Right of Collective
Bargaining" in 1936.[10] The act prohibited infringement
of the right to organize of all types of employees, but it did
not define this right. Consequently, as in Germany, the
question arose as to whether the statute protected both the
positive and the negative freedom to organize. The controversy was settled conclusively by an amendment to the 1936
act, passed in May 1940,[11] which defined the term "right of
association" as the right of employers and employees to
belong to an association, to exercise their rights as members
of the association, and to work for an association or for the
formation of an association. This definition made it clear
that the Swedish legislators intended to place only the
positive freedom to organize under special statutory protection.

In its reply to a questionnaire circulated by the International Labour Office in preparing the 1948 Labour Conference at San Francisco, the Swedish government restated
its policy by declaring that the only way effectively to assure
the right to organize is through legislation securing to
every citizen an unconditional right to establish or join
organizations, the "positive" right to organize. It added
that the "negative" right to organize, that is, the right of

[9] Sweden has a population of approximately 6.7 million people. The unions
affiliated with the Confederation of Trade Unions comprise more than one million members and have been said to have the largest relative membership in
the world. About three out of every four eligible Swedish workers are members
of a union, while in the United States only roughly one out of every six persons
aged 21 years or over belongs to a labor organization. The Swedish Employers'
Federation comprises about 8,600 enterprises, employing some 577,000 wage
earners. The Confederation of Trade Unions is organized on a much wider
basis than the Employers' Federation. The former covers workers employed in
practically every branch of activity, while the majority of the members of the
Employers' Federation are engaged in industry proper. The employers in other
trades, however, follow largely the collective bargaining policy of the Employers'
Federation.

[10] Svensk Författningssamling, Sept. 22, 1936, p. 957.

[11] The same, May 17, 1940, p. 636.

every citizen not to establish or join organizations, should not be regulated by law.[12]

However, as will be discussed later, discrimination against a Swedish worker in regard to employment merely because he is a member of a union other than the one holding an agreement with the employer would constitute an infringement of the positive right of association of the outsider as guaranteed explicitly by the acts of 1936 and 1940.[13] Hereby the right of the individual worker to choose the union to which he wishes to belong is placed under special statutory protection. Employers have held this to mean that the freedom of the worker to choose no union is also protected. Be that as it may, the question is not acute within the significant segment of Swedish industry, in which the exclusive shop has been outlawed by agreement.

In contrast to the Swedish declaration of policy, the French government, in answering questionnaires of the International Labour Office, took the position that the democratic state, as the protector of public liberties, has the duty to ensure the respect of all aspects of the right to organize, "which is one of the fundamental liberties of modern society." Accordingly, the statement emphasized, measures taken to protect this right must not only safeguard the positive freedom of association but also guarantee to wage earners that nonmembership in a union may not be taken into account in relation to engagement, maintenance in employment, or dismissal.[14] In a supplementary declaration the French government added that:

. . . Any provision in a legislative enactment or a collective agreement intended to force a worker to belong or not to belong to a particular trade union, under the threat of not being engaged or of losing his employment, is, especially in those countries in which there exists a plurality of trade unions, incompatible not

[12] International Labour Conference, *Freedom of Association and Protection of the Right to Organise*, Report VII, (1948), p. 51.

[13] P. 223.

[14] International Labour Conference, *Freedom of Association and Protection of the Right to Organise*, Report VII (1948), p. 50.

only with the principle of freedom of association but also with the principle of freedom of work.[15]

Representatives of the United Kingdom government declared recently[16] that a worker should not be deprived of his inherent freedom not to exercise his right to organize, but that the British government was not prepared to legislate on the question of exclusive union agreements or to outlaw strikes by union workers who refuse to work with nonunionists. They pointed out that in the United Kingdom the adoption or nonadoption of union security clauses is settled "in full freedom by collective bargaining."

In the United States, the federal government declared in the Anti-Injunction Act that the worker should have both full freedom of self-organization and the right to decline to associate with his fellows.[17] Provisions to the same effect have been written into state laws. Protection of the positive and negative freedom of association thus has been on American statute books. However, in view of the situation prior to the 1930's, recent public policy in the federal jurisdiction as well as in a considerable number of states was focused for a long time on prevention of compulsion *not* to become or remain a union member rather than on curbing compulsion to join a labor organization. Benevolent neutrality toward pressure in organizing workers, short of overt violence or unlawful threats, spread in the whole of the country. This trend was intensified by the National Labor Relations Act. As passed in 1935, it did not mention the negative freedom of association in its list of rights of employees.[18] On the other hand, though prohibiting management from encouraging membership in a labor

---

15 International Labour Conference, *Industrial Relations*, Report VIII (2) (1948), p. 25.

16 In the debates preceding the adoption by the 1948 session of the International Labour Conference of the convention concerning freedom of association and by the 1949 session of the convention concerning application of the principles of the right to organise and to bargain collectively.

17 Act of Mar. 23, 1932, 47 Stat. 70, sec. 2.

18 Act of July 5, 1935; 49 Stat. 449, sec. 7.

organization, it stated positively that no federal law precluded an employer from making an agreement with a bona
fide union to require as a condition of employment membership therein, if the union was the duly chosen representative of employees. This was authoritatively interpreted as applying to virtually any kind of union security
contract.[19] Corresponding provisions were written into
state labor relations acts patterned after the federal statute.

Not until 1947, when the National Labor Relations Act
was amended by the Labor Management Relations Act, was
the negative right of association explicitly included in the
enumeration of rights of employees in the statute. It is now
specifically set forth that employees also have the right to refrain from self-organization, from forming, joining, or assisting labor organizations, from bargaining collectively,
and from engaging in other concerted activities.[20] A labor
organization or an employer acting as its instrument, which
would restrain or coerce employees in the exercise of their
negative freedom of association now would be guilty of an
unfair labor practice.[21]

The federal government, in writing this provision into
the National Labor Relations Act, has repudiated the
opinion, held by the unions and by a considerable number

[19] Opinion of the NLRB General Counsel, 10 LRRM 1294 (1942). See *Public
Service Company of Colorado* and *Charles G. Smith*, 89 NLRB No. 51 (1950).

[20] National Labor Relations Act, sec. 7.

[21] National Labor Relations Act, sec. 8 (b) (1) (A). This new provision, according to authoritative interpretation, also contains the guarantee of the right to
refrain from striking, that is, to work in the face of a strike. This right has
been defined as including the right to go to and from work without restraint
or coercion while a strike is in progress. *Labor-Management Relations Act, 1947,*
H. Rept. 510, 80 Cong. 1 sess. (1947), p. 42; *International Longshoremen's and
Warehousemen's Union and Sunset Line and Twine Co.*, 79 NLRB 1487 (1948).
The National Labor Relations Board, accordingly, ordered a union, which prevented nonstriking employees from working, to cease restraining or coercing
them in the exercise of their right to refrain from union activity; but it held
that it had no power to direct the union to compensate the nonstriking employees for their loss of pay. *United Furniture Workers and Colonial Hardwood
Flooring Company*, 84 NLRB No. 69 (1949). See also *Local No. 1150, United
Electrical, Radio and Machine Workers of America, CIO, and Cory Corporation*,
84 NLRB 110 (1949). The Board, similarly, ruled that a threat by a union,
holding a security agreement, to strike unless the employer discharged an employee whom it expelled because she crossed its picket line at another company

of foreign governments, that the exercise of the negative freedom to organize ought not to be regulated in special labor statutes since it can be adequately safeguarded by enforcing the provisions of the general civil and penal law protecting freedom of will. Whether this signifies that now any union interference with the individual's full freedom to refrain from participating in concerted activities is to be considered unlawful, even if it is not illicit under traditional principles of law, will depend upon the interpretation of the new provision by administrative agencies and courts. The legislators have been careful to point out that this provision has been worded in a manner intended to make it clear that union interference with the freedom of association of the worker, which does not also constitute restraint or coercion, should not be considered an unfair labor practice.[22] But the act does not define what it understands by "restraint" and "coercion." The National Labor Relations Board thus stated that it will interpret these terms in the light of the legislative history of the 1947 amendments, and further pointed out that it has been interpreting them for many years. Its interpretation, like that of boards applying corresponding provisions of state statutes, by and large, has been that only interference by force, threats of force, and similar wrongful acts, at any rate

---

constituted unlawful interference, restraint, and coercion of an employee exercising her right to refrain from union activity. In this case the Board not only ordered reinstatement but also directed both employer and union to reimburse the employee for any lost wages. *Clara-Val Packing Co.*, 87 NLRB No. 120 (1949).

The National Labor Relations Board left it undecided whether mere concerted refusal of organized workers to work alongside of nonunionists constitutes coercion of the latter to join their union violative of section 8 (b) (1) (A) of the National Labor Relations Act. But the board held the strike an unfair labor practice for other reasons. (*Local 74, United Brotherhood of Carpenters and Joiners of America, A. F. of L., and Ira A. Watson Company*, 80 NLRB 533, 1948). This case deals with the refusal of employees of a unionized employer to work alongside of employees of another—nonunionized—employer. It does not cover concerted refusal of unionized workers to work together with nonunionists hired by the same firm—a union activity on the legality of which opinions were sharply divided in discussions at recent sessions of the International Labour Conference.

22 *Labor-Management Relations Act, 1947*, H. Rept. 510, 80 Cong. 1 sess. (1947), pp. 42-43.

unlawful under existing law, constitute coercion or restraint.[23]

Apart from the fact that interference with the negative freedom of association undertaken by means other than force and threats of force, thus probably will not be considered unlawful, exercise of this freedom by individual workers may still be restricted under some of the provisions of the amended act, for example, under the proviso permitting employers under certain conditions to make a union shop agreement with the union, duly chosen as bargaining representative.[24]

The recent trend in American labor policy toward curbing involuntary unionism has produced a number of state laws designed to outlaw explicitly any kind of abridgment of both the positive and negative freedom of association. American like foreign experience with such provisions, however, has shown that they, too, do not necessarily preclude differences of opinion as to their meaning and scope, unless they are drafted very carefully. The Alabama Bradford Act may serve as an example.[25] It provides in section 8 that every person shall be free to join or to refrain from joining any labor organization, and in the exercise of such freedom shall be free from interference by force, coercion, or intimidation, or by threats of force or coercion, or by intimidation of or injury to his family.[26] The Attorney General of Alabama,[27] the State Department of Labor,[28] and

[23] American views in this respect by and large have corresponded to the British rather than the French concept. See pp. 261 and 267.

A Trial Examiner's report denied the existence of coercion in a case in which employees joined a union for fear of reprisals against their husbands and fathers who were members of the union and had been requested by its officers to make them join. " 'Fear of reprisal'," the report stated, "is different than 'threat of reprisal,' the former being purely subjective while the latter is objective. . . . The Act does not purport to deal with subjective fear nor would it be feasible to do so." *United Mine Workers of America and Union Supply Co.*, Case No. 9-CB-27, rel. Nov. 10, 1949.

[24] See p. 295.

[25] L. 1943, No. 298.

[26] Sec. 16 of the act limits the freedom to organize of executive, administrative, professional, and supervisory employees.

[27] Op. Att. Gen. Nov. 20, 1943.

[28] Administrative Bulletin 3, Nov. 24, 1943.

a number of experts in the field interpreted this provision as outlawing all types of exclusive union security arrangements. The highest state court, however, held that the act does not make the closed shop illegal.[29]

The law of Nevada,[30] to give another example, prohibits agreements which place employees or persons about to enter employment under the obligation either to become or not to become members of a labor organization. The Supreme Court of Nevada, however, held[31] that union members could lawfully picket an employer for the purpose of compelling him to grant a closed shop. Though recognizing that the language of the Nevada provision was similar to that of statutes prohibiting such shops, the court believed that it should not be interpreted as making them unlawful because, when it was enacted in 1907, the legislature probably intended to outlaw only yellow-dog contracts and compulsion to join company-dominated unions.

SCOPE OF LEGITIMATE PRESSURE TO ORGANIZE

Governments which have not settled the question of involuntary unionism conclusively through special enactments have used provisions of the general law in efforts to protect workers against objectionable pressure to organize. In this manner, administrative agencies and courts have established principles defining the line between justifiable and unlawful methods of recruiting union members.

Some governments have appraised the legality of union pressure in the light of its effects upon individuals.

To illustrate governmental efforts of this kind, we may resume the discussion of German policy. The German over-all term for closed, union, and preferential shop clauses is "organization clause." Theory and practice in Germany, as

---

29 *Hotel and Restaurant Employees' International Alliance* v. *Greenwood,* 30 So. (2d) 696 (1947).
30 Compiled Laws, sec. 10473.
31 *State of Nevada* v. *Eighth District Court,* 210 P (2d) 454 (1949).

in other European countries, have distinguished two generic types of "organization clause." Under a "general organization clause" the employer may employ only organized personnel; or he may be bound to grant certain privileges, such as higher pay or paid vacations, to organized employees. The so-called "limited organization clause" lays the employer under the obligation to employ or treat on a preferential basis, exclusively members of a *particular* labor organization. This type of organization clause corresponds to the union security clauses customary in the United States.

The German Conciliation Service (Schlichtungswesen) and the Minister of Labor tended to discourage all types of organization clauses. A recommendation made in governmental conciliation proceedings could, under certain conditions, be declared binding for and against the party which refused to accept it. However, the commissioners of conciliation usually made no use of this authority if a collective agreement including any type of organization clause was involved. The Minister of Labor had the power to declare generally binding any collective agreement which had become the prevailing standard in fixing conditions of employment for the industry in question in the area which it covered. If declared generally binding, the agreement governed within its geographical area all such work as covered by it, even if neither the employer nor the employee affected came originally under its provisions. But the Minister of Labor adopted the policy of refusing to declare an agreement generally binding if it included an organization clause. This attitude of the Ministry of Labor and the Conciliation Service increased the reluctance of unions to write such clauses into collective contracts.

The German Supreme Court defined its position with respect to the closed shop in a decision involving the "limited organization clause."[32] The plaintiff in this case

32 RGZ 104, pp. 327 ff., (1922).

was a well-known actor who was a member of the Alliance of Stage Employees but had given advance notice that he intended to give up his membership. The union was under contract with the German Stage Association, an employers' association to which belonged virtually all important theaters in Germany and Austria. The contract included a clause binding the members of the employers' association to employ exclusively members of the Alliance and, further, obligating the latter to work for nobody except members of the Association. The plaintiff applied for declaratory judgment that neither the employers' nor the employees' organization were entitled to prevent him from appearing on any stage after his resignation from the Alliance. The court granted the petition, declaring the closed-shop clause void under the circumstances of the case. Leaving the question of the constitutional guarantee of freedom not to organize undecided, the Supreme Court judges pointed out that neither the Constitution nor any statute favored compulsory organization. As to pressure tactics by organized labor the court stated that unions have a legitimate interest in enlarging and strengthening their organization and that, in pursuing this objective, they may exert "a certain pressure" upon persons who are not willing to join. But the means applied and the methods used must not violate good morals.[33] Steps undertaken to overcome resistance to unionization, the court continued, violate good morals if the measures as such are immoral, or if the injury inflicted upon the outsider is so considerable as to destroy his economic existence, or if the resulting harm is out of proportion to the advantage sought by the union. The court held that in determining whether a labor organization is violating good morals, the same criteria apply as are used in appraising the conduct of associations in general. Since in the case at bar the closed-shop clause would have

---

[33] Or of course otherwise violate the law. The Swedish Labor Court stated that inducing a person to join an organization is improper only when tactics are used which are contrary to law. *AD dom* 73/ 1937.

deprived the plaintiff of any opportunity to follow his profession, unless he remained a member of the union, it was declared invalid.

After establishment of the labor courts the Supreme Labor Court[34] discussed the question as to whether organized employees act lawfully if they give collective separation notices in order to force the discharge of a nonunion employee. Following essentially the principles of the Supreme Court, the Supreme Labor Court set forth that pressure by a union or its members, that is, the economically stronger, upon an unorganized individual, that is, the economically weaker, violates the law if it is so strong as to menace or endanger seriously his economic existence. Such way of acting, the court said, offends against the sense of propriety of all just and fair thinking persons.[35] In the case at bar the judges found that the organized employees had forced the employer to discharge the plaintiff, knowing that he would not be able to obtain other employment. The court further stated that it did not find any fault with the refusal of the plaintiff to yield to the unlawful union pressure and to surrender his freedom of will by joining a union.[36] Accordingly, judgment was rendered against the organized employees to pay damages to the plaintiff.

Two Swiss decisions dealing with the same issue may be mentioned here because they supplement the conclusions of law of the German court. The Swiss judges declared unlawful threatening with collective separation notices for the purpose of causing a worker to join a labor organization

[34] RAGE 4, pp. 19 ff., 1929.
[35] This is a technical term of the German civil law, which has been defined in a large body of high court decisions.
[36] Art 12 (1) of the "Basic Law for the Federal Republic of Germany" (Bonn Constitution), enacted in 1949 to govern the Federation of western German states (*Laender*) until "the day when a constitution adopted in a free decision by the German people comes into force," states that "all Germans have the right freely to choose their occupation, place of work and place of training." Article 18 provides that whoever abuses, among other basic rights, the freedom of association, shall forfeit this freedom. The forfeiture and its extent shall be pronounced by the Federal Constitutional Court. It remains to be seen whether and how these provisions will affect union demands to exclude nonmembers from opportunities to work.

which—as usual in Europe—is politically not neutral. The opinions denied explicitly the existence of a legally protected individual right to use one's working power without interference by others. "Coercive instigation to dissolve a particular employment relationship," however, was held unlawful, if the advantage which the union tries to attain is contrary to good morals—as, for example, increases in membership of politically interested unions through compulsion—and if, in addition, the interests of the displaced worker, which are affected by the action of the union, are of relatively equal or greater importance than the benefits sought by the union. In the cases under discussion the court found that—aside from the political interest which had to be ignored—the union could have only a weak concern for the discharge of the nonmember since he had not in any way interfered with the interests of the union or its members. He merely wanted to remain a member of his union.[37]

Summarizing, the German and Swiss high courts did not use the concept of a freedom to refrain from joining a union. Nor did they attach great weight to differences between the individual types of closed, union, or similar shops (general or limited organization clause). The German courts, by and large, subjected all kinds of such agreements to the same rules, which were similar to those applied in appraising the legality of boycotts. Since outsiders were more often displaced from their place of work than prevented from obtaining employment at all, cases of enforced discharges prevailed among the relatively few suits which had to be decided. The courts tended to regard concerted efforts of employees to displace a fellow worker as immoral and therefore unlawful, if they endangered or threatened to destroy his economic existence, unless the refusal to work with a fellow employee was justified by his personal conduct in the establishment.

[37] BGE 51 II, pp. 525 ff., 1925; BGE 54 II, pp. 142 ff., 1928.

These examples of German and Swiss policies may suffice to describe government efforts to determine the border line between lawful and unlawful union pressure without resort to the concepts of the negative freedom of association or of the right to work. Differences between American and European official views on the scope of legitimate pressure will be discussed in the following chapters.

CHAPTER VIII

Government Problems and Policies: Freedom of Choice Among Unions

The foregoing discussion indicated that two types of compulsion to organize may be distinguished. The one type is directed solely at unorganized workers and is undertaken to make them take up or maintain membership in any of the existing unions. The end in view is protection of unionism as such without restriction of the freedom of the employee to belong to and to be represented by a bona fide organization of his individual choice. The other type is directed not only at unorganized but also at organized workers and is undertaken to make them join a *particular* union and remain a member of it. The outsider, accordingly, has no freedom of choice. While the former type of compulsion is primarily intended to protect unionism against nonunionism, the latter type, though its supporters consider it likewise a desirable means to promote unionism,[1] gives special protection to the interests of one union against those of rival unions and thus limits free competition among bona fide labor organizations.

EUROPEAN POLICIES

European governments have taken cognizance of these differences between the two kinds of pressure methods. In the United States, however, by and large it has been a foregone conclusion that union security arrangements must give an employment monopoly to the contracting union.

European governments have rejected limitation of individual freedom to choose one's union.

Adherents of that European school of thought, which has appraised pressure to organize in the light of the concept

[1] See John V. Spielman, "Union Security and the Right to Work," *Journal of Political Economy,* December 1949, pp. 537, 539.

of positive and negative freedom of association, have condemned arrangements which place organized workers under the necessity of changing their union affiliation or joining an additional union if they wish to obtain or keep the jobs of their choice. Whether or not they have agreed that the negative freedom is guaranteed by special legislative enactments, they have considered such arrangements an infringement of the *positive* freedom of association because, in their opinion, it includes the right to belong to a union of one's free, individual choosing. Though there has been some dispute as to the legitimacy of exclusion from job opportunities of nonunionists, nearly all German and Swedish writers, for example, have agreed that exclusion of unionists because they do not belong to a contractually prescribed organization is incompatible with freedom to organize.

Since closed-shop and similar agreements were demanded only in relatively rare instances, they were no problem for legislators in the German Republic.[2] For the same reason, the executive and judicial branches of the government had relatively little to do with them. As early as 1920 the national government declared: "Collective agreements which exclude workers from establishments because they belong to a bona fide organization representing another philosophy of life or political opinion are contrary to good morals and possibly may violate Article 159 of the National Constitution."[3]

In keeping with their general tendency, the high courts of the German Republic refrained from applying the con-

---

[2] The Austrian Act of Apr. 5, 1930, "For the Protection of the Right to Work and of Assembly" (Anti-Terror Act; Bundesgesetzblatt, Apr. 14, 1930, p. 546) declared null and void all provisions in collective contracts and other joint agreements between employers and employees if their purpose was directly or indirectly (1) to ensure that no persons other than the members of a specified trade union or other voluntary association should be employed in an undertaking, or (2) to prevent the employment in an establishment of persons who were not members of a trade union or who were members of a specified trade union or other voluntary association. Accordingly, all types of exclusive agreements were unlawful. The act, with few exceptions, also prohibited the check-off.

[3] National Assembly, *Stenographical Report*, Jan. 1, 1920, col. 4408.

cept of positive and negative freedom of association to controversies caused by concerted efforts to make organized
workers join another union as a condition of employment.
They were rather inclined to base decisions on the dogma,
discussed above, that the scope of allowable union pressure
is exceeded when the means applied are contrary to law,
or when the pressure prejudices the interests of the worker
affected in an undue measure. In addition, a strong trend
existed to consider immoral and hence unlawful efforts of
employees to deprive fellow workers of employment opportunities solely because they belonged to another union
or because their opinions or beliefs differed from those of
the other workers.

The Supreme Labor Court in a basic opinion[4] held concerted refusal of members of one union to work with members of another union illegal as a violation of good morals.
Precisely because rivalry among unions means conflict of
opinions, the judges said, the opponent must be respected as
a fellow man. Since everyone has the right to an opinion of
his own and to stand up for it in the appropriate manner, interunion contests must not go so far that the parties carry
them through on the basis of nonobjective, shallow power
policies. Suppression of convictions of others, the court
stated, is generally objectionable. It is so in an even higher
degree, the opinion declared, where the oppressor uses the
weapon of economic injury to endanger and destroy the
existence of the opponent as a human being. Such tactics,
the court concluded, are contrary to the sense of propriety
of all just and fair thinking persons. The general public
and the national economy must be protected against them.

Even prior to the 1940 interpretative amendment of the
Law respecting the Right of Association, the Swedish Labor
Court held that public policy protected all unions alike so
that no individual union had the right to establish a monopoly by making a closed-shop agreement excluding mem-

4 RAGE 3, pp. 125 ff. (1929).

bers of other unions.[5] Under the act of 1940 infringements
of the positive freedom of association are unlawful "even
if the measures in question have been taken under a clause
of a collective agreement or any other contract." In the
light of the Labor Court's interpretation of the right of
association, this provision has been held to mean that,
though closed-shop clauses are valid, an employer who
discriminates under such a clause against a member of a
union other than the one which is a party to the agreement
would be liable for infringement of the outsider's positive
right of association. This tallies in a high degree with German theory. Moreover, the practical effects of prevailing
judicial policy in both countries have been about the same,
despite differences in legal reasoning.

Though closed and union shops of one type or another
have been established sporadically in France, French theory,
administrative practice, and jurisprudence, likewise, have
generally tended to disapprove of them. The agency in
charge of preparing the exhibition of 1937, for example,
distributed a circular, advising the entrepreneurs concerned
to employ exclusively workers referred by the placement
service of the union Employment Exchange of Paris
(Bourse du Travail de Paris). The Council of State held
that this circular infringed upon the right to organize and
declared it void on the ground that the agency had over-
stepped its authority.[6]

Courts have followed a similar policy. The Court of
Chambéry[7] stated that the principle of individual freedom
of work, which is maintained in the public interest, would
be purely imaginary if a worker could not use it without
being threatened with the loss of his work, which more
often than not is his sole means of existence. A newspaper
firm which discharged a proof reader, who had been in its
employ for more than twenty years, for the sole reason that

[5] AD dom 73 (1937) and 24 (1939).
[6] Conseil d'Etat, July 7, 1939. Union Corporative des Travailleurs Français,
Droit Social 1939, p. 376.
[7] Mar. 14, 1893; D 93.2.191.

he refused to join the printers' union, thus was found to have abused a right and to be liable for damages.[8] The Court of Cassation[9] stated that a collective agreement cannot have the legal effect of modifying the relations between an employer and workers already in his employ. Those who are dismissed under the terms of the agreement because they are not unionized, have the right to sue for damages because of "wrongful discharge." The court disregarded the defense of the employer that he was under a contractual obligation to employ only members of the contracting union. The Court of Appeal of Lyon went further. It held[10] that full freedom to choose the union to which a worker wishes to belong must be protected in the same manner as other aspects of the freedom of association. Accordingly, it ruled that a union was entitled to require the cancellation of a clause in a collective agreement between an employer and a rival union, which infringed upon this freedom. The court directed annulment of a contract clause stipulating that the musicians employed by a certain employer must belong to a particular union and that the employment of any musician who resigned or was expelled from this union would be automatically terminated.

The Labor Code, as amended by the law of December 25, 1946[11] now provides explicitly in section 31 (0) that the terms of hiring and discharge which must be laid down in every national collective agreement, must not infringe upon the freedom of the employee to choose his own union.

British decisions have recognized contracts excluding nonmembers of a specific union.

Efforts to compel workers to join a specific union have been made in Britain also. In accordance with the gen-

---

8 Civil Tribunal of the Seine, Nov. 28, 1933. *Journal "Comœdia"* v. *Lacquerrière. Gazette des Tribunaux,* 34.1.294.
9 Mar. 9, 1938; D 38.305.
10 Jan. 19, 1938. D 38.140.
11 J. O. No. 301, Dec. 25, 1946, p. 10,932.

eral trend in legislative, administrative, and judicial practice to interfere less and less with union methods of enrolling members, relatively recent decisions of British agencies and courts display policies quite different from those discussed in the preceding paragraphs. For example, in a case decided under the Unemployment Insurance Act, 1920, and the Trade Disputes and Trade Unions Act, 1927, the Court of Referees and the Umpire found that a lockout was not illegal, the sole purpose of which was enforcement of a collective agreement making membership in a particular union a condition of employment.[12]

The *Reynolds* v. *Shipping Federation* decision[13] dealt at some length with the question of the validity of such an agreement. The court stated:

. . . for many years past no one has questioned the right of a Trade Union to insist, if they are strong enough to do so, under penalty of a strike, that an employer or a group of employers shall employ none but members of the Trade Union. And the result of any such effective combination of workmen has, of course, been to impose on the other workmen in the trade the necessity of joining the Union as a condition of obtaining employment. Here the employers, instead of being forced against their will into employing union men only, have recognised that advantages may arise from adopting such a course voluntarily, and have accordingly made an agreement with the Trade Union to that effect. The incidental result to the other workmen in the trade is the same as if the employers had yielded against their will instead of agreeing voluntarily. But workmen who are unwilling to join the Trade Union have no greater reason to complain of a violation of legal rights in the second case than in the first.[14]

12 Decision of the Umpire No. 10287 (1932), Pamphlet 4, (1932).
13 1 Ch. 48 (1942).
14 It was mentioned above that the Transport and General Workers' Union demanded in 1946 that the members of the rival National Passenger Workers' Union employed by the London Passenger Transport Board be discharged, unless they transferred their membership to the TGWU, and that the Board, taking the view the public should not be asked to suffer because of interunion conflict, granted the TGWU's demand. Five of the members of the National Passenger Workers' Union applied for an interim injunction, restraining the Board from making it a condition of their employment that they should join the Transport and General Workers' Union. This injunction was refused by Mr. Justice Wynn-Parry in the High Court on Sept. 19, 1946. However, he did not base his decision on considerations involving the legality or illegality of closed-shop agreements. The applicants argued that before they were employed by the Board it was either a condition of their contract with their previous employers, whose under-

A Court of Inquiry, appointed on January 13, 1948, to inquire into the causes and circumstances of a dispute between the National Coal Board and the National Union of Colliery Winding Enginemen, dealt with a case of refusal to recognize a union, the founders of which seceded from another organization. The Union of Colliery Winding Enginemen had been formed by a number of winding enginemen who had withdrawn from associations having membership among all classes of colliery enginemen and craftsmen because they felt that their special interests were frequently overlooked by the majority of the members who were not particularly concerned with them. While sympathizing with the motives of the seceding enginemen, the Court held that recognition of the new organization representing only a section of a class in the industry would not be in the interests of orderly relations between the employer and his employees. But the Court felt it imperative that, within the existing organization of craft groups in the National Union of Mineworkers, means should be devised to ensure that, whenever questions affecting the rates and conditions of employment of winding enginemen are to be the subject of negotiations with the employer,

---

takings were transferred to the Board, or a recognized practice, that an employee should not be required to join a trade union, and that he should not be liable to be discharged except for misconduct, age, ill-health or reduction of staff. The applicants contended that these terms had become terms of their employment with the Board. The court agreed that the applicants were not required to join a union either under their previous or their present contracts. Consequently, the court said, if the Board wished that every employee should join a particular union, it must terminate the employment of those who are not willing to do so and replace them by others who accept this condition. The Board had admitted that this was its intention. The court stated that it had nothing to do with the question of the ethics or the morality of the policy of the Board. It further did not consider it desirable to deal with the contention of the applicants that their discharge would involve a breach of contract, because this would be the chief question at the trial of the suit of the applicants. (*Keetch and Others*, v. *London Passenger Transport Board*. The *Times* (London), Sept. 11, 18, 19, 1946.) This suit was for injunction restraining the Board from making the plaintiffs' membership in the TGWU a condition of their employment and ordering the Board to withdraw any such condition, as well as restraining it from dismissing the plaintiffs. In addition, the latter applied for a declaration that any such condition of employment is void and of no effect. When the temporary injunction was refused, the parties did not continue with the action. Therefore, the court had no occasion to decide the basic questions involved.

the union should include among its representatives persons regarded by the winding enginemen themselves as competent to represent their special interests. "Such machinery," the Court added, "of course, can only function successfully if it is established and worked by all concerned in a spirit of co-operation."[15]

The British government rejected the American type of closed and union shop.

Recent events in unionism, coinciding with, and not unrelated to, economic and political postwar changes in Britain, have evoked acute discussion of involuntary unionism. The labor government freed local authorities and public corporations from the statutory prohibition of granting a closed shop, and some of them used the new freedom to make employment, as in the closed shop of the American type, contingent upon membership in particular unions. Although official policy of the Trades Union Congress still rejects such methods, large unions have endeavored to use these events, especially the agreement between the London Passenger Transport Board and the Powerful Transport and General Workers' Union, as a precedent. The strong National Union of Mine Workers, for example, demanded from the National Coal Board a nationwide arrangement under which every worker normally employed by the Board would have been required to be a member of it. In addition, it requested the check-off of union dues.[16]

These developments have made the closed shop an acute British issue. Its importance is aggravated by the fact that

[15] *Report of a Court of Inquiry into a Dispute between the National Coal Board and the National Union of Colliery Winding Enginemen,* ordered by the House of Commons to be printed 28th January 1948.

[16] The union has claimed that it merely demands the introduction of conditions on a nationwide scope, which have existed for some time in a number of mining areas, such as Derbyshire, North Wales, Nottinghamshire, and South Wales. The National Coal Board did not comply with the request for the union shop but consented to the check-off of union dues of those workers who sign a written authorization. (Collective agreement of Feb. 8, 1949.) This is one of the rare instances of a check-off agreement in Europe. It should be noted, however, that it was not entered into with a private employer but with a public board.

it arose in governmentally operated or instituted bodies and at a time of expanding government activities in the economic area. With progressing nationalization of very important and large enterprises, a growing number of workers will come under direct or indirect public employment. If in the future membership in a specific union is generally made a condition of such employment, a considerable portion of workers will be compelled to join particular unions without having a free choice. In addition, strong unions may tend to compel private employers to apply similar rules.[17]

The issue was taken up by the House of Commons in November 1946. An amendment to the King's speech was proposed, expressing regret that the "speech contains no reference to the threat to the personal liberty of workers, members and non-members of trade unions, by the enforcement of the closed shop in industry nor gives any indication of the policy of His Majesty's Government in this grave constitutional matter." As mentioned above, the Minister of Labour, speaking against the amendment and declaring the policy of the government, rejected explicitly the American type of the closed shop. He endeavored to assure the public that there would be no undue compulsion to organize, chiefly by referring to the official policy of the Trade Union Congress "that there shall not be a complete and absolute right of recognition in any industry to any one

---

[17] Whether this type of the closed shop will be established on a large scale in private and public undertakings, as is assumed by a number of people, is at present a matter of conjecture. The Trades Union Congress, so far, does not seem to favor it, and it may be doubted whether the structure of the British labor movement lends itself to such "closed shop unionism."

The economic and social changes going on in Britain are likely to alter, in many respects, functions and policies of unions, which were formed to safeguard the interests of workers under different conditions. The same applies to unions in other European countries in which labor governments, or governments strongly influenced by labor, are planning similar or farther going deviations from the system of free, private enterprise. Though an attempt to analyze the effects which the new course has had, or may in the future have, on the policies of the unions concerned would seem premature, it may be mentioned that it apparently is calling forth a certain trend in union circles to believe that, under the new system, governmental economic planning may offer better prospects for a satisfactory solution of the problem of employment security than exclusive agreements or other traditional restrictive union practices.

union." With respect to nationalized industries, he expressed the opposition of the government to any legislation designating the unions which should be recognized. The essence of the declaration was that the government wants the parties directly concerned to settle the issue on the basis of expediency and without governmental intervention. "We believe," the Minister said, "that we can trust industry. While there may be a little breaking out here and there, no doubt on the part of the employers as well as of the workers, we believe industry wants to find agreements by which it can work with the least possible disruption. . . . " The proposed amendment was rejected by 316 votes to 155.

AMERICAN POLICIES

The foregoing analysis shows that, according to prevailing European view, freedom to organize includes, among other things, the right of every individual, who decides to join a union, to belong to an organization of his free choice. For this reason, a strong trend has existed to condemn arrangements which, by making membership in a certain union a condition of employment, may compel individual workers to change their union affiliation or to belong to a union not to their liking. The trend was noticeable also in the latest, somewhat vague policy declaration of the British government.

Any analysis of prevailing views respecting freedom of choice must take into account the fact that in Europe choosing one's union means choosing one's bargaining agent, but that in the United States, this is not necessarily the case. Under prevailing American public policies, restrictions of the freedom of the individual worker to follow his choice are possible with respect to bargaining representation as well as union membership. Labor relations acts provide that bargaining agents are selected by the majority of the workers concerned, which implies that the choice of members of the minority is disregarded. As to selection of one's union, significant labor statutes recognize the validity of collective agreements which make membership in a specific union a condition of employment so that workers are compelled to join it if they want to obtain or retain a job in the area covered by the contract.

The individual American worker is not necessarily represented by a bargaining agent of his choice.

The National Labor Relations Act[18] presents a good picture of the concept of freedom to organize prevailing in the United States. This act and the corresponding state acts were passed to promote industrial peace and to "encourage that equality of bargaining power which is a prerequisite to equality of opportunity and freedom of contract." The act seeks to achieve these objectives "by encouraging the practice and procedure of collective bargaining and by protecting the exercise by workers of full freedom of association, self-organization, and designation of representatives of their own choosing, for the purpose of negotiating the terms and conditions of their employment or other mutual aid or protection." A comparison of the provisions of the act implementing this program and of European ideologies and policies, as discussed above, shows distinctly the differences in American and European thought as to what constitutes full freedom of association.

Prior to the National Labor Relations Act American workers bargained through their unions, as most European workers still do.[19] This meant that on the side of the workers the negotiating was ordinarily done by unions, and that these unions acted on behalf of their members only. The National Labor Relations Act abolished this system.

18 Act of July 5, 1935, 49 Stat. 449, amended by act of June 23, 1947, 61 Stat. 136.
19 The French Labor Code (Bk. I, Art. 31) and sec. 4 of the Swedish Act Respecting the Right of Association and the Right of Collective Bargaining of Sept. 11, 1936, as amended, (*Författningssamling*, Sept. 22, 1936, p. 957), explicitly designate the occupational organization of employees as the proper bargaining agents of employees. In the United Kingdom the term collective agreement is applied to "arrangements under which the wages and conditions of

It put into practice a new concept in collective bargaining. The union as such, so far considered the "natural" bargaining agent for its members, was replaced by a bargaining agent, which may or may not be a union and which is selected by workers irrespective of membership in a union. Where no union- or closed-shop arrangement applies, no one must join a union in order to be represented directly in collective bargaining. However, American unionism succeeded in preserving its position. Only in relatively few cases have individuals or bodies other than unions been chosen to fill the post of the bargaining representative.

The introduction of this system made it necessary to determine who may take part in the selection of the bargaining representative as well as whom the latter should represent. The act granted the right to designate bargaining agents to a peculiar type of organized labor group, namely, units appropriate for the purposes of collective bargaining (bargaining units). Since as mentioned above, the legislators held that "employees themselves cannot choose these units, because the units must be determined before it can be known what employees are eligible to participate in a choice of any kind," they empowered the National Labor Relations Board to determine appropriate units.[20] Once a

employment are settled by a bargain, in the form of an agreement made between employers and workpeople's organizations." (Ministry of Labour and National Service, *Industrial Relations Handbook*, 1944, p. 18). The law of the German (Weimar) Republic likewise recognized "associations of employees" as the sole representatives of workers for the purposes of collective bargaining. (Order relating to Collective Contracts, Committees of Wage-earning and Salaried Employees, and Conciliation of Labor Disputes," of Dec. 23, 1918, as amended, RGBl. 1918, p. 1456).

20 In practice the appropriate bargaining unit has been determined very often without Board action by direct understanding between employees and employers. Where no dispute exists there will ordinarily be neither need nor occasion for designation of units by the Board. The situation will be different when employees and employers cannot reach agreement. If the Board is invoked to act in case of controversy about who is the duly chosen bargaining representative or about whether or not the duty to bargain collectively has been complied with, a finding as to the appropriate unit to be represented is indispensable to the ultimate decision. It must not be overlooked, however, that the Board can act only after a petition has been filed. With respect to proceedings arising out of alleged refusal to bargain, this has been the case ever since the National Labor Relations Act was passed in 1935. But there was nothing in the original act to prevent the Board from instituting on its own motion an investigation

unit is established, the majority of the workers belonging to
it may choose a bargaining representative, either through

concerning the representation of employees. The Board, however, held that the
power to conduct such an investigation *ex officio* should be exercised sparingly,
if at all, on the theory that, if a controversy concerning representation actually
existed, and if its resolution would facilitate collective bargaining, one of the
labor organizations involved would file a petition. The act, as amended by the
Labor Management Relations Act of 1947, now makes Board investigation of
such a controversy contingent upon the filing of a petition by an employee, a
group of employees, an individual or labor organization acting on their behalf,
or by an employer. Under present law, accordingly, the Board cannot determine
appropriate bargaining units on its own motion even if controversy exists with
respect to recognition of a person or organization as bargaining agent or with
respect to compliance with the statutory duty to bargain collectively.

Owing to this statutory regulation and settled administrative practice, bargaining units and representatives have been chosen in a large number of cases
by the employees, and recognized by the employers, without Board assistance.
But even in case of petition for formal decision the Board has favored direct
settlement between the parties to the dispute, consistent with the policies of
the National Labor Relations Act. A very considerable portion of representation as well as other cases, involving the appropriate unit, thus have been
settled by a variety of informal procedures rather than by formal action. The
majority of existing bargaining units doubtless have not been established by
the Board.

Still, the Board is not bound by every agreement between a union and an
employer defining a bargaining unit (See *Tide Water Associated Oil Co.* 66
NLRB 380, 1946), and it has had to determine units in the cases in which
it was petitioned to do so and no informal settlement could be reached. In
view of its broad discretion under the National Labor Relations Act, the Board
has established administrative policies as to the considerations generally entering
into the designation of a unit. The wishes of the employees concerned have
been declared one of them. Where the considerations favoring a craft unit and
those favoring a more comprehensive unit are of substantially equal weight the
principle was adopted that the desires of employees should be ascertained by
self-determination elections (Globe Doctrine).

From all these facts it follows not only that units frequently have been defined
by employees or the parties immediately concerned, but also that the Board has
tended to consider the desires of employees when making use of its power to
determine the appropriate unit by itself. These practices have been of great
significance. They must be mentioned here to prevent the erroneous impression—to which the ambiguous language of sec. 9 (b) may give rise—that every
single bargaining unit, to be recognized as appropriate, has to be designated by
the Board or that the latter makes its decisions with no regard to the wishes of
the workers (or employers). For the purposes of this study, which is primarily
concerned with a comparison of basic concepts, the statutory principle that a
public authority may make workers involuntary members of a group is of greater
importance than administrative policy to apply the law doctrine in as liberal a
manner as possible.

According to the Canadian Industrial Relations and Disputes Investigation
Act (Bill 195, Fourth Session, Twentieth Parliament, 11-12 George VI, 1947-48,
effective since Sept. 1, 1948) a union claiming to have as members a majority
of employees in a unit appropriate for collective bargaining may make application to the Labor Relations Board to be certified as bargaining agent of the
employees in the unit. The Board determines whether the unit is appropriate.
When it finds that this is the case, it may certify the petitioning union, if it is
satisfied that the majority of the employees in the unit are members in good
standing of the union or have selected the union to be their bargaining representative by majority vote. (Secs. 7 and 9).

election or by other means. If, as is usually the case, a union is chosen, it has under the majority principle the statutory right to represent all the employees in the unit, no matter whether they do or do not belong to this union, whether they are or are not eligible for membership, or whether they expressed themselves in favor of, or against, it.[21]

According to this regulation, majority rule has supplanted freedom of choice on an individual basis. At two stages of this procedure individual workers may be compelled to acquiesce in organization for purposes of collective bargaining without or against their own will in a manner which has not been customary in Europe. They may be incorporated by governmental action in a bargaining unit to which they do not wish to belong; and a union may be designated as their bargaining representative, which they have no desire to join and which they did not authorize to protect their interests, possibly because they are members of a rival union. The concept of a governmentally determined bargaining unit has been as alien to European traditional law and practice as it was to earlier usage in the United States. If European employees wish collective representation, they are generally represented by a union which they join for this purpose. Ordinarily, neither the government nor majority rule is involved.

Congress obviously had to introduce the bargaining unit when it provided for bargaining representatives which are not necessarily unions and which may represent workers irrespective of union affiliation. The introduction of the bargaining unit, in turn, caused the legislators to authorize the National Labor Relations Board to determine, in case of need, the scope of the unit. As to selection of a bargaining

21 Under the Railway Labor Act, the majority of any craft or class of employees has the right to determine who shall be the representative of the craft or class. In the conduct of any election for this purpose the National Mediation Board designates who may participate.

The principle of selection of the bargaining representative by a majority of workers was adopted as a war measure by the National War Labor Board during World War I.

agent, which has taken place under traditional European practice simply by taking up membership in a union, Congress has held that majority rule "by long experience has been discovered best for employers as well as employees," and that making of agreements is impracticable in its absence. This does not tally with prevailing European view, which still tends to construe the freedom of workers to form and join organized bodies and to designate representatives of their own choosing, for the purposes of collective bargaining, as an individual freedom of the worker. European governments have used other methods if substantial obstructions to the smooth functioning of collective bargaining have to be removed.[22] American legislators further pointed out that the majority rule is sanctioned "by the whole philosophy of democratic institutions." But European statutes dealing with collective bargaining have not introduced majority rule of the American type because subjection of minority groups to decision by majority groups generally has not been considered indispensable to safeguard the practice and procedure of collective bargaining.[23]

---

[22] As mentioned above, difficulties which may arise when two or more unions seek to bargain for their members in a given firm or other unit not infrequently have been prevented in Europe through interunion co-operation. The National Labor Relations Board approved of occasional similar efforts of American unions to bargain in conjunction for their members, by certifying them jointly as the exclusive bargaining agent. In such cases the opportunity of the individual workers in the unit to be represented by the union of their choice was preserved in a larger measure. See *Staley Manufacturing Company*, 31 NLRB 946 (1941); *American Car and Foundry Company*, 51 NLRB 1416 (1943); *Fulton Bag and Cotton Mills*, 52 NLRB 464 (1943); *Scullin Steel Company*, 55 NLRB 1461 (1944); *Fairmont Creamery Company*, 61 NLRB 1311 (1945); *The Mead Corporation, Heald Division*, 63 NLRB 1129 (1945); *General Motors Corp., United Motors Service Div., St. Louis Branch*, 67 NLRB 233 (1946).

The Canadian law provides explicitly that two or more unions claiming to have as members in good standing a majority of employees in an appropriate bargaining unit may file an application for joint certification as bargaining agent. Industrial Relations and Disputes Investigation Act, 1948, sec. 7 (5).

[23] As to the functions of the "most representative organizations" in France, see p. 176 n.

The union which bargains for the majority of workers of a certain type in a European enterprise will, in practice, influence the determination of wages and working conditions of nonmembers of the same type employed in the same undertaking in a large, if not decisive, measure. This is partly due to its greater economic power, partly to co-operation between majority and minority unions, partly to the various difficulties that a management would encounter if it

Freedom to belong to a union of one's choice
likewise may be restricted under American statutes.

The National Industrial Recovery Act,[24] one of the statutes ushering in the new period of governmental protection and encouragement of unionism, prescribed that every code of fair competition, agreement, and license to be approved under the act had to provide, among other things, for freedom of employees from employer interference in matters of self-organization. The codes further had to include a provision that no employee and no one seeking employment should be required as a condition of employment to refrain from joining a labor organization of *his own choosing.*[25] The wording of the statute gave rise to protracted controversy about its meaning. Employer interference with the freedom of self-organization, by discriminating against those organized and unorganized workers who are not members of the particular contracting union, has been considered the essence of the closed and union shop of the American type. Moreover, by making membership in this union a condition of employment, individual workers, as discussed above, may be compelled to refrain from joining a union of their own choosing. Since the act did not provide that employer interference was not improper if undertaken in the interest of a union and in compliance with a collective agreement, its language was susceptible to the interpretation that it banned closed-shop and related agreements, though such a ban had not been intended by the legislature. Because of contradictory and ambiguous statements by the administrator of the National Recovery Administration, the controversy about the legal-

---

attempted to operate a plant with different wage scales, hours of work, and other basic conditions of employment for workers performing the same tasks. Accordingly, as far as the determination of employment conditions is concerned, the will of a majority of workers practically is decisive also under European collective bargaining, although it is done under legal and other conditions which differ so much from the American situation.

[24] Approved June 16, 1933, 48 Stat. 195.
[25] Sec. 7 (a) of the act.

ity of union security agreements was not settled until the original National Labor Relations Act declared that no federal statute (except the Railway Labor Act) precluded employers from making an agreement with a bona fide labor organization requiring membership therein as a condition of employment, provided only that the organization was a duly chosen bargaining representative in the meaning of the act at the time when the agreement was made.[26]

The American system created the problem of the maximum period of restriction of freedom of choice.

The federal act thus provided for two important privileges of majority unions. The exclusive right to represent all workers in the bargaining unit and the exclusive right to enter into union security agreements.[27] State legislatures introduced the same principle. The National Labor Relations Act (and state statutes), however, did not fix a period for which the designation of the union as bargaining agent should have legal force.[28] Nor did it regulate the time of validity of collective agreements. This caused numerous disputes involving the question as to whether unions, once

[26] Sec. 8 (3) of the National Labor Relations Act in its original wording. This act became law on July 5, 1935 (49 Stat. 449). Prior to that, in May 1935, the U. S. Supreme Court had declared the National Industrial Recovery Act unconstitutional. The latter act was to expire on June 16, 1935.

[27] The U. S. Senate Committee on Education and Labor emphasized strongly that this regulation did not expand the existing law regarding closed-shop agreements but narrowed it. Its report set forth: "While today an employer may negotiate such an agreement even with a minority union, the bill provides that an employer shall be allowed to make a closed-shop contract only with a labor organization that represents the majority of employees in the appropriate collective-bargaining unit covered by such agreement when made." *National Labor Relations Board,* S. Rept. 573, 74 Cong. 1 sess., p. 12 (1935).

[28] Though European laws have not provided for bargaining representatives of the American type, members of employee representation committees, having functions other than collective bargaining, are elected by methods similar to those prescribed for the selection of the bargaining agent in the United States. Their tenure generally is fixed in a manner resembling the rules governing the term of office of legislators or elected members of other public authorities. The German Works Councils Act and the French Order to Institute Works Committees, for example, prescribed or prescribes, respectively, that all council or committee members hold office for one year, re-election being permissible. The model constitution for Joint Industrial Councils (Whitley Councils), issued by the British Ministry of Labour, similarly states that the council members shall retire annually, and shall be eligible for re-appointment.

they had become bargaining agents, could use their privileged position to restrict the exercise of freedom of choice by workers under their jurisdiction for any length of time.

Since the law was silent with respect to this significant legislative problem, the National Labor Relations Board felt compelled to look for a solution which would make it possible to carry the act through with a minimum of friction. Considering it an anomalous situation that one provision of the act guaranteed employees the right to choose their own union and to select freely their representative for collective bargaining, while other provisions offered inherent possibilities for invasion of these rights,[29] it tried to reconcile freedom to designate representatives with the purpose of the statute to fix the representation of bargaining units for a period of time. Declaring that, to be meaningful, freedom to choose representatives must necessarily include the right to change them, it emphasized that workers could not exercise this right at will. The board did not deny that the certification of a bargaining representative is based on the will of the majority only as of the day of the election and that a change of this will may divest the representative of its majority status at any time after it was chosen; it was held however, that the certification nevertheless must be endowed with a longevity sufficient to accomplish the essential objective of the National Labor Relations Act to bring about a contract binding on both parties with some fair degree of permanence.[30] The board held that employees could not select another representative during the life of a collective agreement, but that the act could not be considered an instrument for depriving them of their right to change bargaining agents for a period succeeding the term embraced by the contract.

As to exclusive contracts in particular, it was stated that

29 Cf. *Colgate-Palmolive-Peet* v. *National Labor Relations Board*, 338 U. S. 355 (1949).
30 See, for example, *Rutland Court Owners, Inc.*, 44 NLRB 587 (1942) and *NLRB* v. *Appalachian Power Co.*, 140 Fed. (2d) 217 (1944).

the union security policy of the act was no reason for holding that security agreements may be made perpetual because validly initiated. But the board did not fix a maximum period for which collective contracts may have legal force. In many decisions too numerous to be cited, it laid down the general policy to regard the selection of a bargaining representative as valid for a "reasonable period," even if the agent loses its majority. Whether or not such a period had elapsed, has been determined according to the specific circumstances of individual dispute cases. The general tendency of the rulings was for a long time to consider one year to be reasonable, unless the situation in an individual case called for another treatment.

Under this policy the board held in numerous cases that a valid contract ordinarily barred investigation of the representation question for a period of one year. In industries in which contracts of longer duration were customary, it considered a longer period reasonable. Agreements which were extended under an automatic renewal clause, according to a number of decisions, continued to preclude a new determination of the representative, unless a rival union had petitioned the board or notified the employer of its claim within the period provided for notice of intention to terminate or amend the contract. Early in 1947 the board stated that, in the light of its experience in administering the act, a contract for a term of two years ordinarily did not unduly limit the right of employees to change their representative, even if contracts of such long duration were not customary in the industry. It was emphasized however, that this statement did not preclude a different decision in cases warranting a longer or shorter period.[31]

As mentioned above[32] exclusive agreements thus could prevent dissident members of the contracting union—even if they constituted a majority of workers in the bargaining

[31] *Reed Roller Bit Co.*, 72 NLRB 927, 1353 (1947).
[32] P. 173.

unit—for a long time from belonging to a union of their own free choice or from working for a change in representation or the termination of the current contract. This raised the problem of "dual unionism." Persons, who joined a union merely because otherwise they would be excluded from employment opportunities, may not have a feeling of allegiance to the organization. Those among them who harbor a predilection for another organization may endeavor to belong at the same time to two unions—voluntarily to the union of their own free choice and involuntarily to the union holding the exclusive contract. They may seek to remain faithful to the group to which they feel attached, while professing allegiance to another to hold their jobs. Unwilling members, no matter whether or not they belong simultaneously to another union, may make efforts to change the situation.

In systems of voluntary unionism and free individual choice of the bargaining representative, there is hardly a reason for such dual unionism, and it is not likely to occur. Dissatisfied workers, who under the prevailing American system were outvoted in a bargaining election and subsequently felt compelled to join the majority union because it made a closed- or union-shop contract, have resorted to dual unionism since under such circumstances it is hardly possible to remove the exclusive position of the union by making moves in membership meetings. Yet, unions, like any private organization, cannot permit members to undermine their position. Majority unions holding exclusive agreements as well as unions with voluntary membership, acccordingly, have tended to expel any member considered disloyal. This has been generally regarded as an internal union matter.[33] But the American worker, who was expelled from a majority union holding an exclusive contract because he promoted a change in representation, was like-

---

[33] The fact that an American union duly chosen as bargaining representative does not perform functions of merely a private nature has had little influence on public policy in this respect. See p. 144.

ly also to lose his job. This the National Labor Relations Board sought to prevent in such cases in which according to its opinion the attempt to bring about a change in the bargaining representation was made at the "appropriate time."

The Board made it settled practice to hold that employees are entitled to engage in activities in behalf of another union when the exclusive agreement is about to expire. Discharge of a worker for the reason that he lost his standing in the union because he exercised this right at that period has been held inconsistent with basic policy of the act. The board, however, has not considered every discharge of this kind to be an unfair labor practice. It ordered reinstatement only in cases in which the employer was aware of the reason for the expulsion from the union. If such knowledge could not be proved, the workers concerned were not protected.[34]

The United States Supreme Court late in 1949, however, repudiated this practice of the National Labor Relations Board in a case involving the discharge of employees on request by a union which had expelled them because they had agitated for a change of bargaining representative after the union had been the bargaining agent and had held a closed-shop contract of indefinite duration for more than four years.[35] The Court did not deny that the discharges had the effect of interfering with the right of employees to self-organization and to collective bargaining through representatives of their own choosing. It also recognized that the discharges had the further effect of discriminating in the tenure of employees, contrary to the statutory prohibition of discrimination because of union activities. But it held that Congress, in passing the original National Labor Rela-

---

[34] See, for example, *Rutland Court Owners, Inc.*, 44 NLRB 587 (1942); *Wallace Corp.*, 50 NLRB 139 (1943) and 323 U. S. 248 (1944); *NLRB* v. *Appalachian Power Co.*, 140 Fed. (2d) 217 (1944); *Portland Lumber Mills*, 64 NLRB 159 (1945); *Diamond T Motor Car Co.*, 64 NLRB 1225 (1945).

[35] *Colgate-Palmolive-Peet* v. *National Labor Relations Board*, 338 U. S. 355 (1949).

tions Act, knew that an exclusive agreement would interfere with freedom of employees to organize in another
union and would, if used, lead inevitably to discrimination
in tenure of employment. It further concluded from the
legislative history of the original act that the legislators
deliberately refused to hamper coercion of employees by
fellow-employees, and that they thought it conducive to
stability of labor relations that parties be required to live
up to a valid exclusive contract regardless of internal dis-
ruptions growing out of agitation for a change in bargaining
representative. No matter whether this congressional policy
was considered correct, the court stated, the Board could
not be permitted, under the guise of administration, to put
limitations in the statute not placed there by the legislators;
only Congress has the power to do that by way of amendment of the statute.

The practical importance of this Supreme Court decision
has been greatly limited by the fact that, prior to its pro-
nouncement, the 1947 amendments of the National Labor
Relations Act, as will be discussed later, had prohibited
unions from demanding the discharge of employees for any
reason other than nonpayment of dues or ordinary initiation fees. But the views expressed by the Court and the
Board reveal interesting details of basic thought behind
American public policies with respect to freedom to organize in general and freedom of choice among unions in
particular, which are of significance for the purpose of this
study.

*The problem of restriction of free choice was
aggravated by changes in American unionism.*

The fact that the policies concerning representation and
union security agreements, as formulated in the original
National Labor Relations Act, led to labor trouble of an
extent not anticipated by the legislators has been due in
part to a relatively recent change in the general structure

of American unionism. When the act was passed, the American Federation of Labor dominated labor organization outside the railroad field. A large number of workers apparently preferred affiliation with the Federation to membership in coexisting independent unions. This high degree of concentration in the union movement, together with the A.F. of L. policy to prevent overlapping jurisdictions, was largely responsible for the belief that the rules pertaining to representation and union security would allay strife rather than provoke it. The whole statutory scheme was based on the trend toward singularism, prevailing at the time when the labor relations bill was discussed in Congress.

This trend, however, changed profoundly after the law came into force. About three years after its enactment the Congress of Industrial Organizations seceded from the A.F. of L., and has represented large numbers of workers ever since. In addition, more employees have formed "independent" unions on a local, industrial, and national scale. A number of these unions established in 1942 the *Confederated Unions of America* (CUA), a central organization which, among other things, seeks "to assist its affiliates in protecting and maintaining their independence, gains and achievements," and to obtain adequate representation of independent unions in all labor agencies. It claimed in 1949 to include seventy-nine important member organizations. The United Mine Workers of America with its catchall union, District 50, has to be added to this list of union groups. If notice is also taken of the fact that central organizations have little disciplinary power over member organizations, it is obvious what a high degree of pluralism exists in the United States. Efforts of all these bodies to exercise full freedom to organize brought them into conflict with each other as well as with provisions of the Labor Relations Act governing representation and union security agreements.

The keenness of these conflicts has not been mitigated by

a working class ideology of the kind prevailing in European countries. Apart from that, though the various American union groups do not represent different social, economic, political, or other philosophies in a manner and extent comparable to European groups, their basic policies now differ in a considerable degree. Individual members, accordingly, have resented increasingly that they may be confronted with the alternative either of changing their union allegiance (or belonging at the same time voluntarily to the union of their own choice and involuntarily to the union holding the exclusive contract) or being excluded from employment at the places of their choice. Membership in a union, not infrequently, has come to mean more than merely retaining an attorney for representation in collective negotiations.

Recent policy changes have limited but not eliminated restrictions of freedom of choice.

American unions generally have made full use of opportunities to attain and maintain privileges offered or sanctioned by the labor relations laws, but have objected to such privileges for other unions when they obstructed their own growth and functioning. Moreover, each union group has complained at some time or other that government agencies, in carrying through the pertinent acts, have given unjustified preference to rival groups. The provisions dealing with bargaining representatives and union security have not only been used to protect unionism, as intended by the legislators, but also to wage interunion warfare on no small scale. The change of the general trend in unionism from near singularism to pluralism, however, has not led to general revision of the basic principles of the National Labor Relations Act.

Those postwar state statutes, which ban all types of exclusive union security agreements, incidentally have reestablished full freedom of the individual worker to belong to a union of his choice (though not necessarily individual freedom to be represented in collective bargaining by this union). Other recent legislation on the subject has maintained the principle that such freedom may be restricted by validly initiated security contracts. The National Labor Relations Act, as amended by the Labor Management Relations Act of 1947, in particular, still admits discrimination against unorganized as well as organized workers under union-shop and maintenance-of-membership agreements, provided that a majority of employees in the bargaining unit concerned authorized the majority union by secret ballot to make such an agreement.[36]

The act, now as before, does not determine a maximum period of validity of union security contracts. But a new section, prohibiting unions, among other things, from demanding the discharge of employees for any reason other than nonpayment of dues or ordinary initiation fees[37] provides protection for workers who are denied membership in, or expelled from, the contracting union because they work for a change in bargaining representation.

Furthermore, the amended statute makes provision for revocation of the certification of a union as bargaining representative if it lost its majority status and at least one year elapsed after its election.[38] The United States Senate Committee on Labor and Public Welfare, however, emphasized that this new provision does not change the rules of decision of the National Labor Relations Board, which militate against a change in bargaining representation while a lawful collective agreement is in effect.[39] This statement

---

[36] National Labor Relations Act as amended, sec. 8 (a) (3).

[37] The same, sec. 8 (b) (2).

[38] The same, sec. 9 (c) (1) (A) and (3).

[39] The rules of the Board are mentioned on p. 238 above. Board members themselves stated that the full exercise of the new right to have a bargaining agent removed also may be restricted by the practice of the Board to permit petitioners to withdraw petitions for decertification in the absence of a showing that prejudice will result. These members pointed out that decertification petitions ordinarily will be filed by loosely-formed groups of dissatisfied employees, who frequently may not have enough strength to resist attempts by unions or other better organized interested parties to coerce abandonment of "their efforts

obviously was motivated by the desire to safeguard maximum stability of the bargaining representative system. The Board thus still may dismiss a petition for decertification, otherwise well-founded, if it holds that according to its settled pre-Labor Management Relations Act practice a collective agreement bars an investigation of representatives.[40] Accordingly, it decided that:

> In resolving the issues of "contract bar" in decertification cases, the Board applies the same rules as have been and still are applied with respect to petitions for investigation and certification. A contract automatically renewed for reasonable term within the certification year is a bar to the petition for certification of representatives, even though notice of a rival claim is given and the expiration date of the original contract may be after the certification year. We shall apply the same principles to a decertification petition.[41]

The amended act also grants employees an opportunity to revoke the authority of the unions to make a "compulsory-membership agreement."[42] If 30 per cent or more of the workers in the bargaining unit covered by the agreement file a petition for rescission of the authority, the Na-

---

to accomplish a protracted expression of their dissatisfaction with the current bargaining representative." In view of the possibility of such coercion, some members of the Board stated that the purpose of the decertification provision can be best effectuated by denying requests for withdrawal of petitions. The majority of the Board, however, held that such denial would be inconsistent with traditional Board practice to permit withdrawals of petitions in the absence of a showing that prejudice will result and to reject offers to prove employer coercion, in representation proceedings. Those asserting that a withdrawal was due to restraint or coercion, the majority stated, may file charges of unfair labor practice under sec. 8 (b) (1) and possibly also 8 (b) (2) of the act. It overruled the argument of the dissenting members that if coercion was sufficiently vigorous to result in a request for withdrawal of a decertification petition, it very likely would be equally effective in dissuading the employees involved from filing an unfair labor practice charge. (*Underwriters Salvage Co. of New York,* 76 NLRB 601, 1948.)

The Canadian *Industrial Relations and Disputes Investigation Act,* 1948, provides that collective agreements generally are deemed to be for a term of one year. If the Labor Relations Board certifies a union as bargaining agent and a collective agreement covering the unit concerned is in force, the newly certified union takes the place of the outgoing union as a party to the agreement. The certification of the old union as bargaining agent is deemed to be revoked by the certification of the new union. Secs. 10 and 20.

[40] *Federal Labor Relations Act of 1947,* S. Rept. 105, 80 Cong. 1 sess. (1947), pp. 10, 25.
[41] *Wilborn Bros. Co.,* 77 NLRB 1026 (1948).
[42] Term used for the union shop in *Federal Labor Relations Act of 1947,* S. Rept. 105, 80 Cong. 1 sess., p. 26; and in other reports.

tional Labor Relations Board will take a secret ballot and certify the result to the union and the employer concerned. The number of such referenda, like that of "decertification" ballots, is limited to one a year.[43] The act, however, does not explain whether or how the revocation of the authority of the union affects a current lawful security agreement.

All this shows that basic American and European public policies respecting the exercise by workers of full freedom of choice in matters of self-organization and designation of bargaining representatives still differ as much as they did prior to the passage of the Labor Management Relations Act of 1947, though American law regarding closed- and union-shop agreements has been narrowed by a number of recent enactments.

[43] National Labor Relations Act, sec. 9 (e) (2) and (3).

CHAPTER IX

Government Problems and Policies:
the Right to Work

The great libertarian movements of the eighteenth and nineteenth centuries aspired to replace medieval restriction by political and economic freedom of the individual. In the wake of this development the concept gained ascendancy that, in his relations to his fellow citizens, every person has the right to dispose of his own labor or his own capital according to his will. "He that hindereth another in his trade or livelihood is liable to an action for so hindering him," stated the British Queen's Bench as early as the beginning of the eighteenth century.[1] The French Revolution of 1789-95 brought the decree of March 2-17, 1791, proclaiming freedom of work, industry, and commerce. This proclamation, and the letter and spirit of the new constitution outlawed interference with liberty in the labor market. Under the new concept the worker became free to sell his labor to any employer of his choice, and the employer gained full freedom to hire anyone as he deemed fit. The principle of freedom of contract further made the determination of the conditions of employment the exclusive concern of the individual employer and employee. Interference with the free exercise of these rights by government, organizations, or individuals was ruled out.

A "right to work" is not mentioned expressly in the United States federal Bill of Rights; nor until quite recently did state constitutions include it explicitly in their lists of fundamental rights. There were, indeed, persons within the area covered by these constitutions, who, in earlier periods, were not regarded as free to choose their employer and to

[1] *Keeble* v. *Hickeringhill,* 11 East 574 n. (1706).

make contracts determining the conditions of their employment. But the existence of a fundamental right to work has been recognized by an ever-increasing number of authorities. They have considered it irrelevant that most constitutions in the United States, including the federal Constitution, do not mention it because their enumerations of basic rights are not regarded as exhaustive.[2] Beyond that, American courts have held that the right of everybody to work, either in employment or independently in business, is incident to the freedom of the individual, which they have considered guaranteed by the Fourteenth Amendment of the federal Constitution and corresponding provisions of state constitutions.[3]

In view of still existing doubts a joint resolution was introduced several times in the United States Congress, proposing to amend the federal Constitution. The proposed amendment, however, did not attempt to state the existence of a right to work or to define it. It dealt merely with one of the many problems which may arise, where a general right to work is guaranteed, namely, the problem of denial of employment because of membership or nonmembership in a union or because of nonpayment of contributions to a labor organization. The proposed joint resolution was not passed.[4]

NATURE OF THE RIGHT TO WORK

It has been chiefly American, British, and French governments that have sought to use the concept of the right to work in dealing with involuntary unionism. In these efforts they have had to answer two basic questions: (1) Is

---

[2] See Federal Constitution, Amendment Nine.

[3] See, for example, *Barbier* v. *Connolly*, 113 U. S. 27 (1884); *Yick Wo* v. *Hopkins*, 118 U. S. 356 (1885); *Berry* v. *Donovan*, 74 NE 603 (1905); *Bautista* v. *Jones*, 155 P (2d) 343 (1944).

[4] See *Right to Work*, Hearings before the House Committee on Education and Labor, 80 Cong. 2 sess. (1948), p. 35.

The term "right to work," not infrequently, has been used in the United States in the more restricted sense of a right to work without regard to membership or nonmembership in a union, or a right to work without union interference during a strike or the like.

unionism at all compatible with this right? (2) Does it constitute an absolute right of every individual to use his labor power free from any interference?

Unionism is not irreconcilable
with the right to work.

There would obviously be hardly any room for concerted activities of workers in the labor market if the right to work were defined as an absolute right of everyone, which the individual could not waive and which would entitle him to dispose of his labor at will, free from interference by groups or individuals. Post-revolutionary liberal governments in France, which were particularly anxious to prevent organization reminiscent of the pre-revolutionary corporate state, indeed rejected unionism as incompatible with the individualistic principle of freedom of work, industry, and commerce. Efforts of labor leaders to convince the government that workers could not make full use of their freedoms without having the right to act in concert were futile for many decades.

Not until 1884, when the Waldeck-Rousseau Act[5] was passed, was the freedom to organize of workers and employers legally recognized. This act, however, did not signify any attempt to deprive the principle of freedom of work and industry of its predominant position in French labor policy. The legislative intent, on the contrary, was merely to acknowledge that freedom to organize is an essential part of individual freedom since individuals have a natural tendency to associate with each other. Compulsory isolation, as it existed prior to the passing of the act, was abandoned because the legislature held that it is no more compatible with individual liberty than is compulsory organization. The purpose of the act, accordingly, was to make individual liberty of the worker complete by recognizing his right to form and join organizations "freely

---

[5] Act of Mar. 21, 1884, J. O. No. 81, Mar. 22, 1884, p. 1577.

and without authorization by the government." Since the
act construed freedom to organize as a phase of the freedom
of any indivdual to pursue his calling as he deems fit, it left
the individual worker free to become a member of a union,
to choose the union to which he wished to belong, to resign
from it at will, or to refrain from organizing altogether.
This policy ruled out compulsion of any kind, including
compulsion to join or not to join an organization, as well
as any obligation to maintain membership. The act stated
explicitly that any member of an occupational organization could at any time resign from it, notwithstanding a
rule to the contrary. The only duty of the quitting member
was payment of his dues for the six months following the
date of his resignation. To forestall any indirect pressure
upon the resigning person, the act further provided that
he retained the right to be a member of old age and other
benefit funds to which he contributed. The statute of
February 25, 1927, later incorporated these provisions of
the Waldeck-Rousseau Act into the Labor Code, which
contains the French law regulating labor matters.

This brief analysis of French policy may serve as an
example of the answer found by a number of liberal governments to the question as to whether unionism is compatible
with individual freedom to dispose of one's labor according
to one's will. The answer has been that the two do not
necessarily conflict and that they even supplement each
other, if no compulsion is involved.

*The right to work is subject to interference
by government or private persons.*

In answering the question as to whether every individual
can be entitled to use his labor power free from any interference, American and foreign public policy has pointed
out that the right to work is no more absolute than other
equally fundamental rights. British decisions, for example,
have stated that every person has not only the right to dis-

pose of his labor according to his will, but that everybody also has the correlative duty to abstain from using it in a manner which would obstruct the exercise of similar rights by others. It has further been emphasized that, since the right to freedom in conducting a trade is only a particular aspect of the citizen's right to personal freedom, statutes and common law may limit it to avoid clashes among the rights of individuals and to safeguard a maximum of individual freedom for everyone. According to this concept, the rights of the employer, for example, are conditioned by the rights of workers to give or withhold their services. Employers, therefore, have to realize that the exercise of the rights of labor may involve some limitation of the freedom of employers in the management of their business. Such interference with a person's business, it has been said, does not constitute a legal wrong, so long as the limitations enforced by law are not contravened.[6] British legal source and scope of the right to dispose freely of one's labor or capital is somewhat obscure, and there has been some disagreement with respect to its enforcement. But its existence has hardly been questioned.

The German (Weimar) Constitution stated that every German shall have the opportunity to earn his living through economic labor and that his necessary maintenance will be supplied if a suitable opportunity to work cannot be given.[7] It was emphasized that the economic order must correspond to the fundamental principles of justice so that *everyone* is guaranteed an existence worthy of a human being.[8]

The preamble to the new French constitution, similarly, states that everyone has the right to a job and that no one may be discriminated against in his work or employment because of his origin, opinions, or creed. It has, however, been generally accepted that a constitutional provision of

[6] House of Lords, *Crofter Harris Tweed Co. v. Veitch*, A. C. 435 (1942).
[7] Art. 163 II.
[8] Art. 151 I. As to the situation under the new (Bonn) Constitution see pp. 45 and 217n.

this kind does not establish any legal claim of an (unemployed) individual to a contract of employment. According to common view, it does not imply a governmental guarantee of opportunities to work sufficient to absorb all job applicants but is to be interpreted as a programmatic directive to the legislators to organize the labor market and to adjust, as far as possible, demand for labor to supply.

The German legislators, for example, sought to follow this directive by means of the public employment service and public works. In addition, they took steps intended to achieve more even distribution of opportunities to work, including legislation providing for sharing of work (for example, introduction of "short-time work"). Moreover, they established the right to protest, possibly at the labor court, against a discharge on the ground, among other reasons, that it appears "to be unjust and involves hardship not caused by the behavior of the employee or the condition of the undertaking." Finally, legislative efforts were made to preserve jobs by limiting the freedom of employers to shut down establishments temporarily or permanently.[9]

The United States Congress declared in 1946 that it is

> . . . the continuing policy and responsibility of the Federal Government to use all practicable means consistent with its needs and obligations and other essential considerations of national policy, with the assistance and cooperation of industry, agriculture, labor,

[9] The German constitution stated not only that everybody had a right to opportunity to earn his living through economic work, but also that, without prejudice to his personal freedom, everyone had the corresponding moral duty to use his mental and physical powers in such a manner as the commonweal demanded (Art. 163 I). The preamble to the new French constitution likewise states that everyone also has the duty to work. Just as the right to work has been defined as a moral rather than a legal right, the duty to work has been construed as a moral rather than a legal obligation. A legal duty to work exists only on grounds of a special legal title, such as a contract of employment or the duty to furnish maintenance to family members, an established general compulsory public service, in the event of imprisonment ordered by a court and the like.

Art. 12 of the Russian constitution may be mentioned in this connection: It declares: "Work in the USSR is a duty and a matter of honor for every able-bodied citizen, in accordance with the principle: 'He who does not work, neither shall he eat.' The principle applied in the USSR is that of socialism: 'From each according to his ability, to each according to his work.'" The principle formerly was stated as "From each according to his ability, to each according to his *need*."

and State and local governments, to coordinate and utilize all its plans, functions, and resources for the purpose of creating and maintaining, in a manner calculated to foster and promote free competitive enterprise and the general welfare, conditions under which there will be afforded useful employment opportunities, including self-employment, for those able, willing, and seeking to work, and to promote maximum employment, production, and purchasing power.[10]

The President has the duty to transmit to Congress economic reports setting forth current and foreseeable trends in the levels of employment, production, and purchasing power and programs for carrying out this policy, together with such recommendations for legislation as he may deem necessary or desirable. A "Council of Economic Advisors" assists the President in the preparation of these reports and renders other expert assistance to the federal government. A permanent "Joint Committee on the Economic Report," composed of seven members of the Senate and seven members of the House of Representatives, studies the reports and ways and means to further public employment policy. It makes reports and recommendations to the legislature.

Courts in the United States have stated that the right to work is safeguarded from legislative action which discriminates against a person or class of persons in respect of opportunities to obtain work or enter into business. Like British and other foreign courts, they have, however, emphasized that the exercise of this right may be restricted by statutes. This has been done, for example, through maximum hour and minimum wage acts, laws establishing age limits for employment, licensing acts, safety regulations, and many more provisions. The right to work also is protected in some degree against arbitrary action by private persons and organizations, including employers and unions. But even its legitimate exercise by a great number of individuals and groups in the same area and at the same time may obstruct its free use. Also, it is subject to inter-

[10] Employment Act of 1946, 60 Stat. 23, sec. 2.

ference by persons or organizations who are acting in the
exercise of an equal or superior right. Such interference,
according to American—like foreign—courts, is not unlawful as long as the persons or organizations concerned keep
within the bounds established by law.

This brief analysis of authoritative definitions of the right
to work shows that it neither guarantees the possibility
to work nor necessarily precludes interference with individual freedom of will in organizational matters. It was
because the right to work traditionally has not been interpreted as establishing a legal claim to a job that unions
called it a right without substance. Since persons able to
work, wishing to work, and dependent upon work for a
livelihood, repeatedly have not been able to obtain employment, governments have undertaken to maintain those
who cannot make use of the right to work until employment
is available. The measures taken under such programs
mitigate the effects of unemployment. But they do not,
and are not intended to, make the right to work and opportunity to work identical concepts.

Recently more or less comprehensive plans have come
into existence in quite a number of countries, designed to
reduce unemployment to a relatively harmless minimum—
popularly called "full employment" programs. Labor
leaders have indicated that governmental assurance of "full
employment at rising standards of living in a free society"
would mean realization of the chief objective which, under
other conditions, their organizations have tried to attain
through restrictive union practices. The British Trades
Union Congress stated, with some qualifications, that a
policy guaranteeing, in the words of Sir William Beveridge,
that "though on any one day there may be some men unemployed there are always more vacant jobs than there are
unemployed men, so that every man whose present job
comes to an end for any reason can find fresh employment

without delay" would establish that type of right to work which the unions have demanded at all times.[11]

Traditional governmental definitions further demonstrate that, apart from not establishing a legal claim to a job, the right to work as such does not necessarily exclude employment of compulsory methods in union efforts to organize workers or to prevent withdrawals. Whether or not such tactics are lawful will depend upon the view of the government as to whether they constitute the legitimate exercise of a right superior to the right to work of individuals; their legality will be contingent on where public policy draws the line between permissible and objectionable interference. As early as about 75 years ago the Supreme Judicial Court of Massachusetts intimated the difficulties involved in establishing this line:

> In the relations existing between labor and capital, the attempt by co-operation on the one side to increase wages by diminishing competition, or on the other to increase the profits due to capital, is within certain limits lawful and proper. It ceases to be so when unlawful coercion is employed to control the freedom of the individual in disposing of his labor or capital. It is not easy to give a definition which shall include every form of such coercion. . . . [12]

In view of this situation, legislatures and courts which have based their policies respecting compulsion to organize on the right to work have sought to do chiefly two things. They have tried to prevent unions from becoming compulsory organizations similar to corporations as they have functioned in corporate states.[13] In addition, they have endeavored to draw lines of demarcation between justifiable and objectionable interference with the right to work. The answers to the question of what shall amount to a

[11] "Interim Report on Post-War Reconstruction," *Report of Proceedings at the 76th Annual Trades Union Congress* (1944), App. D, pp. 393 ff.

[12] *Snow* v. *Wheeler,* 113 Mass. 179 (1873).

[13] This has included efforts to prevent the establishment of the principle of the closed shop on the ground that it would signify the revival of a principle, characteristic of the guild system, in a modern version adapted to unionism.

justification have been based chiefly on considerations of policy and of social advantage.[14] It requires no elaboration that they have differed with time and place.

EUROPEAN ATTEMPTS TO DEFINE LAWFUL AND UNLAWFUL INTERFERENCE

Ever since the Waldeck-Rousseau Act was passed, the French legislators have endeavored to co-ordinate the activities of unions and the freedom to work; in other words, to harmonize collective and individual liberty. In 1936 the Blum administration, like a few years earlier the Roosevelt administration in the United States, submitted to the legislators a national recovery program to overcome economic emergency conditions. Improvement of labor relations was part of the program in both countries. In contradistinction to the course of events in the United States, French organized management and labor concluded on June 7, 1936, a master agreement to form the basis of industrial relations in the future. This strategy was reminiscent of the tactics used by Swedish employers and unions, which resulted in such a master agreement thirty years earlier.[15]

The French agreement (Matignon Agreement), like comparable master agreements in Sweden, Germany, and other European countries, was in a large measure an attempt to eliminate without, or with a minimum of, governmental intervention industrial unrest which had been caused by obstructions to the exercise of full freedom of association

14 Compare Justice Oliver Wendell Holmes, dissenting in *Vegelahn* v. *Guntner*, 44 N. E. 1077, 1080 (1896).

15 See pp. 31, 76, 163, 207.

Basic agreements between central federations of employers' associations and unions, designed to settle fundamental issues and to forestall or minimize government intervention have been made in several other European countries. In Denmark such an agreement guaranteed the right to organize and established rules for the settlement of industrial disputes as early as 1898. A similar agreement was concluded in Norway in the mid-thirties.

The German employers' associations and central federations of unions entered into a master agreement on Nov. 15, 1918, five days after the revolution. The agreement declared inadmissible any restrictions of the freedom of employees to organize. Furthermore, the unions were recognized as the appropriate representatives of employees. Finally, it was stipulated that the employment conditions of all employees should be determined by collective agreements with the organizations of the employees. This agreement formed the basis of the subsequent labor law of the German (Weimar) Republic.

and collective bargaining. In the absence of such direct understanding between management and labor, regulation of this matter was initiated by legislative action in the United States. French management promised explicitly to respect the right of workers to organize and bargain collectively. The employers, further, agreed to the immediate preparation of collective contracts—something many of them had tried to avoid up to that time. Moreover, they declared that:

> . . . as it is the duty of all citizens to obey the law, the employers acknowledge the right of freedom of opinion and the right of all workers freely to join and belong to a trade union. . . . The employers undertake that in arriving at decisions in regard to hiring, conduct or distribution of work, disciplinary measures or dismissal, they will not take into consideration the workers' membership or non-membership in a union. . . . The exercise of the right of association may not give rise to acts contrary to law.

This was a clear recognition by management and labor of the right to join or not to join a union and an equally clear rejection of any compulsion to organize.

French laws treat exclusive arrangements
as incompatible with freedom to work.

On the basis of the Matignon agreement the government issued on June 24 of the same year an act modifying and supplementing the collective bargaining provisions of the Labor Code. The act prescribed that any collective agreement regulating the relations between employers and employees in a particular branch of industry or commerce or for the whole national territory had to include a clause safeguarding freedom of association and of opinion for the employees—freedom of opinion of course meaning freedom of the worker to choose the union to which he desires to belong. Similarly, the act of December 31, 1936, introducing compulsory arbitration of collective labor disputes, mentioned individual liberty, freedom to work, and freedom of association among the factors which arbitrators have to respect.

The draft of the new French constitution, which was rejected for other reasons in the popular referendum of May 5, 1946, stated in Article 30 of its Declaration of the Rights of Man that "everyone may belong to the union *of his choice* or not belong to any union at all." The present constitution, as adopted in September 1946, "reaffirms the rights and freedoms of man and of the citizen consecrated by the Declaration of Rights of 1789 and the fundamental principles recognized by the laws of the Republic." These principles include the freedoms of work, industry, and commerce, which, according to prevailing French view, preclude compulsion to organize. The preamble to the constitution restates that everyone may defend his rights and interests by union action and may join the union *of his choice.* Moreover, it mentions among the political, economic, and social principles "most vital in our time" the 1ight to obtain employment, adding that no one may suffer in his work or his employment because of his origin, *his opinions,* or his creed.

Finally, the act of December 23, 1946[16] amending the part of the Labor Code regulating collective bargaining, prescribes again that national collective agreements must contain provisions concerning freedom of association *and of opinion* for the employees.[17] Contractual regulation of hiring and discharge in a manner which prejudices the freedom of workers to join unions of their own choice is explicitly prohibited.

French courts have rejected exclusive arrangements as interference with the right to work.

The principle that freedom of association, as a phase of freedom of work, must not impair individual freedom of will in union matters and in choosing a place of employ-

16 J. O. No. 301, Dec. 23, 1946, p. 10932.
17 Regional and local agreements may be concluded to adapt national agreements or certain of their provisions to the particular conditions of employment in the region or locality.

ment has pervaded French labor policy from the days of the great revolution to the present time. Consistent application of this theory, however, has frequently proved a Herculean task. It has been subject to attacks from all directions. As in other democracies the freedom of association has clashed with other equally fundamental freedoms such as, for example, the freedom of contract. Moreover, it has been very difficult to maintain some kind of equilibrium between the basically individualistic spirit of French law and society and the fundamentally collectivistic and not infrequently socialistic philosophy of the unions. Certain characteristic practices of unionists were bound to cause conflicts with government policy. French unions like others have endeavored, if possible, to organize whole trades and industries and to acquire not only the actual power but also the right to represent all the workers belonging to various trades and industries in the manner of semipublic institutions. This obviously, has been contrary to the spirit and the letter of the Waldeck-Rousseau Act and subsequent statutes, which reflected the liberalism and individualism of their time and conceived of unions as strictly private associations.

Union policy of this kind further enhanced tendencies among unionists to apply direct or indirect compulsion in efforts to make outsiders join their organizations. Attempts have been made to force employers to refrain from hiring nonunionists or to discharge unorganized employees. In a few scattered instances, for example, in the book-printing industry, organized workers even have endeavored to secure vacant jobs for members of their union to the exclusion of members of other unions. It was mentioned above that top union leadership denied to have inspired tactics of this kind, and their use, indeed, has not been common.

At the time of the split between the General Confederation of labor and the (communist) General Confederation of United Labor, for example, members of both organizations, worked side by side even in the printing shops, while

still refusing to work together with nonunionists.[18] This
attitude of labor prevented union security policy of the
American type from becoming a significant issue in France.
In view of the government policy of protecting individual
freedom of work, pressure tactics employed against unorganized workers, however, raised some problems.

In this protracted contest between traditional liberalistic
individualism and growing collectivism the French government, like other governments, has been compelled to make
compromises. The right of unions to represent interests of
groups as such and not only of their members as individuals
apparently is no longer seriously disputed. The legislators
themselves, by conferring special privileges upon "the most

18 The General Confederation of Labor (Confédération Générale du Travail,
C.G.T.) was formed in 1895. Differences between adherents of the socialist and
communist parties in the organization resulted in the secession of the communist
group in 1921. It formed the General Confederation of United Labor (Confédération Général du Travail Unitaire, C.G.T.U.), but re-entered the General Confederation of Labor in 1935 in connection with the establishment of the Popular
Front. The attitude of the communists with respect to the Soviet-German pact,
however, gave rise to their expulsion in 1940. Co-operation of socialist and communist organized workers in the resistance movement after Russia's entry into
the war on the side of the Allies prepared the way for a rapprochement. Thus,
both groups reconstituted the General Confederation of Labor after the war
(1943).
The communists now, however, were in the majority. This caused the non-
communist faction to leave the organization late in 1947 and to form a central
federation of their own, called the General Confederation of Labor—Workers
Force (CGT—Force Ouvrière, F.O.). As the name of the new organization indicates, it considers itself to be the true representative of the traditional policy of
the General Confederation of Labor, as laid down in the latter's Amiens Charter
of 1906. According to the Workers Force, 1,435 delegates from 35 industrial
federations and 90 regional unions, representing an estimated 1 to 1.5 million
workers, attended its first convention in April 1948. The General Confederation
of Labor and the Workers Force comprise the majority of French organized
workers.
The Christian unions, which adhere to the social doctrine as embodied in the
papal encyclical Rerum Novarum, form the other leading French union group.
The movement has existed in France for over sixty years. Its central organization is the French Confederation of Christian Workers, formed in 1919, (Confédération Française des Travailleurs Chrétiéns, C.F.T.C.). It claimed in 1947
to represent 3,181 permanently constituted unions.
Several other unions were formed after the war. They may be classified in
three major groups: the independent unions which organized into a General
Committee for Independent Unionism (Comité Général du Syndicalisme Indé-
pendant, C.G.S.I.), the autonomous unions which united into the Federation of
Autonomous Unions (Fédération des Syndicats Autonomes, F.S.A.), and a number of unions without any political allegiance which are quite numerous. In
addition, a National Federation of Labor (Confédération Nationale du Travail,
C.N.T) was established. Up to now it has only a few thousand members in
Paris and a few provincial cities, especially Lyon.

representative unions," have disturbed full equality among unions and have made membership in such privileged organizations advisable. These and other developments have strengthened collective tendencies in industrial relations and administration of the labor law at the expense of traditional individual freedom.[19] Nevertheless, the courts generally have striven to harmonize union collectivism with traditional freedom of the individual and to avoid sacrificing the latter for the former. These efforts have been based on penal and civil law.

Articles 414 and 415 of the Penal Code provide that anyone is to be punished with fines and/or imprisonment who by means of violence, assault, threats, or fraudulent actions causes, or causes to continue, or attempts to cause or cause to continue, a concerted stoppage of work for the purpose of forcing wages up or down or of impairing the freedom of industry or work. Heavier punishment is provided in case this is done by means of a concerted plan. These provisions punish not only violence and fraudulent maneuvers but also threats, and they cover not only physical but also so-called moral violence. The latter concept, courts have said, must be construed in its natural and broadest sense. Threats have been regarded as coming under Article 414 if they are sufficiently impressive to induce a normally vigorous man to act against his own will and to do something he does not wish to do.[20]

Accordingly, a number of decisions declared illegal threats against management and workers to cause a concerted stoppage of work for the purpose of compelling the discharge of nonunion workers, or the employment of mem-

---

[19] "It is the duty of the courts to respect trade-union rights, while at the same time respecting the right of an individual to join a union or to withdraw from one if he so desires. The attempts by trade unions to organize all the workers in their industry, however, and the growing recognition of the unions' right to represent the workers result in an indirect limitation of the freedom to stay out of the union. Non-union workers find themselves unable to take part in the organization of professional life, and are progressively giving up abstention." French Embassy, Press and Information Service, New York, "French Trade Unions and their Membership," Document, November 1949, p. 2.

[20] Court of Appeal, Lyon, July 8, 1931. Gaz. Pal., 31.2.738.

bers of a particular union. Such threats were held to constitute a punishable attack on the freedom of work by means of moral violence. The discharge of a musician, not a member of the musicians' union, in order to avert a threatened strike by the organized members of the orchestra was held a punishable infringement of the right to dispose freely of one's labor.[21] In another case a union had threatened immediate strike action unless nonunion workers were discharged at once and hiring preference given, under union control, to holders of the union card. This action was regarded as intimidation by arousing fear of difficulties, characteristic of moral violence in the meaning of Article 414 of the Penal Code.[22] The court held that such moral violence constituted a punishable infringement of the freedom of work. The nonunion employees concerned were compelled to apply for the union card in order to make a living, while the employer was forced to yield to the union demands in order to be able to comply with his business obligations. Exercising or threatening to exercise the freedom to strike in such a manner, according to the Court of Appeal of Bordeaux, is punishable because it tends to nullify the employer's right to choose his own workers without distinguishing between unionists and nonunionists and because it compels workers to join a union. The court sentenced the representatives of the union—a longshoremen's union—to prison terms ranging from two to three months, declaring that "the gravity of this offense necessitates and justifies severe punishment."

Since the repeal of Article 416 of the Penal Code by the Waldeck-Rousseau Act of 1884, however, it is no longer an unlawful and punishable act "to impair the freedom of industry or work by means of fines, prohibitions, restrictions, or interdictions, pronounced under a concerted plan." Unions may now use these means with impunity to prevent

---

21 Court of Cassation, Dec. 17, 1926. Rev. Quest. Prud. 1927, p. 56.
22 Bordeaux, Apr. 24, 1929; Gaz. Pal. 29.1.776. See also Civil Tribunal of the Seine, Jan. 18, 1929; Gaz. Pal. 29.1.686, and other decisions.

members from working in a particular enterprise and thereby to compel an employer indirectly not to employ a certain worker. Customary belligerent activities in defense of occupational interests, which the union has the purpose to safeguard, expose the union or the acting persons to prosecution under criminal law only if they are accompanied by acts forbidden under Article 414.[23]

But this does not mean that French unions or workers who undertake industrial warfare may not, under certain circumstances, be responsible for damage resulting from breach of contract or from a civil delict, that is, a tort. Freedom of unions to employ belligerent tactics to increase membership and for many more purposes does not exempt them from the general responsibility for injury inflicted upon others by improper use of rights.[24] This is a basic principle which a number of liberal governments have applied, in some from or other, in efforts to co-ordinate opposing collective and individual freedoms.[25]

Though the basis of civil liability has not been precisely the same everywhere, the general use of this doctrine has shifted the emphasis in labor policy from prohibition and punishment to responsibility under civil law for wrongful use of rights. As in other countries, it is well settled in France that unions or their members are under no duty to make compensation for injury caused by the normal exercise of their rights. It has, however, been held that liability for damage exists if these rights are abused. In judging whether a right was exercised in a proper or improper manner, the intent of the legislators in granting it is of course of

[23] See Court of Cassation, July 12, 1921; Sir. 22.1.148. It is obviously a complicated judicial task to distinguish these different elements and to determine their significance for the action as a whole.

[24] According to the French general theory of abuse of rights, the limit of the legitimate use of rights by employers, employees, or unions is at the point where the acting person (or organization) ceases to exercise his right to protect his personal interest and makes use of it solely to inflict harm upon others.

[25] The House of Lords applied this doctrine in the Taff Vale case, mentioned on p. 37 above; but it was expressly abolished by the British Trade Disputes Act of 1906. The United States Supreme Court based its decision in the fundamental *United Mine Workers of America* v. *Coronado Coal Company* case on the same principle, 259 U. S. 344, 390 (1922).

primary importance. Apart from that, the decision depends upon the motive behind the action of the union. By and large, the opinion has prevailed among French judges that a union which acts with malicious intentions commits a civil wrong even though the measures taken may be lawful as such. As at times in British and American jurisprudence otherwise lawful union activities have been considered malicious where it was held that they were prompted solely or predominantly by animosity against others rather than merely by the desire to defend occupational interests of members.

In applying this doctrine to enlistment of union members under pressure, courts have passed judgment for damages against unions which they found to have *maliciously* prevented an employer from hiring personnel as he deems fit. Damages also have been awarded in cases in which courts have held that unions had, with malicious intent, violated the freedom of workers to sell their labor to an employer of their choice, to join a union of their own choosing, to resign from it at will, or to refrain from joining any union. The decision as to whether unions abused a right thus will frequently depend upon the opinion of the court on their guiding motives in the particular case. Again, this is a complex judicial task. Consequently, decisions have not always been uniform, and there have even been some contradictions. As in other countries, the difficulty of ascertaining the true motive of union actions and, if malice is involved, to appraise its significance in relation to other factors has caused a certain tendency toward determining the propriety of union measures on the basis of visible effects rather than on the basis of frequently not determinable motives.

In the well-known basic case *Joost* v. *Union of Printers on Fabrics of Bourgoin-Jallieu* the court of original jurisdiction[26] stated that a strike to compel the discharge of a worker who was not a member of a union was the legitimate

[26] Grenoble, Oct. 28, 1890, D. 92.1.281.

exercise of a right and therefore did not justify prosecution of the union either under criminal or civil law. The Court of Cassation[27] reversed the decision, holding that concerted action to force the dismissal of an employee because he withdrew from, or refused to become a member of, a union constitutes an attack on the rights of other persons which makes the attacker liable for damages. The principle of individual freedom of work, the preservation of which is necessary in the public interest, another court stated, would be purely imaginary if a worker could not use it without being threatened with the loss of his work.[28]

In a case decided in 1916,[29] however, the Court of Cassation treated a contract clause requiring an employer to hire only organized workers as lawful on the ground that its period of validity was limited and that it was motivated by the mutual desire for conciliation and protection of justified occupational interests rather than by any intent to cause prejudice to other workers. Comparing this opinion with the earlier *Joost* v. *Union of Printers* decision, commentators have interpreted it as indicative of the trend toward recognition of increased rights of unions at the expense of traditional individual freedom of workers. But the decision has remained an isolated case. French writers and courts generally have continued to reject exclusive union-management agreements, especially of the American type, as incompatible with the right to work and freedom to organize.[30] It is widely held that the statments on freedom to organize in the 1946 Constitution are merely a re-statement of this policy.

*No British statute outlaws
exclusive contracts.*

The British law, like the law in the United States, rests not only on constitutional principles and on a statutes, but

[27] June 22, 1892, D. 92.1.449.
[28] Chambéry, Mar. 14, 1893, D. 93.2.191.
[29] Oct. 24, 1916, D. 16.1.246.
[30] See pp. 223-24 above.

also on common law. Decisions rendered under British common law have not established fixed rules defining generally the limits of justifiable union interference with the freedom to work and to carry on one's business. Nor have they determined unequivocally the legal remedies for unlawful interference. As to legislation, the over-all trend has been to exempt unions increasingly from liability for interference with individual freedom of will. At present no statute prohibits expressly closed or similar shops.

The Combination Act of 1799 declared illegal and punishable contracts between "any journeymen manufacturers or other workmen, or other persons," designed to prevent or hinder "any person or persons from employing whomsoever he, she, or they shall think proper to employ in his, her, or their manufacture, trade or business."[31] After the repeal of all Combination Acts in 1824, the Combination Laws Repeal Act Amendment Act of 1825 reintroduced some limitation upon the activities of unions. Among the restrictive provisions was one[32] prohibiting violence, threats, intimidation, molestation or obstruction for the purpose of forcing or inducing a worker to belong to a union or to contribute to any common fund, or to force an employer to alter his mode of conducting his business. Compulsion by such means also was outlawed if it was used to exact a fine or penalty because a person did not belong to a union or did not observe a union rule. Noncompliance with these prohibitions was punishable by imprisonment.

In 1871 the act of 1825 was repealed by the Criminal Law Amendment Act which contained a provision punishing with imprisonment and hard labor the use of violence, threats, and certain types of molestation or obstruction, to exert compulsion upon other persons for trade purposes. Molestation or obstruction was outlawed, in particular, when it was used to compel an employer to discharge a worker or to refuse employment to him or "to alter the

---

[31] Sec. 1.
[32] Sec. III.

mode of carrying on his business, or the number or description of any persons employed by him," or when its purpose was to force employees to belong or not to belong to specific organizations. The Conspiracy and Protection of Property Act, which replaced the Criminal Law Amendment Act in 1875, put employer-union relations on a civil basis. But it still includes some penal provisions. Violence or intimidation to compel a person to abstain from doing, or to do, any act which he has a legal right to do or abstain from doing is declared punishable by fine or imprisonment.[33] In contrast to French jurisprudence, English courts, however, have not regarded arousing fear of difficulties as punishable intimidation. Threats that work will be stopped by concerted action, not accompanied by personal violence, have not been considered a violation of this statute.[34]

The Trade Disputes Act of 1906 extended the immunities granted unions by the act of 1875. It declares acts done in contemplation or furtherance of a labor dispute not actionable on the ground only that they constitute interference with the trade, business, or employment of some other person, or with his right to dispose of his capital or labor as he wills.[35] In addition, the act bars civil actions against any union for tortious acts.[36] The British legislators thus went further than the French lawmakers. The latter, similarly removed through the Waldeck-Rousseau Act criminal liability for interference with the freedom of work and industry in the course of legitimate industrial warfare, but they did not exempt unions, or individuals acting for them, from the general duty to pay damages for tortious acts.

The Trade Disputes and Trade Unions Act of 1927 contained the only instance of direct statutory proscription of

[33] Sec. 7.
[34] See, for example, R. v. McKeevit (1890), cited by Lord Coleridge, C. J., in Gibson v. Lawson, 2 Q. B. 545 (1891); and R. v. M'Carthy, 2 L. R. 146 (1903).
[35] Sec. 3.
[36] Sec. 4.

the closed shop in Great Britain. It prohibited local or other public authorities from making union membership or non-membership a condition of employment and from discriminating against workers in some other manner because they were or were not organized. Public authorities, further, were not allowed to make it a condition of a contract that persons to be employed by any party should or should not be members of a union.[37] These prohibitions, which were revoked by the repeal of the act in 1946, had the purpose of securing neutrality of public authorities in hiring employees and making contracts and of forestalling pressure on governments by political and economic groups.[38]

*British courts have dismissed damage suits
for violation of the right to work.*

The *Allen* v. *Flood* decision, rendered by the House of Lords in 1898,[39] was an early British judicial answer to the question whether unions may compel employers to discharge outsiders. The plaintiffs in this case, Flood and Taylor, were two unionized shipwrights, who were presently engaged in repairing the wood work of a ship but had done iron work on a ship for another firm. They were dismissed under pressure of a strike-threat by iron workers, members of the United Society of Boilermakers and Iron Shipbuilders, which opposed employment of shipwrights on iron work. The lower courts and the minority of the Lords held that the right of the discharged workers to pursue their calling unmolested had been infringed upon and that therefore Allen, the union representative in charge of

---

[37] Sec. 6.

[38] A number of court decisions in the United States, similarly, held that municipalities should not limit bidding to contractors who employ union labor, or accept bids only from unionized contractors. Such practices were considered unjust discrimination in favor of members of a union or between classes of citizens. Policies of this kind were rejected on the ground that they create monopolies, restrict competition in public bidding, and may increase expenses for work and supplies. Some more recent judgments disavowed this concept and held that its application may result in delays and added expense caused by labor trouble. See for details and decisions: Charles S. Rhyne, *Labor Unions and Municipal Employe Law* (1946), pp. 65-69.

[39] A. C. 1.

the matter, was responsible for the damage caused to the dismissed employees. The majority of the Lords, however, saw no cause for a damage suit because "whether we approve or disapprove of such attempted trade restrictions, it was entirely within the right of the iron-workers to take any steps, not unlawful, to prevent any of the work which they regarded as legitimately theirs being entrusted to other hands." This view obviously is the reverse of the position taken by French high courts in the similar cases, discussed above.

In a subsequent decision[40] the majority of the Lords came nearer to sharing French judicial opinion. Plaintiff in this case was a butcher who employed nonunionists. Officers of a butchers' union, which maintained a policy of demanding employment for its members in preference to nonunion men, asked the plaintiff to hire his help exclusively from among the members of their organization. The plaintiff offered to have his workers join the union and to pay their fines and admission fees. The union rejected this offer and stated that, if the plaintiff's men became members of the union, they must give up their jobs and wait for their turn to get employment in accordance with the union rules. The plaintiff refused to discharge his workers, whereupon the union forced his best customer by threat of a strike to cease doing business with him.

In this case the majority of the Lords affirmed the judgment of the lower court which had awarded damages to the plaintiff. The House of Lords, through Lord Brampton, stated that:

. . . the real and substantial cause of [this] action is an unlawful conspiracy to molest the plaintiff, a trader, in carrying on his business, and by so doing to invade his undoubted right, thus described by Alderson B. in delivering the judgment of the Exchequer Chamber in *Hilton* v. *Eckersley* (6 E. and B. 74): *Prima facie* it is the privilege of a trader in a free country in all matters not contrary to law to regulate his own mode of carrying it on according to his own discretion and choice. If the law has in any matter regulated or re-

40 *Quinn* v. *Leatham*, A. C. 495 (1901).

strained his mode of doing this, the law must be obeyed. But no power short of the general law ought to restrain his free discretion.

The doctrine contained in this decision, together with the law of the Taff Vale decision[41] that unions may be sued for damages caused by tortious acts of their officers and agents, contributed much to the enactment of the Trade Disputes Act of 1906. This act, as mentioned above, now bars damage suits on the ground alone that measures taken in contemplation or furtherance of a labor dispute interfered with the right to dispose of one's labor or capital according to one's will. Such interference is actionable only when it is done by unlawful acts. But according to the same statute, even unlawful, that is tortious, acts, if committed by or on behalf of a union, generally do not afford ground for an action at law against the union as such, or against any of its officers or members in their capacity of representatives of the union.

In recent years British courts have generally tended to accept the view that no liability exists if a "just cause or excuse" for interference with another person's rights can be proved. The doctrine has been applied to suits brought against individual unionists who allegedly had interfered with another person's business or employment by unlawful acts. This jurisprudence, however, has not established hard and fast rules as to what constitutes a "just cause or excuse." Judges rather have endeavored to determine in the light of the circumstances of each particular case whether or not the specific acts of the defendants can be considered justified. The decisive factor frequently has been whether their primary intent had been to inflict harm to the injured or to promote legitimate union interests.[42]

---

[41] House of Lords, A. C. 426 (1901). This decision was rendered two weeks before the *Quinn* v. *Leatham* decision.

[42] In this respect British judicial policy has not infrequently been similar to that of French courts. Yet application of this basic policy in the two countries appears to have been different in many cases and to have produced different results in a number of instances. This is especially true with respect to recognition and protection of freedom of the worker to choose the union to which he

The *Crofter Harris Tweed Co.* v. *Veitch* case[43] may serve as an example of this judicial practice. It involved a damage suit of a company operating a spinning mill on the Island of Lewis against officers of a union representing 90 per cent of the spinners employed in the island mills. The company obtained its yarn from the mainland and sent the tweed cloth woven from it to the mainland for finishing, because it was charged lower prices there. The union regarded these practices (which were also applied by some other firms) as a serious interference with its purposes. They tended to keep the costs of the company lower than those of competitors who bought their yarn in the island and did the finishing in their own plants. This rendered it more difficult for the latter to comply with demands for the closed shop and wage increases. Acting in combination with some producers, the union therefore directed the dockers in the island port, all of whom were members of it, to cease handling yarn arriving for the company or tweeds coming from it.

The court found that the chief objective of the union in imposing the embargo was to further the interests of its members by eliminating undercutting and by regulating competition on the island. The House of Lords stated that "a combination with such an object is not unlawful, because the object is the legitimate promotion of the interests of the combiners, and because the damage necessarily inflicted on the applicants is not inflicted by criminal or tortious means and is not 'the real purpose' of the combination." In this case the union officers had interfered with the individual freedom of an employer; but the opinion

---

desires to belong. British legislation prohibiting actions for tort against unions as such and restricting liability under civil law for interfering with another person's business or employment of course has contributed a great deal to differences in jurisprudence. Also, the coexistence of several labor movements in France and the prevailing singularism in Britain have influenced judicial opinion.

[43] House of Lords, A. C. 435 (1942).

contains the general doctrine on union interference also with other freedoms, including the right of workers to dispose freely of their labor.

The foregoing discussion shows that British public policy has granted unions far-reaching immunity from liability for interference with the trade, business, or employment of other persons. Yet, as discussed above, the British Trades Union Congress has discountenanced the idea of using this immunity to practice union security policies of the type traditional in the United States. Unionists have exerted vigorous pressure upon *unorganized* workers to join a union. But contracts excluding them from employment opportunities have been made in only a few fields, such as, for example, in shipping and co-operative enterprises. There has been little contractual or other pressure to make *organized* workers join another union.[44]

AMERICAN ATTEMPTS TO DEFINE LAWFUL AND UNLAWFUL INTERFERENCE

American legislators and courts, like foreign lawmakers and judges, have rejected compulsion to organize by outright force, such as violence, extortion, fraud, and other generally unlawful acts. However, most courts gradually developed a tendency to regard as lawful, compulsion to organize short of such acts.

JUDICIAL POLICY PRIOR TO 1947

Most cases dealing with involuntary unionism involved the closed shop. But principles developed in these cases have been generally held relevant to other types of union

---

[44] An attempt of the British Actors' Equity Association to introduce the closed shop at a London West End theater led in 1935 to the establishment of the London Theatre Council. It is composed of ten representatives each of management and artists, under neutral chairmanship. The Council maintains a register of approved managers and artists; and only registered artists may be hired. All members of the affiliated organizations are registered during their membership. Where all artists are registered and employed under a standard contract approved by the Council, it is provided that no action shall be taken to impede or endanger the production or run of a play.

security.[45] The fact that a large number of American unions vigorously sought to establish closed or union shops was in no small measure responsible for judicial antagonism in the nineteenth century. After many decades of declining resistance to involuntary union membership,[46] however, judicial opposition to closed-shop and similar contracts had all but disappeared by the time of World War II. By the late thirties and early forties, American judges considered them generally unlawful in only relatively few cases. Frequently, they did so for reasons similar to those advanced by European colleagues.

Some American courts until recently
opposed exclusive contracts.

A few courts held that the closed-shop contract fell under the condemnation of state constitutions because it constituted discrimination between different classes of citizens. It was considered a violation of the fifth and fourteenth amendments of the Constitution of the United States, which provide that no person shall be deprived of life, liberty, or property without due process of law, and that no state shall deprive any person of life, liberty, or property without due process of law, *nor deny to any person within its jurisdiction the equal protection of the laws.* Some courts, defining labor as property, held that the closed-shop principle deprived workers of property without due process of law, and some courts declared it must be rejected as inimical to the freedom of individual pursuit guaranteed by the fundamental law.[47]

45 An opinion delivered in 1941 by the general counsel of the National Labor Relations Board, for example, stated that the exemption from prosecution for encouragement or discouragement of membership in a labor organization, which sec. 8 (3) of the National Labor Relations Act granted such employers who acted to comply with a closed-shop agreement, was not confined to the closed-shop variety of contract. See 10 LRRM 1294 (1942).

46 Massachusetts and New York have been considered leading states in this movement.

47 See, for example, *Curran v. Galen,* 46 N. E. 297, 298, 299 (1897); *O'Brien v. People,* 75 N. E. 108, 116 (1905); *International Ticket Co. v. Wendrich,* 193 A 808, 810 (1937).

More often judges found specific closed- or union-shop contracts void because of the special circumstances of the particular case. Their decisions, too, not infrequently reflected a philosophy similar to that of European judges. Some courts, for example, declared illegal closed or union shops tending to establish an employment monopoly for the members of the union concerned, holding that such arrangements were contrary to public policy or a common-law prinicple which, in their opinion, generally prohibits restraint of trade.[48] Some judges tended to consider the closed shop justified and lawful, if it was limited to a single establishment, but subjected it to special legal treatment, if it covered an entire industry through a considerable area. A number of decisions endeavored to distinguish, in the latter case, between a closed shop sought by a union as a protective measure and one sought in order to establish a monopoly of labor infringing upon "the utmost freedom of the individual to pursue his lawful trade or business." Courts, making this distinction, held the latter type of contract to be against public policy. As to a closed shop in substantially an entire industry based on motives intrinsically self-protective, the decisions were conflicting.[49]

A number of courts were particularly opposed to closed- and union-shop contracts, if they were made by so-called closed unions. This type of labor organization, with which European courts have hardly had to deal, limits admission of new members in general, or of certain persons in particular, through high initiation fees, requirement of family relationship, or other restrictive membership provisions. Closed unions do not seek a closed shop to force nonmem-

[48] See, for example, *McCord* v. *Thompson-Starrett Co.*, 113 N. Y. 385 (1908) and 92 N. E. 1090 (1910); and *Anderson* v. *Shipowners Association*, 272 U. S. 359 (1926).

[49] See, for example, *Connors* v. *Conolly*, 86 A 600, 603, 604 (1913); *International Ticket Co.* v. *Wendrich*, 193 A 808, 810 (1937); *Four Plating Co.* v. *Mako*, 194 A 53, 55 (1937); *Williams* v. *Quill*, 12 N. E. (2d) 547 (1938); *Dorrington* v. *Manning*, 4 A (2d) 886, 890, 892 (1939); *Feast* v. *United Oystermen's Union*, 15 A (2d) 129, 132, 133 (1940); *Christiansen* v. *Local 680*, 10 A (2d) 168 (1940); *Brown* v. *Lehman*, 15 A (2d) 513 (1940). Also, see note at 95 A.L.R. 18.

bers into its ranks, but primarily to secure certain job opportunities exclusively for its present members and a relatively small number of special proteges. Apart from pressure upon present members to maintain membership and upon the privileged to apply for admission, this is, strictly speaking, the reverse of compulsion to organize. But it may carry the exclusion of workers from job opportunities to extremes; the excluded workers cannot obtain the jobs even by joining the union. Therefore, courts applied the principles mentioned before very strictly to closed-shop contracts made by unions in which membership was not open to applicants on "reasonable" terms. The demand by a union holding a closed-shop contract to discharge workers whose admission it had refused without giving reasons, was held an intentional and malicious violation of the right to work, lacking any legal or social justification.[50] It was said that protection against arbitrary and discriminatory exclusion from union membership is essential to the validity of closed-shop agreements. Hence a number of decisions held that the closed shop combined with the closed union was incompatible with public policy.[51] "A union," stated a New Jersey court, "may restrict its membership at pleasure; it may, under certain conditions, lawfully contract with employers that all work shall be given to its members. But it cannot do both."[52]

*Judicial opposition to exclusive contracts had
nearly disappeared by the late thirties.*

These examples show that, until rather recently, some American courts held union security agreements invalid, at least under certain circumstances. Except for relatively few states, in which certain types of contracts were proscribed, the general judicial trend, however, was toward

[50] *Dorrington* v. *Manning*, 4 A (2d) 886, 890, 892 (1939).
[51] *Williams* v. *International Brotherhood of Boilermakers*, 165 P (2d) 903 (1946), relying largely on *James* v. *Marinship Corp.*, 155 P (2d) 329 (1944), and *Railway Mail Ass'n* v. *Corsi*, 326 U. S. 88 (1945). Cf. *Betts* v. *Easley*, 169 P (2d) 831 (1946).
[52] *Wilson* v. *Newspaper Union*, 197 A 720 (1938).

recognition of virtually all kinds of such agreements and labor activities to obtain them. Efforts of courts to outlaw closed- and union-shop contracts establishing a labor monopoly for a union in substantially an entire industry through an area, did not produce a uniform body of principles. No general agreement could be reached, particularly on the basic question as to how many establishments had to be covered to make the contract a monopolistic one. The method was used less and less, as judicial disapproval of such labor monopolies subsided.[53]

Growing opposition to the doctrine that the legality of any labor activity must be tested by the character of its motives, moreover, caused increasing abandonment of the practice of making the validity of union security agreements dependent upon the view of the court on the propriety of the intent of the union.[54] In addition, the view spread that under closed- and union-shop agreements fellow workers rather than employers compel employees to join a union and that pressure upon workers to organize is not contrary to public policy if it is exerted not by employers but by employees.[55] It also happened that a closed-shop contract was held valid although in the opinion of the court

[53] See, for example, *Williams* v. *Quill*, 12 N. E. (2d) 547 (1938) and *Domanick* v *Triboro Coach Corporation*, 18 N. Y. Supp. (2d) 650 (1940).

[54] See "The All-Union Shop in the Courts," 6 *International Juridical Association Bulletin* 147 ff. (1938).

[55] See, for example, *Shafer* v. *Registered Pharmacists Union*, 106 P (2d) 403 (1940).

Mr. Justice Jackson, dissenting in *Wallace Corporation* v. *National Labor Relations Board* (323 U. S. 248, 1944), explained this doctrine, stating that while "acts of influence or pressure on workmen are unfair when exerted by the employer in his own interest, they are fair and lawful when enforced by him as an instrument of the union itself. A closed shop is the ultimate goal of most union endeavor, and not a few employers have found it a stabilizer of labor relations by putting out of their shops men who were antagonistic to the dominant union, thus ending strife for domination. It puts the employment office under a veto of the union, which uses its own membership standards as a basis on which to exclude men from employment." Despite this influence of union membership policies on employment opportunities of workers, Justice Jackson continued, "neither the National Labor Relations Act nor any other Act of Congress expressly or by implication gives to the [National Labor Relations] Board any power to supervise union membership or to deal with union practices, however unfair they may be to members, to applicants, to minorities, to other unions, or to employers. This may or may not have been a mistake, but it was no oversight."

membership in the contracting union was not permitted on reasonable terms.[56]

Most American courts either did not recognize or did not give any thought at all to the various other considerations applied by European courts in testing the legality of pressure to organize. The United States Supreme Court stated its position with regard to the customary union security devices implicitly rather than expressly. It became obvious, however, that the court held them lawful when it declared the National Labor Relations Act constitutional together with the proviso in section 8 (3) of the statute. That proviso exempted the employer from prosecution for encouragement or discouragement of membership in a union if he acted in performance of a union security agreement entered into with a union which represented a majority of the employees in an appropriate bargaining unit at the time the contract was made. Furthermore, the union had to have attained its majority status without employer assistance, considered an unfair labor practice by the statute. These qualifications applied to all types of union security agreements, including the check-off. They still govern those security contracts which are considered lawful as such after recent changes in federal and state laws.

POLICY IN THE FIELD OF PUBLIC EMPLOYMENT

The National Labor Relations Act and almost all state labor relations acts exclude from their scope employment relations with the United States, the states, and their political subdivisions. In this field, as mentioned above, legislators have done little to formulate a general policy respecting the right to organize and to bargain collectively. A number of public authorities have entered into collective contracts with unions. Some of these contracts have provided for exclusive bargaining rights for specific unions, the union shop, or other union security plans. Judicial

[56] *Stockwell* v. *Vinstrand Theatres*, 8 LRRM 1072 (1941).

opinion as to whether the mere making of collective agreements by governmental agencies is or is not contrary to
public policy has been divided.

*A marked trend has existed to reject exclusive
contracts in public employment.*

It has been widely held that collective agreements in the
area of government service, if at all legitimate, must not go
beyond giving unions the opportunity of acting as bargaining representative for their members, leaving to other employees the full right to deal with their employer on their
own behalf either singly or through other organizations of
their choice—a principle which has prevailed in Europe
in employer-employee relations of any type.

The supporters of this policy have been guided chiefly
by the consideration that union security agreements of the
kind customary in private employment would not be compatible with the character and requirements of the public
service. They have held that, in this field, granting of pref-
erences to a union in whatever form would involve illegal
delegation of disciplinary authority, of legislative power,
or of the discretion of public officers; that it would constitute illegal discrimination between different classes of
citizens, disable government employees from performing
their duty, result in divided allegiance, be detrimental to
the public welfare, and subversive of the public service.[57]
Courts, further, have emphasized that, under civil service
conditions, appointments and promotions must be determined upon merit and fitness rather than membership in
a labor organization; and that persons having civil service
status may be discharged only for causes listed in the law
but not for refusing to join a union or to remain a member.[58]

Moreover, it has been pointed out that government

[57] See, for example, *Mugford v. Baltimore,* 8 CCH Lab. Cas. 66,147 (1945);
9 CCH Lab. Cas. 66,996 (1944); 10 CCH Lab. Cas. 68,362 (1945).
[58] See *Petrucci v. Hogan,* 27 N. Y. Supp. (2d) 718 (1941).

exists for the benefit of all, and that it has a responsibility to all of its inhabitants alike.[59] Therefore, it was said, there can be no question of union jurisdiction in the public service. In this field no exclusive or preferred position can be established either for any individual or for any group or organization. It would be a breach of these fundamental principles to discriminate against or to deny employment opportunity to any qualified employee or prospective employee because of his membership or nonmembership in any organization.[60]

The automatic check-off has been outlawed likewise. It was said that union dues could not be deducted merely upon the request of the union. But there has been a trend to admit the voluntary and revocable check-off where it has been the general policy of the public agency concerned to grant employees' requests to withhold from their wages sums to be applied to pensions, war loans, donations, and the like.[61]

LEGISLATIVE POLICY PRIOR TO 1947

Apart from the field of public employment, prevailing judicial policy in recent decades changed from rejection through conditional acceptance to far-reaching recognition of involuntary union membership. This was due partly to general developments, partly to the position taken by federal and state legislators.

The National Labor Relations Act expressly admitted exclusive contracts.

As discussed above, the Congress of the United States implied in the National Labor Relations Act that it did not oppose exclusive union security agreements on principle.

[59] See Ludwig Teller, *Labor Disputes and Collective Bargaining* (1940), 1947 supp., sec. 171.

[60] *Mugford* v. *Baltimore*, 9 CCH Lab. Cas. 66,996 (1944), aff'd in 10 CCH Lab. Cas. 68,362 (1945).

[61] See for example, *Mugford* v. *Baltimore*, 10 CCH Lab. Cas. 68,362 (1945).

It is true, the statute made it an unfair labor practice for an employer by discrimination to encourage or discourage membership in any labor organization. However, to eliminate the possible repetition of "doubts and misconstructions" in regard to this provision, such as had been caused by the similar wording of section 7 (a) of the National Industrial Recovery Act, the legislators wrote it explicitly into the original act that nothing in any federal statute should illegalize a closed-shop agreement between an employer and a bona fide labor organization which is the legitimate bargaining agent of employees.[62] As mentioned before, this has been interpreted authoritatively also to cover union security devices other than the closed shop.

According to the Senate Report on the act,[63] it was not intended either to make the closed shop legal in states where it might be considered illegal, or to facilitate the making of closed-shop contracts. Denying any desire to favor such agreements, the legislators pointed out that they even narrowed the then existing law. As mentioned above, section 8 (3) of the statute prescribed that from now on exclusive contracts should be treated as legal only if they were concluded with a labor organization which was not employer-dominated and which, further, represented the majority of employees in the appropriate bargaining unit covered by the agreement when it was made. Both Houses of Congress rejected all demands to proscribe compulsion to organize not only if exercised by employers but also if exerted by employees. The legislators made it clear that they wanted to deal with employer-employee relations but not with relations among and between employees and unions. "To prohibit employees from 'coercing' their own side," the House and Senate committees on labor stated, "would not merely outlaw the undesirable activi-

---

[62] See *National Labor Relations Board*, H. Rept. 969, 74 Cong. 1 sess. (1935), p. 17.

[63] *National Labor Relations Board*, S. Rept. 573, 74 Cong. 1 sess. (1935), pp. 11-12.

tives which the words connote to the layman, but would raise in federal law the ghosts of many much-criticized injunctions issued by courts of equity against activities of labor organizations, ghosts which it was supposed Congress had laid low in the Norris-LaGuardia Act."[64] The Senate report declared that, with the one exception just mentioned, the act did not interfere with the *status quo* on the debatable subject but left the way open to such closed-shop agreements as could be legally consummated at the time the law was passed.

In practice, however, this policy contributed much to the growth of indulgent public policies with respect to involuntary union membership and to the large increase in exclusive contracts described above. Conferment to majority unions of a monopoly of representation, and their explicit statutory authorization to continue establishing employment monopolies, restricted considerably competition among bona fide unions and freedom of individual workers "to decline to associate with their fellows" or to become or remain members of unions of their own uncontrolled choice.

A few federal statutes of the thirties
outlawed involuntary unionism.

Federal policy moved in a different direction in only few areas. An amendment to the Bankruptcy Act of 1898[65] prohibited judges, trustees, and receivers from requiring a job-seeker to sign any promise to join a labor organization. Moreover, they had to cease giving effect to existing contracts, containing such a promise.[66]

[64] See *National Labor Relations Board,* H. Rept. 1147, 75 Cong. 1 sess. (1935), p. 16.
[65] 47 Stat. 1467, sec. 77 (q).
[66] This section subsequently was amended to read: "The right of employees or of persons seeking employment on the property of the debtor under the jurisdiction of the court to join a labor organization of their choice, or to refuse to join or remain members of a company union, shall be free from interference, restraint, or coercion by the court, a debtor or trustee. It shall be the duty of a debtor or trustee to report to the judge any agreement restricting or interfering

At the request of the standard unions in the railway field, this provision of the Bankruptcy Act was incorporated verbally and extended to railroads under private management in the Emergency Railroad Transportation Act, 1933.[67] The request of the unions was motivated by the desire to eliminate the closed shop as a device by which employers could maintain company-dominated unions, rather than by antagonism to the closed shop as a matter of principle. Accordingly, when the Railway Labor Act was amended in 1934, union representatives demanded that the proscription of the closed shop should be limited to company unions. The legislators in this case, however, followed the policy that "if genuine freedom of choice is to be the basis of labor relations under the Railway Labor Act as it should be, then the yellow dog contract, *and* its corollary, the closed shop, . . . have no place in the picture," as the Federal Co-ordinator of Transportation put it.[68]

The railroad unions attached more importance to elmination of company unions than to the closed shop. The legislators provided that employers subject to the Railway Labor Act commit a misdemeanor if they require a job applicant to sign an agreement promising to join (or not to join) a labor organization or if they influence or coerce employees in an effort to induce them to become or remain members of a union.[69] This also covers union security devices other than the closed shop. The act also outlaws the check-off.[70]

---

with such right, and the judge shall thereupon enter an appropriate order for the termination of such agreement and for notice to the employees that the same is no longer binding upon them." (USC., title 11, sec. 627). However, Section 15 of the National Labor Relations Act provides that, if the application of these rules conflicts with the application of the National Labor Relations Act, the latter shall prevail.

67 48 Stat. 211, sec. 7 (e).

68 Hearings on S. 3266 before the Senate Committee on Interstate Commerce, 73 Cong. 2 sess. (1934), p. 150.

69 An Act to amend the Railway Labor Act approved May 20, 1926, and to provide for the prompt disposition of disputes between carriers and their employees, 48 Stat. 1185, sec. 3.

70 Sec. 2, Fourth. See *Brotherhood of R. R. Shop Crafts of America, Rock Island System v. Lowden,* 86 Fed. (2d) 458 (1936).

Few states proscribed involuntary
unionism prior to World War II.

While federal policy, with only few exceptions and qualifications, admitted involuntary union membership, a number of prewar state statutes curbed certain types of union
security agreements in one way or another. In addition to
proclaiming full freedom of individual employees in
organizational matters, some states declared void and unen-
forcible contract clauses in which a worker promised to
join or remain a member of a labor organization. But at
the same time other statutes of these states might provide
that union security agreements, at least with majority
unions, were valid. There also was some legislative action
to outlaw the check-off without the consent of the workers
concerned.

A considerable number of states, however, had no laws
pertaining to involuntary unionism in general or the
closed shop in particular. State labor relations acts, like the
national act, ordinarily set forth explicitly that they did
not illegalize closed-shop and similar agreements with a
bona fide labor organization, which was the duly chosen
bargaining representative of employees. Only a few statutes
sought to reduce the number of involuntary union members, for example, by making the validity of closed and
union shops contingent upon an affirmative referendum
of the workers. Most of the states which had taken any
action with respect to union security devices treated them
as lawful about the time of World War II.

PUBLIC POLICY AFTER THE END OF WORLD WAR II

After the war, movements to place restrictions on union
activities in general and to eliminate or limit involuntary
unionism in particular sprang up in a steadily increasing
number of states. While at first only a few statutes were
passed, issued chiefly in states considered less industrial-

ized,[71] the trend grew so strong that now at least 18 states have provisions of this type in their constitutions or statute books.

Some postwar state statutes made
exclusive contracts illegal.

Most of these state laws which contain an explanation as to the reasons for outlawing or restricting involuntary union membership cite as their ideological and constitutional basis the "right to work." Appraised in terms of the "right to work" doctrine, labor policy in virtually the whole of the United States, for some time has carried exclusion of nonmembers from employment opportunities on the list of legitimate measures which unions, duly chosen as bargaining representatives, may take in exercising their right to organize. As to restriction of the individual freedom of outsiders, which might result therefrom, this right of such unions has been held equal or superior to the right of individuals to opportunity to work at their chosen place.

This doctrine has been modified or abandoned, in those states which recently re-evaluated the relative significance of the two rights and, as a result, reduced the area of legitimate union pressure. The concept that majority unions may make arrangements compelling outsiders to join them and that, accordingly, compulsion to organize by an employer is not unlawful when undertaken in carrying out an agreement with such a union has been discarded where the right to work at one's chosen place has been declared without qualification superior to the right of unions to organize.

Most of the states which re-evaluated the relative significance of the right to organize and the right to opportunity to work at the place of one's choice did so by outlawing one specific type of interference with the latter, namely, deny-

[71] Since unionism in these states was relatively weak, the new restrictive legislation was criticized by its opponents as being an attempt to prevent the growth of it.

ing or abridging it on account of nonmembership in a labor organization. The North Carolina statute declares more generally that the exercise of this right must be maintained free from *any undue* restraint and outlaws closed-shop, union-shop, and maintenance-of-membership clauses on the ground that they constitute one type of such restraint. Only the Texas law went further and declared—obviously in contrast to generally accepted theory—that not only organizations but also legislators are precluded from interfering with the right of a person to work. Arkansas based the prohibition of closed, union, and maintenance-of-membership shops on the freedom of contract by declaring "freedom of organized labor to bargain collectively, and freedom of unorganized labor to bargain individually" the public policy of the state.

The states have retained proscription of the yellow-dog contract, which makes it a condition of employment that employees do not join a union. On the other hand, more states declared that workers should be free to refrain from joining a union, or that no employee should be compelled by employers, unions, or fellow workers to become a member of a labor organization. Not all governments which enacted statutes to protect freedom to organize, however, banned closed shop and similar devices altogether.[72] Those that did proscribe all or some of them usually treat as unlawful not only *agreements* providing for outlawed forms of union security but also denial, without a contractual obligation, of opportunity to obtain or retain employment, which would *in fact* give a union a position proscribed by the law. None of the state governments, which took action to settle the closed-shop issue, chose the intermediate solu-

[72] The Pennsylvania Labor Relations Act, for example, was amended in 1947. Prior to the amendment, coercion of an employee for the purpose of compelling him to join or refrain from joining a union was an unfair labor practice only if it was undertaken by means of threats of force or violence. Now an employer or labor organization commits an unfair labor practice if he or it intimidates, restrains, or coerces an employee for such purpose, even if no threats of force or violence are made. But the act still includes a proviso in favor of union security agreements.

tion tried in some European areas, namely, rejection of undertakings making membership in a specified union a condition of employment, but toleration, possibly with qualifications, of arrangements or usage reserving employment opportunities in single establishments for workers belonging to some union, no matter which one. Where such policy has been attempted in Europe, the intent has been to protect unionism as a whole without giving special protection to individual business interests of specified organizations.[73] Finally, the new state laws treat the closed and union shop alike, obviously because, as discussed above, there is no significant difference between the two as far as pressure on workers is concerned. Some statutes even use a common term for both, namely, all-union agreement.

A number of state courts have declared new "anti-closed shop laws" constitutional as within the police power of the states. They have rejected assertions that the statutes constituted arbitrary or unreasonable exercise of that power and that they, therefore, were in conflict with due process provisions of state constitutions or the federal Constitution. These decisions also denied that the acts were contrary to the policy of the National Labor Relations Act or the Labor Management Relations Act, 1947. They set forth that this matter has been left outside the scope of the federal law.

The United States Supreme Court declared that neither the Arizona and Nebraska constitutional amendments nor the North Carolina "anti-closed shop law" violate the federal Constitution.[74] In a subsequent decision the court

---

[73] Sec. 30 of the (repealed) Delaware Act Regulating Labor Unions and Relations Between Employers and Employees, Members of Labor Unions (L. 1947, H. B. 212) declared that "every agreement . . . whereby a party undertakes or promises to join or remain a member of some *specific* labor organization . . . to be contrary to public policy." This language was susceptible to the interpretation that a contract was not contrary to public policy if it required employees to belong to a union but did not require them to belong to a *specific* union. But there is reason to believe that the state legislature did not interpret the provision in this manner.

[74] *Lincoln Union* v. *Northwestern*, 335 U. S. 525 (1949); *A. F. of L.* v. *American Sash Co.*, 335 U. S. 538 (1949).

further held that the National Labor Relations Act permits both regulation and prohibition of exclusive agreements by the states.[75] The validity of state laws, providing that no person shall be denied an opportunity to obtain or retain employment because he is or is not a member of a labor organization thus seems to be beyond question. The unions concerned attacked the constitutionality of the enactments on the ground that insofar as they attempt to protect non-union members from discrimination, they are in violation of the right of freedom of speech, of assembly, and of petition, and deprive unions and employers of equal protection and due process of law.

The Supreme Court rejected all these contentions. Denying that the language of the laws indicates a purpose to prohibit speech, assembly, or petition, it pointed out that "precisely what these state laws do is to forbid employers acting alone or in concert with labor organizations deliberately to restrict employment to none but union members." The constitutional right of workers to assemble, to discuss and formulate plans for furthering their own self-interest in jobs, the judges held, cannot be construed as a constitutional guarantee that none shall get and hold jobs except those who will join the organization or will agree to abide by its plans. Though not denying that the attacked laws may weaken the bargaining power of unions and may correspondingly strengthen the power of employers, the Court emphasized that they do not deny but, on the contrary, grant equal protection to all labor organizations, union and nonunion workers; that they provide, in particular, protection for union members equal to that provided for non-union members by forbidding employers to discriminate against unionists and nonunionists and thus commanding equal employment opportunities for both groups of workers. Finally, rejecting the union contention that the federal Constitution affords protection against discrimina-

75 *Algoma Plywood Co.* v. *Wisconsin Employment Relations Board,* 336 U. S. 301, 314 (1949).

tion to union members but that it nevertheless forbids a state from providing the same protection to nonunion members, the decision concludes with the statement: "Just as we have held that the due process clause erects no obstacle to block legislative protection of union members, we now hold that legislative protection can be afforded non-union workers." Justice Frankfurter, concurring, added a statement reminiscent of the basic policy of the German and Swiss supreme courts, mentioned above: "The right of association, like any other right," he said, "carried to its extreme, encounters limiting principles. At the point where the mutual advantage of association demands too much individual disadvantage, a compromise must be struck. When that point has been reached—where the intersection should fall—is plainly a question within the special province of the legislature."

Several states prohibit the closed, union,
and maintenance-of-membership shop.

Arizona, Arkansas, Florida, Nebraska, and South Dakota have embodied proscription of the closed, union, and maintenance-of-membership shop in their constitutions.[76] The provision in the Florida constitution, outlawing all three types of union security devices, has not been implemented by further legislation for enforcement.

The "anti-closed shop laws" of Arizona,[77] Arkansas,[78] Georgia,[79] Iowa,[80] Nebraska,[81] North Carolina,[82] North Dakota,[83] South Dakota,[84] Tennessee,[85] Texas,[86] and Vir-

---

[76] A bill proposing a constitutional ban of the same kind, passed by the New Mexico legislature in 1947 (H.J.R. 15), was submitted to a plebiscite at the general election in 1948 and rejected by the voters.

[77] L. 1947, c. 81, sec. 2.

[78] L. 1947, act 101, secs. 2, 3.

[79] L. 1947, H. B. 72, sec. 4.

[80] L. 1947, S. B. 109, secs. 2, 3.

[81] L. 1947, L. B. 344, sec. 1.

[82] L. 1947, H. B. 229, secs. 2, 3.

[83] L. 1947, H. B. 151.

[84] L. 1945, H. B. 78, sec. 1, and L. 1947, S. B. 224, secs. 1, 2.

[85] L. 1947, S. B. 367, secs. 1, 2.

[86] L. 1947, H. B. 23, secs. 2, 3.

ginia,[87] proscribe, so far as pertinent here, denying or abridging the opportunity to obtain or retain employment because of nonmembership in a labor organization. Consequently, they prohibit employers and associations of any kind from entering into agreements which would exclude any person from employment for this reason. This means that the closed-shop, union-shop, and maintenance-of-membership clauses are equally unlawful.

Some statutes, such as those of Arkansas, Iowa, Nebraska, and Tennessee, mention explicitly that this also covers workers who withdraw, or are excluded, from a union. The Arizona law, further, outlaws expressly collective refusal to work with an unorganized employee in order to cause discharge or denial of employment to him because of his nonunion status. The law of Maryland does not use the language of the acts, mentioned so far; but it declares any promise to join, or remain a member of, a specific labor organization to be contrary to public policy and unenforceable in court.[88] The Nevada Criminal Code declares unlawful promises or agreements to become, or continue to be, a member of a labor organization as a condition of employment.[89]

The states of Arkansas, Georgia, Iowa, Nebraska, South Dakota, and Tennessee have made noncompliance with provisions discussed above and below a misdemeanor. Penalties range from not less than $100 nor more than $500 in Nebraska[90] to fines not to exceed $1,000, imprisonment up to six months, or work in the chain gang not to exceed 12 months in Georgia.[91] Other methods provided for enforcement may be injunctive relief, suit for damages, or subjection to the consequences of an unfair labor practice. In North Carolina and Virginia, where union security agreements have been declared illegal combinations or conspira-

---

87 L. 1947, H. B. 5, secs. 2, 3.
88 Ann. Code 1939, Art. 100.
89 Criminal Code, sec. 10473.
90 L. 1947, L. B. 344, sec. 3.
91 L. 1947, H. B. 72, sec. 9; Code of Ga. 1933, sec. 27-2506.

cies, civil and criminal liability as well as injunctive relief apply.

Several states qualify the
legality of exclusive agreements.

Under the Colorado Labor Peace Act[92] an employer may enter into an all-union agreement with a union representing a bargaining unit only if three quarters or more of the employees in the unit have voted for it. The Industrial Commission has the duty to declare the agreement terminated when it finds that membership has been denied to an employee of the contracting employer. Similarly, Kansas prohibits bargaining representatives from making an all-union agreement unless a majority of the affected employees authorized them to do so.[93]

The Massachusetts Labor Relations Act includes a proviso in favor of the three types of union security agreements similar to the original national act. However, it exempts from the application of such agreements those employees who are not eligible for full membership and voting rights in the contracting union. An employer who would discharge or otherwise discriminate against a worker because he is not a member in good standing of the union, would commit an unfair labor practice, unless the union certified that the employee was denied admission or lost his membership in good standing as a result of a bona fide occupational disqualification or disciplinary measure and has exhausted the remedies available to him within the organization. The Labor Relations Commission determines whether these statutory conditions of a lawful discharge are present.[94] The Pennsylvania Labor Relations Act also contains a proviso

92 Sec. 6 (1) (c).
93 L. 1943, S. B. 264, sec. 8 (4).
94 State Labor Relations Act, sec. 4 (3) and (6). Sec. 4A (2c) of this act, further, makes it an unfair labor practice for any person and union to authorize or engage in any concerted cessation of work or boycott for the purpose of interfering with employees in their choice or rejection of bargaining representatives after the State Labor Relations Commission determined that such employees do not desire to be represented by the union.

in favor of union security agreements, patterned after the original federal act, but, similar to the Massachusetts law, requires further that the union must not deny membership to persons who are employed by the contracting employer at the time when the agreement is made.[95]

The Wisconsin Employment Peace Act, which includes the same proviso admitting union security agreements as the Massachusetts and Pennsylvania statutes, makes the validity of such agreements further contingent upon an affirmative vote of two thirds or more of the employees, constituting at least a majority of the workers in the bargaining unit concerned, in a secret ballot conducted by the Employment Relations Board. The provision that this board has to declare the agreement terminated whenever it finds that the contracting union unreasonably refused to receive as a member any employee of the contracting employer, expresses policy similar to that of the corresponding provision in the Pennsylvania Labor Relations Act. In contrast to the latter, however, it mentions explicitly that only unreasonable refusal makes the contract unlawful.[96]

A number of states also have qualified
the legality of the check-off.

The check-off agreement, the purpose of which is preserving membership by securing payment of dues rather than increasing the number of members, has been subjected to some limitation in at least twelve states. Under the North Carolina[97] Tennessee,[98] and Virginia[99] laws, no person may be required as a condition of employment to pay any fee or assessment to a labor organization. A considerable number of states now ban the automatic but permit the voluntary check-off under certain conditions. In Penn-

[95] Provided the employee was not employed in violation of a previously existing agreement with the same union. State Labor Relations Act, sec. 6 (1) (c).
[96] Wisconsin Employment Peace Act, sec. 111.06 (1) (c).
[97] L. 1947, H. B. 229, sec. 5.
[98] L. 1947, c. 36, sec. 3.
[99] L. 1947, H. B. 5, sec. 5.

sylvania, for example, an employer is guilty of an unfair labor practice if he checks off union dues without being authorized to do so by a majority vote of all the employees in the bargaining unit concerned, and further by each employee individually whose wages are affected.[100] Many statutes require individual, voluntary authorization by each worker concerned. Such statutes were enacted in Arkansas,[101] Colorado,[102] Connecticut,[103] Georgia,[104] Indiana,[105] Iowa,[106] Massachusetts,[107] Rhode Island,[108] Texas,[109] and Wisconsin.[110] Some states, for example Arkansas, Colorado, Connecticut, Indiana, Iowa, Massachusetts, and Texas, prescribe explicitly the written form of such consent. Under the law of Iowa it must be countersigned by the employee's spouse if he or she is married. In Georgia and Indiana the authorization has to be revocable at the will of the worker concerned; in other states advanced notice must be provided for, the period of which is fixed by law. The Colorado law requires that such notice must be permissible at any time. The Wisconsin law demands that the employee must have the right to give notice at the end of any year of his life. The Indiana statute states explicitly that the provisions permitting the check-off under certain conditions apply only to dues to be paid to a union of which the employee is a member. As mentioned above[111] Alabama, Delaware, Georgia, Iowa, Massachusetts, New Hampshire, North Carolina, Tennessee, Texas, and Virginia have declared it unlawful to require a *nonunion* worker, as a

---

[100] Labor Relations Act, sec. 6 (1) (f).
[101] L. 1947, act 101.
[102] Labor Peace Act, sec. 6 (1) (i).
[103] General Statutes, sec. 1414 (e), 1939 Supp., as amended by 1945 Supp., sec. 1004 (h), and D.A.G. Mar. 29, 1947.
[104] L. 1947, sec. 6.
[105] L. 1947, c. 330.
[106] L. 1947, S. B. 109, sec. 5.
[107] L. 1939, c. 96. (L. 1948, c. 119.)
[108] L. 1947, c. 1944. Otherwise the employer must comply with the law concerning the assignment of wages.
[109] L. 1947, H. B. 22.
[110] Employment Peace Act, sec. 111.06 (1) (i).
[111] P. 153n.

condition of employment, to make periodic payments to a labor organization.

The Labor Management Relations Act curbs involuntary unionism.

Postwar state legislation dealing with certain effects of labor relations acts and other problems of industrial relations increased demands for federal legislation of this kind.[112] The Congress of the United States complied with them by passing in June 1947 the Labor Management Relations Act.[113] The declared intent of the lawmakers was to enact a bill of rights in industrial relations, defining clearly the rights of employers and employees, in keeping with the protection of the paramount public interest, and thereby to reduce the number of strikes and to bring about industrial peace. With respect to involuntary unionism, the House Committee on Education and Labor set forth:

> . . . For the last 14 years, as a result of labor laws ill-conceived and disastrously executed, the American workingman has been deprived of his dignity as an individual. He has been cajoled, coerced, intimidated, and on many occasions beaten up, in the name of the splendid aims set forth in section 1 of the National Labor Relations Act. His whole economic life has been subject to the complete domination and control of unregulated monopolists. He has on many occasions had to pay them tribute to get a job. He has been forced into labor organizations against his will. At other times when he has desired to join a particular labor organization he has been prevented from doing so and forced to join another one. . . . In short, his mind, his soul, and his very life have been subject to a tyranny more despotic than one could think possible in a free country.[114]

The Senate Committee on Labor and Public Welfare stated that abuses of the National Labor Relations Act had

112 As early as April 1938, President Franklin D. Roosevelt stated that "The Wagner Act ought to have various amendments made to it." But he expressed apprehension that it would be impossible to keep party politics out of any discussion of amendments, and that the legislators thus may go to extremes. "The Continuing Struggle for Liberalism," *The Public Papers and Addresses of Franklin D. Roosevelt* (1938 Vol), (1941), p. 288.

113 Act of June 23, 1947, 61 Stat. 136, passed over the President's veto.

114 *Labor-Management Relations Act, 1947,* H. Rept. 245, 80 Cong. 1 sess. (1947), p. 4.

become too serious and numerous to justify permitting the law to remain unchanged. Concentrating on the closed shop, it declared that it creates too great a barrier to free employment to be longer tolerated.[115]

The legislation passed as a result of these considerations, like corresponding statutes in the states, has been based on the right to work.[116] A new line of demarcation between justifiable and objectionable interference with this right has been drawn, and the area of compulsion to organize considered lawful has been reduced. It has been specifically provided that employees have the right not only to participate but also to refrain from participating in concerted activities with their fellow workers. Employers no longer enjoy immunity under the National Labor Relations Act if they discriminate against workers in carrying through a closed shop, preferential shop, hiring hall, or other preferential hiring agreement. In so far as union security agreements, such as union-shop and maintenance-of-membership contracts, still justify otherwise unlawful discrimination against workers, exemption of employers from the consequences of an unfair labor practice has been qualified in order to protect individual workers against certain union actions. In addition, as mentioned above, provisions have been added, designed to enable workers to terminate at some time involuntary union allegiance resulting from provisions of the act or contracts.[117]

Federal legislators have made it clear that, in their opinion, all types of agreements making union membership a condition of employment are "compulsory unionism" or "compulsory-membership agreements." However, Congress has not drawn the line between justifiable and objectionable interference with the right to work in a manner precluding all forms of "compulsory membership agree-

---

[115] *Federal Labor Relations Act of 1947*, S. Rept. 105, 80 Cong. 1 sess. (1947), pp. 6-7.
[116] See, for example, *Labor-Management Relations Act, 1947*, H. Rept. 245, 80 Cong. 1 sess. (1947), p. 34.
[117] See p. 244.

ments" from legal recognition under the act. An employer, who would discriminate against otherwise qualified job applicants under the terms of a closed-shop agreement, entered into after the new provisions came into force, would be directed by the National Labor Relations Board to give them the jobs and to pay back wages if a charge is filed.[118] If the Board decides that the union is responsible for the discrimination, it may assess back pay against the union.

Yet, now as before, the employer is permitted to use non-membership in the contracting union as a reason for refusing employment under an agreement requiring all the employees in a bargaining unit to become members thirty days after being hired, if the union is the duly chosen representative of the unit and if, further, the National Labor Relations Board has certified that at least a majority of employees eligible to vote have voted to authorize it to make such an agreement.[119] Though the requirement of this ballot now prevents the making of a union security agreement without asking the employees concerned whether they want it, interference with the right to opportunity to work under the terms of a union-shop or maintenance-of-membership agreement arrived at in compliance with the provisions of the amended National Labor Relations Act is still lawful.

In order to forestall some of the practices which the legislators intended to eliminate, however, the act provides that even in the case of a legitimate exclusive agreement, the employer must not discriminate against an employee if

118 The National Labor Relations Board is not authorized to act unless a complaint is made to it. It is ordinarily very difficult for an individual worker to challenge agreements entered into, formally or informally, by employers and powerful unions. This also applies to contracts making union membership a condition of employment in violation of the National Labor Relations Act. Without complaints being made, however, the regulations concerning exclusive agreements cannot be enforced. Their effectiveness, like that of the provisions dealing with "decertification" of bargaining representatives, depends largely upon whether individual employees have sufficient initiative as well as interest and economic strength to resist joint union-management pressure and to enforce their rights in time-consuming proceedings. (See p. 244 n.)

119 The act does not require the employer to enter into a union-shop agreement if the employees authorize the union to bargain for it.

he has reasonable grounds for believing (1) that membership in the union was not available to the worker on the same terms as to other members, or (2) that membership was denied or terminated for reasons other than failure to pay the initiation fee or dues.[120] The National Labor Relations Board interpreted the second of these two provisions as extending protection to any employee who tenders dues and initiation fees but is denied membership for any reason, even though that reason is not discriminatory in the sense of the first provision. If the union imposes qualifications and conditions for membership with which the employee is unwilling to comply, the Board stated, he may not be entitled to membership, but he is entitled to keep his job.[121]

The prohibition of discharge for loss of union membership in case the employer has reason to believe that the employee was expelled for reasons other than dues delinquency may make it less precarious for members of unions holding exclusive agreements to work for a change in bargaining representation or for termination of the exclusive contract. It also enables involuntary members of such unions to belong simultaneously to the union of their own choice if they only pay their dues to the contracting union. Misuse of the right to demand the discharge of workers who fail to pay the initiation fee or dues is forestalled by a new provision which prohibits unions and their agents from requiring the payment of excessive or discriminatory contributions.[122]

Unless excused by a recognized union security agreement, an employer now as ever commits an unfair labor practice if he discriminates in regard to hire or tenure or any condition of employment for the purpose of encouraging or dis-

---

120 National Labor Relations Act, sec. 8 (a) (3).
121 "Congress carefully limited the sphere of permissible union security, and even in that limited sphere accorded the union no power to effect the discharge of nonmembers except to protect itself against 'free rides.'" *Union Starch & Refining Co. and John Ralph*, 87 NLRB No. 137 (1949).
122 National Labor Relations Act, sec. 8 (b) (5).

couraging membership in a labor organization.[123] This provision has been supplemented by the prohibition of attempts by a union or its agents to cause an employer to commit this unfair labor practice.[124]

As mentioned above, congressional reports repeatedly have characterized any type of exclusive union security device as compulsory unionism. Senator Robert A. Taft, one of the sponsors of the Labor Management Relations Bill of 1947, stated expressly that "there is no difference in constitutional principle" between a closed and a union shop.[125] Moreover, he and a number of other senators set forth that no reason can be seen why *union* coercion of employees should not be subject to the same rules as *employer* coercion of employees. "We believe that the freedom of the individual workman should be protected from duress from the union as well as from duress by the employer."[126] But Congress, in formulating the new federal policy with respect to the borderline between proper and improper interference with the right to work, did not go so far as to declare any type of involuntary unionism contrary to public policy.[127] The legislators were content with trying to remedy only what they considered "the most serious abuses of compulsory union membership and yet give employers and unions who feel that such agreements promoted stabili-

123 The Pennsylvania Supreme Court held in an action for damages that in the absence of any definite or specific contract of employment employees may be dismissed at any time with or without cause and that refusal to join a union may be a cause for discharge since an employer may on his own initiative adopt the policy of favoring and encouraging membership in a union in order to maintain harmonious labor relations and to eliminate the necessity of dealing with individuals. *Polk* v. *Steel Workers Organizing Committee*, 62A (2d) 850 (1949).

124 National Labor Relations Act, sec. 8 (a) (3) and 8 (b) (2).

125 See *Congressional Record*, daily ed., May 9, 1947, p. 5088.

126 Supplemental views on S. 1126 in *Federal Labor Relations Act of 1947*, S. Rept. 105, 80 Cong. 1 sess. (1947), p. 50.

127 In this connection a statement of the Norwegian government may be mentioned, made in reply to an inquiry undertaken by the International Labour Office in preparing an international convention. Answering the question as to whether it considered that the international regulations should include a provision to the effect that legislation—or a collective agreement concluded in conformity with legislation—requiring membership in a given union as a previous condition to engagement, or as a condition to maintenance in employment, is not incompatible with the fundamental principles of freedom of association as

ty by eliminating 'free riders' the right to continue such agreements."[128] This indicates that there was apparently no inclination to consider methods, tried in some areas abroad, to eliminate "free riders" without making membership in a *specific* union a condition of employment. Official approbation of such methods might have necessitated changing basic policy of the National Labor Relations Act— something Congress did not intend to do.

Though the federal legislators thus reduced but did not eliminate the possibility of compulsory membership, they emphasized that they did not wish to "deprive the States of their powers to prevent compulsory unionism" altogether. Section 14 (b) states that nothing in the act is to be construed as authorizing any closed shop, union shop, maintenance-of-membership, or other form of "compulsory unionism agreement" in any state where its execution or application would be contrary to state law.[129] Thus it has been made clear that the states may regulate "compulsory unionism" concurrently with the federal government, notwithstanding that agreements affect interstate commerce and notwithstanding that the state laws limit involuntary

---

laid down in the present regulations, the government set forth: "In Norway it is an established system that trade union membership is not a previous condition to engagement, and the Government will not recommend that the Convention permit the practice of closed shop clauses. Nor are union shop clauses at present practiced in Norway, but the Government will not oppose a formulation of the Convention which will render possible such a system in countries wanting it." Like members of the U. S. Congress, the Norwegian government apparently was seeking to facilitate the acceptance of the proposed measure by suggesting a compromise solution. International Labour Conference, *Industrial Relations,* Report VIII (2), 1948, p. 26.

[128] See *Federal Labor Relations Act of 1947,* S. Rept. 105, 80 Cong. 1 sess., p. 7 (1947).

"As more and more unions seek [union-shop] authorizations through the democratic procedure of an election," the first report of the Congressional Joint Committee on Labor-Management Relations stated, "they are discovering that *enforced* members are *better* satisfied members when knowing that it is by virtue of majority choice. They are also discovering that the reluctance of many employers to enter into such contracts disappears after the majority of the employees have demonstrated that this is what they desire." *Labor-Management Relations,* S. Rept. 986, 80 Cong. 2 sess., Mar. 15, 1948, pp. 24-25. (Italics supplied.)

[129] See *Labor-Management Relations Act, 1947,* H. Rept. 510, 80 Cong. 1 sess. (1947), p. 60.

unionism more drastically than does federal law.[130] As mentioned above, Arizona, Arkansas, Florida, Georgia, Iowa, Nebraska, Nevada, North Carolina, North Dakota, South Dakota, Tennessee, Texas, and Virginia have enacted statutes more stringent than the federal act.

The Labor Management Relations Act qualifies the legality of the check-off.

The Labor Management Relations Act of 1947 also has restricted freedom of employers to deduct amounts from wages and to pay them to bargaining representatives. It is now unlawful to withold union levies, such as fines. The automatic check-off has been outlawed likewise. But the check-off of union *dues* is still permitted for any length of time under a legitimate collective agreement, provided that the employer received a written authorization from each worker whose wage is affected.[131] This authorization, however, must not be irrevocable for a period exceeding one year. Under no circumstances can it be irrevocable beyond the termination date of the collective agreement even if this means that the period of irrevocability is shorter than one year.[132]

So far as noncompliance with rules here discussed has been made an unfair labor practice, the National Labor Relations Board is empowered to adjudicate charges of violation filed by individuals or organizations. Employees who were discharged for participating in prohibited activities will not be entitled to reinstatement. Furthermore, the board may seek a temporary injunction enjoining unfair practices pending its decision on the merits of the charge. If breach of a collective contract is involved, the

[130] *Labor-Management Relations Act, 1947,* H. Rept. 245, 80 Cong. 1 sess. (1947), p. 34.

[131] The Attorney General, in an opinion dated May 13, 1948, stated that initiation fees and assessments are incidents of membership and therefore should be considered as falling within the classification of "membership dues."

[132] Labor-Management Relations Act, sec. 302.

injured party may bring action for damages.[133] Employers
and employee representatives who offend willfully against
the check-off provisions, commit a misdemeanor and are
subject to fines, or imprisonment, or both, and to injunctions.

[133] The same, sec. 301.

CHAPTER X

Summary

Modern times relieved the wage earner from restrictions to which governments, guilds, and custom had subjected him during the Middle Ages. He became free to work at any place where he could find a job and to settle the conditions of his employment directly with the employer. On the other hand, the new industrial era placed him in a new type of wage-earning class, to which—more often than not—he would belong for his whole life. Soon more and more workers came to recognize that the introduction of freedom of competition and of contract did not have the beneficial effects for the mass of employees that had been generally expected. They found, in particular, that the prevailing trend toward over-supply of labor tended to keep the position of the individual employee so weak that, as Adam Smith pointed out, the employer ordinarily could force him into compliance with his terms. To strengthen the position of the worker in his relations to the employer and to give him a better chance to attain conditions of employment which he, too, deemed proper, increasing numbers of wage-earners began to advocate substitution of collective for individual action.

Their efforts to put this idea into practice, especially by forming and operating unions, however, brought them into conflict with prevailing social, political, economic, and legal tenets of the time. Public policy in nearly all countries tried hard to suppress the movement. But this proved impossible everywhere. Apart from that, unionism grew up in a period in which traditional ways of life and thinking were undergoing profound changes. Governmental attitude toward combinations of workers thus sooner or later changed from unconditional hostility to willingness to tolerate though not to protect them. Not until rather recently was freedom of workers to act in concert recognized and granted protection as a fundamental right.

The development, however, has not come to an end with the recognition of the right to form, join, and operate unions. Additional types of labor organization have come into existence and have been recognized by the law. They are permanent machineries to protect the interests of employees, and to ensure employer-employee relations making for maximum efficiency, *at the level of the individual establishment.* In a number of countries the establishment of such institutions has been made compulsory. This most recent phase of the evolution of labor organization has brought into being novel corporate bodies such as works committees and councils; the wage-earning employees unit, the salary-earning employees unit, the employees (staff) unit in Germany, and the bargaining unit in the United States.

Recognition of the right to organize has brought division of opinion on its nature and scope.

In the present stage of the development the freedom of wage and salary earners to combine for collective action is no longer seriously questioned, at least not in nontotalitarian countries. In recent times friction between governments and labor or management, or between employers and employees, arising in connection with the exercise of this freedom, ordinarily has been due to conflicting views on its meaning and scope rather than to flat denial of its existence. Efforts therefore have been made to define the nature and limits of this freedom. Though these efforts have produced a number of basic principles which may be considered universally accepted, marked differences of opinion still exist, especially with respect to categories of persons and types of actions which come under the guarantee of full freedom of workers to organize and to engage in other concerted activities.

*Freedom to organize means freedom to engage in
various individual and concerted activities.*

There is general agreement that the freedom of workers to organize includes quite a number of freedoms. As most fundamental have been regarded the freedom of individuals to form and join unions and the freedom of labor organizations to formulate and carry through their programs without interference by public authorities or private persons as long as they act in conformity with the law of the land.

*American and European methods of protecting
exercise of the freedom are not the same.*

Prevailing European and American views, however, differ with regard to the desirable method of protecting these freedoms. Governments on the other side of the Atlantic have relied for prevention and redress of interference primarily on the general civil law concerning wrongful acts or breach of contract. As to the procedure to be followed, they also have adhered to the ordinary principles. Since the court is the authority that generally settles disputes about rights, it has been regarded as the proper place to turn to in case of violation of the right to organize as well. Where special courts of justice exist to handle labor litigation—labor courts—their jurisdiction includes controversies about interference with labor's right of association. In the United States, on the other hand, it has been considered necessary to enact special provisions for the protection of this right and to give special administrative agencies exclusive jurisdiction to enforce the observance of them. Courts, by and large, participate in the procedure only when petitioned to review or enforce decisions of the administrative agencies.

*Some countries do not give equal protection to
unionism of managerial and other employees.*

The union movement originated among rank and file
workers. In the course of time, however, it spread among
managerial employees. Increasing numbers of the latter
have come to believe that their interests as employees,
which at times may conflict with those of the employer,
can, like the interests of other employees, be better protected by concerted than by individual action. The ensuing
movement toward unionization, while at first limited mainly
to foremen, in a number of countries, now has reached
supervisory and executive personnel at higher levels of
authority. It has met with opposition not only from outside but also from inside the ranks of the managerial employees. The chief objection has been that union membership of supervisors and executives is likely to interfere
with the efficient and unbiased performance of their functions. This reasoning, though not putting a stop to unionization, has been one of the factors that have caused a strong
trend toward formation of associations which are unaffiliated with organizations of nonmanagerial salary or wage
earners. But not a few managerial employees belong to
organizations admitting also rank and file workers, or
unions of such workers.

Employer opposition to membership of foremen in rank
and file unions caused the Swedish legislature to provide
that a contract clause prohibiting foremen from belonging to an organization protecting the interests of their
subordinates does not constitute an unlawful infringement
of the right to organize. The United States Congress went
further and in 1947 excluded supervisory employees explicitly from the coverage of the National Labor Relations
Act, the basic statute providing for special protection of
full freedom of self-organization. But in none of the countries discussed in this study have managerial employees

been denied this freedom in general, or the right to organize into unions in particular.

Differences in status of government personnel caused differences in views on its right to organize.

There has been opposition to unionization not only of managerial but also of government personnel. In both cases it has been said that the persons concerned do not need protection by unions and that the nature of their positions precludes exercise of full or even any freedom to organize. As to individuals working for a government, it has further been pointed out that the notion of the right to organize and its corollaries pertains, for historical and conceptual reasons, only to the private economy and that the considerations which caused labor to demand and legislators to grant special protection of the exercise of this right do not apply to the relations between a government and its personnel. Quite a few opponents of freedom to organize in the field of public service actually have objected less to unionization as such than to recognition of a right to bargain collectively or even to engage in concerted work stoppages. But they have feared that persons in this field would claim these rights if they were permitted to form and join unions.

These considerations have played an important role in the determination of pertinent public policies. The governments covered by this study, like other governments, now generally no longer seek to prevent their personnel from establishing or joining unions. But they maintain that the right to bargain collectively, as recognized in private industry, cannot be transplanted into the field of public employment, at least not without careful adaptation to the character of the public service. Concerted work stoppages are generally considered contrary to public policy.

In Europe a tendency has existed to distinguish in this respect between government employees and civil servants. Government employees are persons who work for a public authority under conditions of employment which resemble more or less those of private employees. Civil servants have a quite different status in that they are not hired but appointed, do not work under a contract of employment, as a rule cannot be discharged in the manner customary in private employment, and enjoy other important privileges. There appears to have been less opposition to collective bargaining by public employees than to collective bargaining by civil servants because it has been widely held that the employment conditions of the former—as contrasted with those of the latter—justify the desire to protect their interests by collective action. In the European countries here discussed, moreover, no statutes deal with the question as to whether government employees may or may not strike. A number of writers have held that they could not in justice be flatly denied the freedom to resort to militant tactics, which other employees have who work under similar conditions of employment. Public authorities on all levels, however, have made vigorous efforts to prevent them from engaging in concerted work stoppages.

As to European civil servants, who ordinarily take care of the sovereign functions of the governments, it is generally accepted that tacit or explicit recognition of their right to exercise freedom of association has not implied recognition of the right to bargain collectively in the manner customary and lawful in the private economy. But in the sense of election of personnel representatives, collective representation and adjustment of grievances, or establishment of advisory staff committees or joint machinery for the purpose of discussing general problems or individual cases, collective bargaining would seem to have become a regular feature of most civil service systems in Europe. This, however, has not led to recognition of a right of civil servants to use other than peaceable tactics to attain compliance with requests. Disciplinary penalties for a work stoppage or for any refusal to carry out orders are so heavy as to make it clear that strikes by civil servants are contrary to public policy, though in the countries discussed in this study no statutes outlaw them explicitly.

The overwhelming majority of persons working for governments in the United States are employees rather than civil servants in the strictly technical sense of the term, no matter whether they carry out sovereign or proprietary governmental functions. In interpreting the scope of their freedom of association, there has been a strong trend by and large to apply the principles governing the right to organize of European *civil servants*. As to militant tactics, a number of American legislative bodies, including the United States Congress, have gone further than European governments and have expressly prohibited strikes against public authorities. Whether government employees have a right to bargain collectively is still a controversial question. Some public agencies have entered into collective contracts of types customary in the private economy. But prevailing practice appears to be the same as in European civil service systems.

American and European labor leaders have appraised differently union restriction of freedom to organize.

Recognition of the right to organize has given rise not only to controversies as to whether its basic principles apply equally to all wage and salary earners, but also to great differences of opinion as to what types of concerted activities it covers. Among the activities which have caused polemics as to whether they come under the principles of freedom of association have been union practices to recruit members by methods more vigorous than mere persuasion, especially arrangements making union membership a condition of employment. Unions have demanded that no outsiders be hired (closed shop) or that outsiders be required to join after they were hired (union shop). There are two types of this technique for compelling outsiders to become union members if they want to get or keep the jobs of their choice. One type is directed solely at *unorganized workers,* and its intended effect is to make them take up or maintain membership in *any* union, no matter which one; the outsider has free choice among the existing unions. The other type is directed not only at unorganized but also at organized workers and is used to make them become and remain members of a *specific* union, namely, the contracting union; the outsider accordingly has no freedom of choice.

So far as European organized labor has at all insisted upon arrangements of this kind—generally known as union security arrangements—it has in the majority of cases employed the first technique. American unions, on the other hand, have used the second type. Many unionists in the United States maintain that their policy does not involve coercive or undue pressure. They emphasize that their security devices do not force anyone to become or remain a union member since nobody is compelled to accept work in or to stay with a firm operating under a union security plan not to his liking. Other American unionists do not deny that their customary closed- and union-shop arrangements may—and are intended to—compel nonunionists and members of other unions to become and remain members of the contracting union irrespective of their personal wishes. But they have insisted that this is no reason for condemning such arrangements, because the outsider is required to join up for his own benefit and because union membership of the maximum of workers also is desirable in the public interest. In addition, probably all labor leaders in the United States have maintained that the conditions under which American unions operate compel them to insist on the right to exclude both organized and unorganized nonmembers from the areas covered by their contracts. They have pointed out that otherwise they either would not be able to carry through their legitimate programs or to perform the functions which the American labor relations laws have assigned to them, or could do so only with great difficulty.

European unions, too, have made vigorous efforts to bring the maximum of workers into the fold and to protect themselves against the possibility that employers might undermine their strength by discriminating in favor of outsiders or by other hostile actions. The views of labor leadership on the significance of the closed and union shop for success in these efforts, however, have not been the same on both sides of the Atlantic. Most European in contrast to American union leaders have shown considerable reluctance to use these devices because they have been apprehensive of potential undesirable effects of involuntary unionism. But even when they have tried to employ them, they have only seldom sought exclusion of members of another bona fide organization who do not join the contracting union. Accordingly, they have been relieved of the whole problem of exclusive agreements in some industrial areas in which the majority of the employers have adopted the practice of giving hiring preference to members of unions even without any contractual obligation to do so.

European unionists have disliked nonunionists at least as much as has American organized labor. This has led to not a few instances of refusal to work with them. Also, attempts by fellow workers to organize them have not necessarily been of a gentle nature. But most union leaders on higher levels, though doing their best to reduce the number of unorganized workers, have displayed marked disinclination to force them into a union by confronting them with the alternative of joining or being excluded from jobs of their choice. They have held that, since strength and security of unionism in their countries rests upon its fighting power rather than on governmental protection, and since its fighting power, in turn, springs from voluntary adherence and free choice of one's union, systematic compulsion to organize would weaken union power.

There also has been apprehension that compulsion might impair union strength for an additional reason. Many labor leaders in Europe have believed that, if substantial numbers of workers would be excluded from job opportunities unless they join a union, governments might think it necessary to regulate internal affairs of the unions in order to ensure to everyone the opportunity to become and remain a member under terms which the government considers equitable. Even if such compulsory government regulation would establish fair rules, it has been argued, it would not only restrict the freedom of unions to draw up their own rules and to organize their administration and activities, to which they have been entitled as voluntary associations, but it also might have other effects considered detrimental by prevailing European union view. Labor leaders have expressed fear that legislators might grant privileges to individual organizations and thus destroy legal equality among unions and among workers; statutes might determine which organization should and which should not be recognized, so that freedom to organize would be restricted. Individual organizations might try to obtain special favors from legislators and thus jeopardize union morale and solidarity; and governments might obtain the possibility of restricting or suppressing union freedom of economic and political thought.

Accordingly, European unions have shown considerable reluctance to insist upon agreements excluding unorganized workers from employment opportunities. Demands for exclusion of unionists who do not join the contracting organization have been still more uncommon. This has been due chiefly to prevailing union ideology and to the structure of the labor movements on the other side of the Atlantic. The dogma of the class war, or strong belief in working class solidarity, or their concept of democracy has prevented most labor leaders from supporting plans under which members of any bona fide union may be deprived of opportunities to work merely because of their union affiliation. The same factors have caused aversion to plans which give an exclusive right to organize and represent employees to one union where other unions too organized workers and want to represent their interests.

Such self-restraint as has existed in European interunion competition, however, has resulted not only from ideological considerations but also from considerations of expediency. No matter whether in a single country most of the significant unions have been affiliated with one principal organization or whether — as in the United States — the labor movement has been divided in several organized factions, the vast majority of union policy makers have believed that recognition of exclusive privileges of any one union at any place would unduly obstruct the exercise of full freedom of association and lead to so much union disunity as to weaken organized labor and correspondingly strengthen management. In the many countries, in which movements with profoundly differing social, economic, political, or other philosophies compete with each other, labor leaders have disliked compulsion to join a specific organization for the additional reason that application for membership presupposes — at least theoretically — faith in the official ideology of the union, which cannot be expected from workers who join merely to obtain or hold their jobs. Enforced membership, it has been stated, makes usually for indifference and lower morale; but involuntary membership of many adherents of a diametrically opposed philosophy could prevent the union entirely from carrying out its program.

American and European management policies
regarding exclusive contracts are different.

Closed-shop and similar exclusive agreements not only restrict the freedom of the worker to work for any employer who is willing to employ him but also limit the freedom of the employer to select those whom he wishes to employ (or discharge). His managerial liberty may be affected beyond that. Employers on both sides of the Atlantic, therefore, have objected to all types of arrangements making union membership a condition of employment. Only relatively few European employers have signed exclusive agreements, most of which have been directed solely against unorganized workers. Those employers who—with or without formal agreement—have consented to the exclusion of nonunionists have done so primarily to avoid losses which may be caused by friction between their organized and unorganized employees. But the majority of European managements steadfastly have approached the problem of exclusive agreements as a matter of principle rather than expediency.

Prevailing policy of American employers has differed from that of their European colleagues at least in two respects. They have signed a large number of exclusive agreements, especially in recent times. Moreover, they have closed their establishments, or parts of them, not only to unorganized but also to such organized workers as do not belong to, or do not wish to join, a particular union, namely, the contracting one. Not a few American employers adopted this policy in order to escape costly controversies with unions. They also have sought to avoid trouble with the National Labor Relations Board. For the latter has regarded demands for exclusive union security agreements, made in conformity with the Labor Relations Act, as one of the subjects coming under the statutory obligation to bargain collectively; and, in case no agreement is reached on such a subject, the Board has been reluctant to recognize that the employer complied fully with this duty. However, management policy in the United States has been determined also by other factors. There has been an increase in the number of American employers who hold that union security agreements are not only useful to avoid labor trouble but also bring positive benefits for their businesses.

Public policy in most countries is based on the
principle that union membership is voluntary.

Some countries have statutes under which employees in individual establishments are automatically members of, or can be incorporated into, collective bodies *other than unions,* for example, the staff unit in Germany and the bargaining unit in the United States. But in the vast majority of liberal nations the law does not compel workers to join a *union.* Efforts of organized labor to do that by insisting on exclusion from opportunities to work of non-unionists, and possibly also unionists not belonging to a specific organization, have given rise to legislative or judicial action. Recognizing as a rule that unions cannot exist and function effectively without liberty to exert certain pressure upon persons who are not willing to join, legislators and courts have tried to define how far they may go without acting contrary to public policy. Without attaching decisive weight to the highly controversial question as to whether compulsory unionism impairs efficiency in production, they have sought to fix the line of demarcation between justifiable and objectionable pressure on the basis of fundamental national philosophy and of general principles, especially the dogma of freedom to refrain from joining a union, or the right to work, or individual freedom to choose one's union. They also have been strongly influenced by considerations of social advantage. All governments have held that, as a matter of course, union practices must not violate the general criminal law, the relevant provisions of which are similar in all countries discussed. But as to the propriety of union pressure tactics not coming clearly under provisions of the general penal law, opinions of American and European governmental authorities have differed in several respects.

*Views differ regarding protection of
the right to refrain from joining a union.*

Nearly all liberal governments recognize that full freedom to organize includes not only freedom to form and join unions—positive freedom of association—but also freedom to refrain from such activities—negative freedom of association. This doctrine also has been generally accepted by management and labor. The true issue involved in controversies about the "right to refrain from joining a union" has not been its existence but rather the question whether the labor law should protect its exercise in precisely the same extent and manner as the freedom to join a union.

A number of European and of American (state) legislatures have answered this question in the affirmative; they have enacted special statutes providing explicitly for equal protection of both freedoms, and outlawing, in particular, interference with the negative freedom by means of closed- and union-shop arrangements. Other governments, for example the Swedish government, have held that the labor law must make provision for protection of the positive right to organize, but that the negative right to organize should not be regulated by special statutes. Between these two extremes have been pertinent foreign and American legislative enactments which have guaranteed freedom of self-organization without any mention of its two aspects and thus have left it to interpretation whether or not they cover the freedom not to establish or join labor organizations at all. Moreover, there have been legal systems which, though expressly guaranteeing both freedoms, have permitted arrangements devised to compel workers to join a union; sometimes their legality has been made dependent upon compliance with certain conditions, for example, that they are agreed upon freely and with labor organizations deemed truly representative of the workers directly concerned. The American National Labor Relations Act may be cited as illustrative.

This indicates that, in practice, the doctrine of the negative freedom of association has not prevented the rise of contradictory and sometimes vague policies respecting the limits of justifiable pressure to organize. Moreover, the relative position of the two somewhat antithetical freedoms to join and not to join a union has been the subject of much controversy. There has been marked disinclination to place

protection of both on precisely the same footing. In some
countries this reluctance has been due to the relative in-
frequency of interference with the negative right to organize. In others the view has prevailed that pressure to join
a union is less dangerous from the angle of over-all policy
and social advantage than pressure not to join a union.
Moreover, not a few governments have feared that emphasis
on protection of the negative freedom of association might
weaken the positive freedom of association.

Finally, it has been widely held that the enactment of
special provisions is necessary to protect the right to form,
join, and operate unions but not to safeguard the right to
refrain from doing so. The former right, governments have
pointed out, has been interfered with chiefly by employers,
the latter almost exclusively by unions or their members.
Most actions which employers have undertaken to prevent
workers from exercising their right to form and join labor
organizations, it has been explained, would still be legal
without amendment of the traditional law. In contrast,
unions and organized workers, according to this legislative
school of thought, ordinarily cannot interfere with the negative freedom of association without committing acts which
have been unlawful at all times, so that infringement of this
freedom now as ever can be prevented or remedied adequately by enforcing existing general legal principles.

*Many governments have used other approaches to
prevent objectionable pressure to organize.*

Many legislatures and courts, for all these reasons, have
sought to fix the dividing line between justifiable and improper pressure to organize with the help of broader concepts than that of the negative freedom of association. In
some European countries, for example, Germany and
Switzerland, the legality of steps to overcome unwillingness
to unionize by making membership a condition of employ-

ment has been judged on the basis of their effects upon the individuals affected in the specific cases rather than of hard and fast general rules. Such steps have been considered unlawful if they seriously endanger the economic existence of outsiders or if they inflict harm on others out of proportion to the advantage sought by the union. In efforts to establish generally valid rules, however, the concept of the right to work has played an important role in Europe as well as the United States.

Use of the "right to work" principle has not resulted in uniform definition of improper pressure.

Under the concept of the right to work freedom of the individual includes the right to dispose of his own labor according to his will either in employment or independently in business. According to common view this right is no more absolute than other equally fundamental rights and therefore is subject to interference by the government or by private persons. Its exercise has been restricted by a variety of statutes in every country. Also, the governments have recognized that interference with it by persons or organizations acting in the exercise of an equal or superior right is not unlawful as long as they keep within the bounds of the general law. Accordingly, the right to work as such does not necessarily preclude the use of the closed shop or similar devices confronting workers with the alternative of joining a union or being excluded from opportunities to work. The propriety of such devices rather depends on whether or not public policy considers the right of unions to organize equal or superior to the right of individuals to opportunity to work at the place of their choice or, more specifically, whether it regards such interference with the right of others to work as a legitimate method of exercising the right to organize.

In the area specifically examined in this study, it has

been chiefly American, British, and French governmental authorities that have dealt with the problem of the relative significance of the two rights. France has treated exclusive union-management arrangements as contrary to the right to work (and freedom to organize) ever since the days of the Great Revolution. Though in more recent times a certain trend has developed to recognize increases in union power at the expense of traditional individual freedom of workers, closed and union shops are still strongly opposed. A number of British administrative and judicial rulings have treated closed-shop contracts of both types as valid. But such contracts have been relatively rare. Thus, the British government is obviously inclined to take no strong stand with respect to the issue but to leave its settlement to the parties immediately concerned.

Public policy in the United States, until quite recently, supposed that exclusive union-management agreements do not violate the right to work. There were only few exceptions to this rule. A considerable number of statutes, federal and state, mentioned expressly the admissibility of such agreements, provided only that they were entered into with bona fide unions duly chosen as bargaining representatives in conformity with the pertinent legal provisions. After World War II, however, a steadily increasing number of states began to treat exclusion of nonmembers of contracting unions from employment opportunities as incompatible with the right to work. At present, at least 18 states have laws prohibiting closed, union, and similar shops, or qualifying their legality, for this reason. In 1947 the United States Congress also accepted this doctrine, at least in part. In amending the basic National Labor Relations Act, it outlawed the closed shop. The act, however, still permits the union-shop agreement, provided that it is made with a bona fide union which was duly chosen as bargaining representative and authorized to negotiate such agreement by a majority of the employees concerned.

*In Europe the right to choose one's union and
bargaining representative is an individual right.*

Still more striking than the differences between American and European views on the relative position of the right to organize, on the one hand, and the right to work and the right to refrain from organizing, on the other hand, has been the sharp division of opinion concerning the meaning of full freedom to choose one's union. The liberal governments on the European continent regard freedom of every worker to belong to the union of his individual, free choice and to be represented by it as an essential part of freedom of association. Accordingly, such pressure upon workers to join a *specific* union, as exists under closed- and union-shop agreements of the type customary in the United States, has in most European continental countries been treated as unlawful, chiefly on the ground that it violates the *positive* freedom to organize, occasionally on the theory that it is immoral. A considerable number of continental court rulings have categorically rejected especially contracts which place organized workers under the necessity of changing their union affiliation or joining an additional union if they wish to obtain or keep the jobs of their choice. A number of British judicial and administrative decisions, conversely, have not objected to such contracts. Nor does any statute of the United Kingdom prohibit them. Declarations of public policy, like policy statements of the British Trades Union Congress, however, have disapproved of such arrangements.

*In the United States individual choice
has been replaced by majority rule.*

Public policy in the United States, on the other hand, has been quite different. Under the American system choosing one's union does not necessarily mean choosing one's bargaining agent, as it ordinarily does in Europe. The problem of freedom of choice thus may come up not only as the problem of freedom to choose one's union, but also as the problem of freedom to designate one's bargaining representative. When and where legislators and judges began to recognize union security agreements, they accepted prevailing American opinion that such agreements, as a matter of course, must give an employment monopoly to the members of the contracting union. Subsequent federal and state legislation did not change this basic policy, though it sought to reserve the right to demand union security contracts to labor organizations representative of at least a majority of the workers affected. The National Labor Relations Act of 1935 and similar state labor relations acts thus have provided that a union security agreement can be validly made only by a bona fide labor organization which, at the time of its conclusion, represents the majority of the employees to be covered by it. To prevent such organizations from entering into an exclusive agreement without asking the employees whether they want it, the act, since its amendment in 1947, makes the validity of union and maintenance-of-membership contracts (the only types of exclusive union security agreements still permitted within its purview) dependent upon previous authorization of the union by at least a majority of the workers directly concerned. Some state laws contain similar regulations. Though such statutory provisions have curbed the freedom of employers and unions to enter into exclusive arrangements, they have not removed or narrowed the difference between the American and the prevailing European concept of freedom of choice.

This difference also is conspicuous in the American provisions concerning the designation of bargaining representatives. Labor relations acts in the United States recognize as valid only those collective agreements which were made with bargaining agents selected by the majority of the employees in units appropriate for the purposes of collective bargaining. In addition, these acts generally empower special administrative agencies to decide, in case of need, which unit is appropriate. Under this system then individual American workers may be incorporated in a bargaining unit to which they do not wish to belong, and employees who did not vote for the union that obtained the majority in the selection of a bargaining agent are nevertheless represented by it. The concept of a bargaining unit, which may be determined by a governmental authority, is unknown in Europe. Nor does the selection of the union which acts as bargaining representative take place under majority rule. Any European worker who wishes to have a representative may join a union of his own choosing, and this union then will take care of his interests vis-a-vis his employer. No law prevents a bona fide labor organization from representing its members in any establishment. The American legislators, however, have held that collective bargaining would be impracticable, without both the bargaining unit and the majority rule principles. American labor and management appear to share this view and to be satisfied with the system.

British policy is following a middle course.

Summing up, the foregoing analysis shows that considerable differences exist between present American and continental European policies with respect to freedom to organize in general and the propriety of exclusive arrangements in particular. British authorities have been maintaining a kind of middle course somewhere between the governmental attitudes prevailing on either continent. Legislators and judges in the United Kingdom have tended for many years past to refrain from interfering with closed- and union-shop arrangements. This is concordant with policies followed in recent years by many public authorities in the United States, at least prior to the rise of the postwar movement to outlaw or curb exclusive arrangements. Official policy declarations of the British government (and the Trades Union Congress) however, have tallied with prevailing continental European policies in that they have rejected recognition of any one union as exclusive representative of workers and have disapproved of the type of closed and union shop traditional in the United States which excludes any nonmember of the contracting union from work in the area covered by the agreement, no matter whether he is unorganized or a member of another bona fide union.

TABLE OF CASES

United States

PAGE

Foreign

GENERAL INDEX

Alabama, 88, 123, 153, 213
All-union agreement, 286
American Federation of Labor, 159
American Plan Movement, 189
Antitrust laws (United States), 14, 33-36
Arizona, 88, 288
Arkansas, 88, 285, 288, 292
Armed forces, freedom to organize of members of, 113 ff
Attlee, Clement R., 160
Australia, 129n, 159n
  compulsory unionism, 129n
Austria, 221
Auxiliary Service Act (Germany), 43, 53

Bargaining representative (United States), 61, 172, 176n, 231, 236, 244
  change of, 173-74, 240, 244, 296; selection of, 229 ff
Bargaining unit (United States), 62, 70, 171, 172, 231 ff
Belgium, 154, 201
Bernstein, Irving, 60
Beveridge, Sir William, 254
Bonn Constitution (Germany), 44, 217n
Britain, See United Kingdom
British Trades Union Congress, 152, 158n, 160, 161, 228
  Interim Report on Post-War Reconstruction, 1944, 12, 254

Canada, 232, 234n, 245n
Capitalistic system
  American union attitude toward, 13 ff; European union attitude toward, 12-13
Central Organization of Salaried Employees (TCO) (Sweden), 42, 158
Check-off agreement, 137, 140, 150, 153n, 192, 227, 277, 279, 282, 283, 291-93, 299
Christian unions, 10
Civil servants
  definition of, 91; freedom to organize of, 101, 105 ff, 113n
Civil Servants, Act Concerning the General Status of (France), 106
Civil Service Act (United States), 94

Civil Service Arbitration Tribunal (Britain), 109
Civil Service Retirement Act (United States), 96
Class solidarity, 11
Classification Act (United States), 95
Class-war philosophy, 11, 14
Closed shop, attitude toward,
  American employers, 187, 188, 191-94; American government, 201, 210-14, 229-46, 272-99; American union, 135n, 140, 141 ff, 173 ff, 178 ff; British employers, 190; British government, 210, 224-29, 265-72; British union, 160 ff, 169; employers, 184 ff; European union, 149 ff, 164 ff, 175 ff, 179-80; French employers, 189, 257; French government, 201, 209-10, 223-25, 256-65; French union, 164, 168; German government, 206-07, 214-17, 221-22; German union, 168-69; Swedish employers, 163, 189, 190; Swedish government, 207-09, 222-23; Swedish union, 163; Swiss government, 217-18; Swiss union, 164-65, 169-70; See also Exclusive agreement, Freedom to refrain from joining a union, Freedom of choice among unions, and Right to work
Closed shop, American type of, 133 ff, 166
Closed union, 274
Collective Agreements, Act Respecting (France), 154, 176n
Collective Contracts, Committees of Wage-earning and Salaried Employees, and Conciliation of Labor Disputes, Order Relating to (Germany), 230n
Colorado, 87, 290, 292
Combination Acts (Britain), 23, 266
Combination Laws Repeal Act, 1824 (Britain), 23
Combination Laws Repeal Act Amendment Act, 1825 (Britain), 23, 266
Competition among unions, 159 ff, 170 ff
Compulsion, definition of, 127
Compulsory devices to unionize workers, 130 ff